The Big Steal

The Big Steal

Tony Marzano

with

Painter E. Powell

BOSTON

Houghton Mifflin Company

1980

To Marsha Fischer and Terry

Library of Congress Cataloging in Publication Data

Marzano, Tony.
The big steal.

1. Robbery—Illinois—Chicago—Case studies.
I. Powell, Painter E., joint author. II. Title.
HV6661.I32 1974.M37   364.1'62'0977311   80-17472
ISBN 0-395-28150-4

Printed in the United States of America

S 10 9 8 7 6 5 4 3 2 1

The Big Steal

Always on Sunday

If you can't make it in Chicago, you can't make it anywhere.

— Anonymous

October 13, 1974. Another damn Sunday.

Tony Marzano's hands were tense on the wheel, though the streets were more or less deserted and the weather was mild. He had stopped on the West Side to pick up his cousin Charlie a few minutes ago. Charlie had got into the car without looking at Tony and had grunted something that might or might not have been a hello. East for just about thirty minutes, then take a left, through the Loop, and onto North La Salle.

It was the fourth Sunday since early September that they had made this drive at exactly the same time and over the same route. By now, Tony had memorized the looks of every building along North La Salle, knew where every hole in the pavement was, had a sixth sense for the squad car in the neighborhood.

At 6:30, they passed the checkpoint that signaled "go," and Charlie pulled a walkie-talkie out of his jacket, turned it on, and sat hunched with the black box close to his ear.

"Take it slow, now," he said.

Tony slowed and checked the rearview mirror again. Then, about a block ahead of them, he saw the squat cement building. The Chicago office of Purolator Security. No sign on the outside. Six months ago, he'd never even heard of Purolator. He slowed the car to a crawl and strained to hear. For a minute or two, there was nothing but the sandpaper sound of static from the box.

There was a clicking noise and then the voice came.

"Forget it."

Charlie clicked the box off and slammed it down on the seat. "Fuck, fuck, fuck," he said.

"This ain't never goin' down," Tony said. "We make this trip one more time and we get busted for wearing ruts in La Salle Street." He leaned over the wheel and hunched his shoulders up and down to try to relax them. "Who fucked up this time?" He glanced at Charlie and saw the pulse dancing in his temple.

"Maybe not much money. Somebody else in the building. How the fuck should I know?"

Tony speeded up a little and Purolator, like an oblong, ugly pot of gold, receded in the distance. Tony took a right onto Chicago and then another right for the silent journey home.

Tony remembered their first Sunday drive in September when he'd first heard the box speak. "Hey, I bet I can guess who's talkin' on the other end."

"No shit," Charlie had said and had gone silent.

"It sounds like Ralphie. Tell him to order two fried eggs and bacon and I'll know for sure."

For the past six months, almost every morning, Ralph Marrera had been coming over to sit with them when they had breakfast at Connie's diner.

"He ain't hungry," Charlie said.

"He inside the building?" Tony had persisted.

"Night guard."

It was then that Tony had known that this was going down for sure. Before that, it seemed like Charlie's big talk about a big score. No details and nothing solid. Now there was an inside man, and everybody knew that a good inside man could mean a really big score.

Still, everything had to click into place just right. And tonight, again, something went clack instead of click. Tony was depressed.

When they got to Charlie's house, Tony cut the motor. "Come in," Charlie said as he put the walkie-talkie under his jacket again.

"I guess," Tony said. He followed Charlie up the walk to the neat bungalow.

When they were inside, Charlie headed for the kitchen and, in a minute, came back to the living room with a loaf of Italian bread under his arm and two cans of Budweiser. "Kay and the kids are at her mother's for dinner," he said. He handed Tony one of the beers and sat down. Now that he was back home, he seemed perfectly cheerful again. There were the Little League trophies, won by the team Charlie coached, up there on the shelf. There was the clean and well-kept Sears furniture. Charlie dropped easily back into type, the good family man proud of his wife and kids.

Tony couldn't do it. All his muscles ached from the tension of the drive and then the letdown, like stepping on a step that isn't there.

Charlie went over to the television set, turned it on, and began searching through the channels. Tony paced up and down the room. He began to wonder, If Charlie was a rich man, how rich? Nothing he saw around him in the house showed it. After that gold robbery a few years ago, the police, from what Tony heard, had watched Charlie very,

very closely. But they never did get enough evidence to indict. And Charlie's way of spending stayed just the same. No new car, no trips to Vegas, no investments. He kept wearing the too-short double-knit pants and that sweater. He drank Kool-Aid or beer. The only women he knew were the ones he was related to. A life of nickels and dimes.

Charlie had found his program, something with a family in a living room a lot bigger than this one snapping one-liners at one another. Charlie lay down on the couch to enjoy it. He tore off a chunk of bread and began to chew. "Siddown, Tony, this is good," he said.

Tony finished his beer in a gulp. "O.K., you watch them fuckin' yo-yos. I'm goin'." Charlie raised a hand, but his eyes were full on the screen. As Tony closed the door, the studio audience laughed wildly.

He drove through the dusk back in the direction they had just come from, the irritation of the dry run still nagging him. Ordinarily, he would have gone east to Lake Shore Drive — the quick way north to where he was headed — but, instead, he found himself taking La Salle for another look at Purolator.

A few blocks north and east of the Purolator building, Lake Shore Drive sweeps grandly along the edge of Lake Michigan, lined by the towers of the Gold Coast. There are the Hancock Building, the apartments designed by Mies van der Rohe, the Drake Towers, the Carlyle. This lakeside strip, as distinct from most of Chicago, is the land of the rich. The exclusive shops, the art galleries, the fine restaurants are here. Because it's where the wealth is — but not necessarily the cash.

La Salle Street is a little more representative of Chicago. In the Loop it is a downtown canyon with an array of banks and buildings that house great law firms. The dignity falls off as it leads north across the Chicago River, and there it becomes the shabby western border of the Gold Coast. To the west lie acres of urban decay and the newly built black slums of Cabrini Green.

But that boxy, nondescript concrete building at Huron and La Salle was the Chicago headquarters of the world's largest armored-car service, and that's where the cash was. In very big numbers.

Tony sighed as he drove past, nodded once, and aimed for Rush Street, another distinct stretch of Chicago's vast geography. This was not where Tony came from but where he was heading if things turned out right. The quarter of singles bars, striptease spots, fancy restaurants, nightclubs, and discos. Later on, the rest of America would get a view of it as the movie setting for *Looking for Mr. Goodbar.* Here the conventioneers came looking for Mr. Kelly's, Rally Alley, or The Store. Affluent Chicagoans would be trying to get a table at Arnie's or, a few blocks farther north on State, crowding into Eugene's. But the place for Tony was Faces. It cost a $300 membership fee to see and be seen there.

Tony pulled into a NO PARKING spot on Oak Street and sat there for a minute or two, the afterimage of Purolator still in his mind. When Tony was a kid on Taylor Street, one of the big dreams was to bust open an armored car. Everybody his age talked about it. Just like hitting the biggest slot machine that ever was. Gushers of silver dollars spouting out of holes, avalanches of hundred-dollar bills. Now, he and Charlie were thinking the same way about the home base of all the armored cars, about the treasure vault where it all ended up.

He sighed. It sure took a lot of patience and a lot of nerve.

He crossed the street and headed for Faces. At the door was Jake, in tuxedo as usual, and Tony nodded. Jake omitted the usual membership-card routine and waved Tony on

toward the black, upholstered tunnel, something like a huge
velvet culvert. At the other end of it came the music, the
dance floor like a shining black lake, and the bar. Strobes
like heat lightning flashed intermittently in the large room.

Tony went through the mezzanine that surrounded the
dance floor, passed the row of banquettes, and made his
way to the bar. There were not many people around yet and
Faces wasn't in full swing. Later on, when the crowd had
come and the place was full of sound, the disc jockey would
play a smoky piece and, sure enough, clouds of artificial
smoke would rise from the dance floor.

Tony ordered a vodka and drank it. Then another. He
was getting into that kind of suspended state he liked, neither excited nor depressed. He could stand back a little; he
could drink for a long time without getting drunk.

There were always some old friends from Taylor Street or
Bridgeport around Faces on a night like this, guys Tony had
known for years. At Faces, they would turn up with girls
who didn't come from Taylor Street, girls who used to be
cheerleaders or homecoming queens in Evanston or Wau-
kegan. Now they were beauticians or convention models.
Tony suddenly heard the thump of a glass on the bar next to
him and he turned to see Vince Pasquesi. Vince didn't pause
for a hello.

"You heard they run Sal in? Put him in a line-up with a
fuckin' nylon stocking over his head and some crazy lady
fingers him. He isn't even in town at the time. But it costs
ten, maybe fifteen grand could be, just to beat it." Vince
shook his head and drank. All the injustice around seemed
to make him thirsty.

"His luck," Tony said and signaled the bartender for a
refill. Just then two girls came out of the tunnel and stood
for a moment, looking the room over. Then the blonde said
something to the dark-haired one and they steered over to

the bar and perched on stools. They looked as if they were really talking to each other and not checking the place out some more.

"So I been workin' on this thing," Vince was saying. "This big score goin' down and my crew put together almost. Any day. Guy with a bunch of furs we could borrow easy and then sell him back. No fences. Hundred percent." He leaned against Tony's arm. "You interested?"

Tony's stomach always got tight when he heard the words *big score*. But Vince, with his load of shitty furs, didn't know big. Big was Purolator.

But so far Purolator was only driving around on Sunday night and going crazy when Ralphie told them to pass. Nothing coming down. And then drinking every night of the week because he couldn't sleep.

"You listenin' Tony? I said, you want in?"

Tony shook his head. "I don't need it."

Vince looked at him incredulously. "You know, you're fuckin' crazy." Over another round of drinks, he tried to talk Tony in. Then he went off to recruit somewhere else. Vince always had a good story, you had to give him that, but he talked too much and too loud and the big scores were mostly in his head.

Tony got another drink. Pete, the DJ, had turned the music up so much that it was pushing the ceiling. Tony looked at the big glass tanks around the bar. Can fish hear? If they can, these fish must be deaf by this time. Couples were beginning to dance, their bodies turning instantly white in the strobes, then to shadow. Tony saw the blonde who'd been at the bar and she was dancing now, no bra and all of her in motion. When the strobe hit her breasts, the nipples looked like thimbles.

So, this was William Anthony Marzano standing there at the bar in Faces: thirty-three years old, an easy-smiling man with a thick black mustache. Women were always telling him he looked like Burt Reynolds and, in the light of the strobes, he almost did.

The looks were a help, but it was a quick mind and a flawless line that made a scam a success. Unlike a lot of the men he'd grown up with, Tony never used a gun. Give him a chance to talk, and then a lot of people would keep insisting that Tony take their money.

Tony had several pretty friends who used quite a bit of that money to buy ultrasuede jackets or Dior lingerie in the Michigan Avenue boutiques. Sometimes Tony would take a trip to Vegas and one of them would go along, just for luck. Looking at the dance floor, he could picture the blonde in a shortie black nightgown. The room, now heavy with perfume and cigarette smoke, was filling up with dancers.

Tony went to the men's room, and when he came back he saw Mickey Vena ushering the blonde to a barstool right by his. Funny, Mickey must have been the guy dancing with her but Tony had missed him.

"Tony! Hey, where's the harem?" Mickey said. He slapped Tony on the shoulder.

"Gave them the night off."

"Ain't you goin' to dance?"

"Not with you."

The blonde giggled and slipped onto a stool — not the one on the other side of Mickey but the one next to Tony. Mickey shoved an empty glass to the back of the bar and ordered three drinks.

"Tony, meet Sheila."

"Any place she says." Tony gave her his best smile.

Sheila gave her little laugh again and dropped her shoe. When she had stopped wiggling on the barstool, her leg was pressed lightly against Tony's.

For the next five minutes, he ignored her while he talked

with Mickey. But he kept up a little pressure against her leg, just to let her know she shouldn't go away. Mickey was complaining and complaining about a horse he'd bet on.

"Like they say in the TV commercials, it was troubled with irregularity."

"O.K., I'm your straight man," Tony said. "What does that mean?"

"Too fuckin' constipated to trot."

Tony pretended to be thinking about that in silence for a few moments. Then he looked up and asked, "No shit?"

Tony turned to the blonde. "I seen you here before?"

"Well, I only came here twice before, with a friend of mine who belongs." She smiled and showed perfect teeth. "I don't believe I saw you."

"Sometimes I come in disguise. You ever notice somebody you thought was Howard Hughes?"

The blonde smiled as if she didn't know whether to believe him or not.

"He thinks he lives here," Mickey said. "They have to throw him out when they close up. Hey, did you know that Tony says he's gonna buy Faces. Tells everybody that. *And* when he learns to write, he's gonna give 'em a check!"

Buy Faces — Tony's favorite dream. He stared over the girl's shoulder for a minute. He was back in the car, his hands gripping the wheel, with Charlie listening for Marrera inside. And the door was opening and Tony could see inside, and the place was just like a greenhouse full of bills. He set his glass down carefully on the bar because he'd felt his hand begin to tremble and had heard the ice cubes click like dice. Forget it. For now.

Mickey had turned and looked off toward the other end of the room. "Hey, I see a guy I got to talk to over there. You keep an eye on Sheila."

"What guy?" asked Tony.

"Old high-school buddy of mine. Got successful and got promoted. Now he's the fuckin' king of England. Gotta buy him a drink." He gave Tony a punch on the arm, winked, and walked away. A striking-looking black-haired woman in a silvery dress had just come out of the tunnel entrance and they watched as Mickey went over to her. She smiled as she saw him, as if he was the man she'd been looking for, and she reached out and took his arm.

Tony turned to Sheila. "Mickey gets lost easy. Don't blame him — no sense of direction at all. And now the poor king has to get drunk all by himself."

"I think you're putting me on," she said.

It turned out that Sheila had moved to Chicago from Ann Arbor just two months ago. She had got a job as a receptionist in one of the big law firms down on La Salle Street. She sat all day in a big paneled room and asked clients their names and whom did they wish to see, please, and did they have an appointment? She shared an apartment on Bellevue Street with another Ann Arbor girl, but Pat had gone home for the weekend.

"Hey, nice," Tony said, looking around at the plants, pillows, and throw rugs in that apartment when they arrived there later. Sheila was putting some music on. Sheila was putting some vodka on the rocks in two glasses. Sheila was taking the barrette out and letting her blonde hair fall free.

Not as good as counting a million bucks on Sunday night, Tony thought, but the next best thing. At least it wasn't a dry run.

2

Ready or Not

All thieves wear medals of Saint Dismas.

— J.D.

October 20, 1974. Sunday again. Around noon Tony dragged himself out of bed to pick up his son and daughter from their mother's. Then he stopped by Charlie's to ask if he'd be at Therese's for a two o'clock dinner.

Charlie's wife and kids weren't home from church yet, but Charlie reassured him. "Tell your sister we'll be there. Then we'll take another little ride."

So they were going to run through it again. "My kids'll need a lift home," Tony told him, motioning to the two children waiting in the car.

Charlie said not to worry; his wife would take them later that evening. If.

As Tony climbed back into his car, his stomach told him it wasn't "if." Whether it was Charlie's voice, or a now-or-never feeling, he couldn't pin it down. The kids were reporting on school and friends and their most recent arguments as he said, "Yeah, yeah," — but he couldn't concentrate. Pretty soon he realized they must have caught on, because they shut up. He turned the radio on and told the boy to pick a station. Throughout the rest of the ride he felt as if he were under water.

At Therese's his old friend Gino Martelli, out of prison just two weeks, stopped by. He and Tony opened a couple of beers and sat in the kitchen. Gino was full of gossip, cell talk. He was more than six feet tall, with a face that had been almost pretty before jail. Now the eyes squinted, hidden in their bony sockets. His cheeks and chest looked caved in. Tony let him rattle on.

"Hey," Gino said to Therese when she finally shooed them out of the kitchen. "You're a beautician. How do you like the way the state did me? Didn't have to tip neither."

"It'll grow. Just sprinkle a little beer on it once in a while," she said, laughing, as she moved the centerpiece of orange flowers to the buffet and set the table for twelve. She had heard all the beautician jokes an ex-con can come up with his first days out when he's still hyper around women.

Gino cornered Therese's husband and Tony by the front window. "I gotta tell you the wildest story this guy in my cellblock swears is true. He's a professional burglar. Goes all over. One night he's in this big house like a castle, all covered with ivy, the maid's off, and the baby in the room next to the parents starts crying. So, to keep the kid from wakin' them up, he takes him downstairs, roots in the refrigerator, finds a bottle, heats it, tests it on the wrist and all, you know? And he gives the kid a bottle and puts it back in bed. Got two of his own, you know? Then he gets into the parents' bedroom where he's been tipped the jewels are — he only takes jewels and he knows which ones. Suddenly, he hears a change in breathin' and he looks around and sees the broad. Before he can move, she shakes her head and puts her finger to her mouth like she won't say nothin' or scream and she waves him closer and whispers in his ear. Says she'll give him cash if he kills her old man. So the guy looks over and her old man is sleeping like a baby. So he says if she'll give him the cash, he'll come back and do it, 'cause he can't do it on a burglary, and he gives her some reasons, which she buys. So he gets the cash and leaves. Course he doesn't go back, though he says it crosses his mind to give it to *her*."

The brother-in-law howled, cueing Tony, who had nodded first, until he saw Gino was waiting for a bigger response. But it was as if he was hearing them from the bottom of a well.

Gino made another try. "Who you workin' with, Tony? I gotta keep clean six more months for parole. Then I'm home free. I'll be looking about that time."

"Not working," Tony told him. "Nothin' going down."

Gino nodded; he knew the signs. He left early. Tony said he'd get back to him the middle of next week. It was as if he carried an invisible force field around him that others needed to bump into only once or twice to recognize — and keep their distance.

Charlie arrived, the pulse in his forehead giving away his own state of nerves. He and Tony barely covered their plates with food. Both assured Therese that it wasn't her spaghetti. Something must be going around. At times Tony was thinking with painful clarity. Contingency plans formed and faded in his mind as kids bickered in the background and Therese and Kay exchanged recipes and carried dishes back and forth. If he should be wounded; safety deposit boxes; his lawyer's number; answers for surprise questions; Charlie; Ralphie. Suppose Fargo decided to come over? Or the other guard came back? Playing with gasoline. If they got stopped before.

"No," he said. "I don't need any dessert."

They all laughed but no one asked questions. What you don't know you can't beef on.

At 5:30 Charlie said, "You ready to go?"

Tony replied, "Yeah, ready to go."

They left as they had arrived. Unaware of anything but a cube of steel inside a cube of stone. Tony's chest was tight, his mouth like the morning after, tongue sprouting fuzz. He tried to swallow and tasted oregano.

"Got to get something from my car, put it in yours," Charlie said when they reached the street. He returned with four walkie-talkies and a satchel. In the car, he announced he had a couple of .45s in it.

Tony zipped open the case and glanced at the pistols in the light of the setting sun. So we're equipped for anything. When a bullet from a .45 slams into a man, he stops. For good. Blows a hole as big as a window. Tony didn't much like it. This was supposed to be a class-con operation, but too late for changes now. Maybe something new came up.

The car seemed to find the route by itself. As they left Congress Expressway to get on the Kennedy, Charlie plugged in the scanner. Their tension increased. Tony lit his third cigarette. Finally the Ohio exit. Almost 6:30. Ralphie was expecting them.

They moved past Wells Fargo on the corner of Ohio and Wells. Its buildings were as unimposing as Purolator's, but the Western-style sign tried its best to conjure up the century-old history of gold shipments, stage coaches, horses, and armed guards who always came through. But not tonight, Tony hoped. Not tonight. Neither he nor Charlie said anything as they passed by, but they were thinking the same thing, Tony knew.

Finally they turned on La Salle. They were on the last lap. Charlie had his walkie-talkie on and ready. They stood at a red light. An old lady with a string shopping bag crossed slowly in front of them. The light changed and Tony eased his foot off the brake just as the box shot off some static.

"It's O.K." a voice croaked then.

"I'm going to get the stuff," Charlie said into his box.

"O.K." And the voice went silent.

Charlie put the box on the seat.

This was it.

They turned two corners and then went back south, re-tracing the last six blocks.

"He set off the alarm yet?" Tony asked.

"How the fuck should I know?"

Tony remembered Charlie's comment. "You'd think being a guard's boring enough, they'd jump at the chance to get out. But the lazy bastards. They won't. Nobody wants to work."

And tonight it was going down. Alarm and all. Tony reached over to flick the radio on, but Charlie stopped him. He was feeling it, too. Neither of them liked guns. In 1959, Charlie's brother, Daniel, had died from being shot all to pieces. Charlie, getting five bullets pumped into him at the time, had barely survived. With guns, always a chance of somebody gettin' killed. Tony hadn't used a gun for a long while—didn't like the weight of it in his hand. Guns change the whole feeling, he believed. Once you take a gun out, you're stuck. It's not the same anymore. True, it's easier than being a good burglar. That takes time, planning, alarms know-how, watching and waiting, maybe getting a tip. With a gun you just go in and out. Instant success. Easier, but dangerous. Some guys maybe like the action. But you can end up killing someone when you don't have to. And if you don't get killed yourself, you can get twenty-five years for thirty bucks. It's not worth it. Not when people's natural greed will do the job for you. A little phony I.D. A bargain. An inside man.

But it was too late for new plans. And it was Charlie's show. Tony almost wished he were back living off his fruit stand and printing fake airline tickets. He'd done well. Gino wouldn't have been sent down if he'd stopped when Tony did. Too greedy. No scam goes on forever. But partners won't always listen.

"Charlie, how come you brought in Gushi in the first place?"

"He's a real funny guy. I get a kick being around him. Got great stories to go with that laugh of his, even when we was both back in the Patch."

"You cut him in just for his stories?"

"Hell, no, something as big as this, it don't hurt to have an animal. He can be scary, you know. Keeps people in line. And he brought us Louie."

"Does he know anything?"

"Only to stay by his phone," Charlie said, adding, "Hang a left at Forty-third."

"Wanna tell me when to shit?"

They drove around the block twice before stopping at the garage on Forty-third. Charlie opened the door while Tony parked the car. He closed the garage door behind him and then helped Charlie finish loading the Econoline van. It was already nearly filled with the army duffels, fuses, wicks, cheap suitcases, and a second set of walkie-talkies. The last things they loaded were the plastic bags that Charlie had filled with about one and a half gallons of gasoline each. They took the shape of large hot-water bottles. The sharp smell still hung in the air, and Tony could smell it on his hands. The plastic containers, stacked in shopping bags, rocked gently as Charlie closed first one door and then the other.

"Follow me, but don't talk on the box," Charlie said as he climbed into the van. "Just drive and when we get there sit where I told you. And don't use the box under *any* circumstances. You got it?"

"Try to miss my car backing out," Tony said. He opened

the garage door for Charlie to leave, then shut it behind him. He climbed into his own car, aware of the pistols on the seat beside him. He knew they wouldn't do any good if they got trapped in the vault. Only Pete Gushi'd be crazy enough to try a movie stunt. But Charlie said the guns might come in handy if they ran into any thieves. Afterward. On both sides of the law.

Tony's car stalled once before lurching out into the street behind Charlie. He needed a cigarette. But he could still smell gasoline. Suddenly, Tony's box made a squawk. He worriedly searched the street for what Charlie had seen, felt around the seat for the talkie, and then hit the button.

"What's wrong for Chrissake?"

"How do I look?" Charlie asked.

"What the fuck you mean 'look'?" Tony peered at the dirty back windows of the van, then realized that Charlie was pointing to the cap on his head, just like the one that Purolator drivers wore.

"Oh. Just like the real thing," Tony said. A small detail, but no detail is too small, Tony thought. Thinking about details is what puts the real pro up there above the street thief.

When they were a few blocks away from Purolator, Tony held his box close to wait for Charlie's exchange with Ralphie. The slushy sound of the transmitter filled the car like sick breathing. Slowly they passed the alley leading to a Purolator garage entrance. Tony could barely see the dim outline of the huge doors through which millions of dollars passed daily. Finally the van pulled out of sight as it circled the block again, leaving Tony alone, parked now on Huron facing west. Purolator was behind him, across La Salle. Charlie was on his own.

Minutes later Charlie's voice broke out of the walkie-talkie making Tony start.

"One to two. I'm ready." His words were tense, strung

together on an invisible wire of energy between the van and Ralphie guarding all that money inside.

Ralphie didn't answer.

Charlie couldn't enter that blind alley until Ralphie had signaled permission. Tony put his foot a fraction closer to the gas pedal. He edged nearer the window to see Charlie turning the corner onto Huron, going past the front entrance.

"One to two." That would probably be Charlie's last attempt to reach Ralphie. His voice sounded as if he might be close to cracking. Silence.

Then Ralphie's voice. "Two to one."

"I'm right here," Charlie said, as the van turned south on La Salle out of Tony's sight. He could imagine it pulling up to the door. Seconds ticked. Then Charlie once more.

"Is everything O.K.?"

Ralph: "Yes."

"I'm right here. Open the fuckin' door right now. Right now."

Was the second "right now" to keep Ralphie from backing out at the last minute? Tony could almost see the metal door slowly open, the olive green van disappear as if the building itself had sucked it in. He watched the building in his rearview mirror. Would the van come right on out again, or not?

The waiting began.

As Tony clicked off his ignition he realized he'd been holding his breath and let out a long sigh. If there was one thing he'd learned from cons, it was how to wait. No. It's different, he thought. Damn different when you got two automatics in the car and another guy's I.D. And Huron is one creepy street at night when you're sitting in it all alone. Waiting. The back of your neck a target.

He didn't like the idea that Purolator was only one block

over from the police station, four blocks away from Wells Fargo. Their lights must be flashing by now. Would they come? Just to break the pattern of not showing up?

He could feel the muscles in his neck cramp but he couldn't drag his eyes away from the rearview mirror. Nothing there yet. Not a word from Charlie. *Wells Fargo was staying home.* The vault must be open by now.

Christ, he thought. This is for real. *We're in.*

Then he saw a car turn onto Huron two blocks back. His hands tensed on the wheel as he identified it as an unmarked police car. Out cruising. Passing Purolator now, getting closer. In the light of the streetlamp he could see that one of the cops, maybe both, was black. That was a big help. Black cops didn't like to ask a white guy what he was doing when he didn't look like he was doing anything.

He forced himself to look straight ahead, past the mirror. What if they stopped? Damn guns. His shirt was sticking to his back and he cursed his leather jacket. Now they were about even with him, still crawling — like a cat-and-mouse game. He could feel their eyes on him, taking in the car, the closed offices, and the shuttered businesses. They rolled past, then backed up. Trying to get a make on the plates? On him? He forced himself to glance their way. Three seconds he held their gaze, then looked straight ahead. Forced himself to swallow. Finally they pulled away but took a right at the corner. Good chance they'd be back. And he couldn't leave. They might be waiting right around the corner to see if they'd scared him off or something. Then they'd know. And Charlie locked inside. He'd have to stay and sweat it out. But not with the heat for company.

Tony pushed the door open and reached for the guns under the seat. The case came out with a half-eaten Clark bar sticking to it. Damn kids. If he'd told them once . . . he threw the candy in the gutter and looked frantically around for a place to stash the pistols and the walkie-talkies. He'd be clean if the cops came back for a closer look. He hesitated about removing the walkie-talkies, then decided if Charlie called him with the cops there he couldn't have one on anyway. Not worth taking the chance of having him squawk in the middle of it all.

He had to move. He grabbed Charlie's sweater, wallet, and I.D. and dumped them with the other stuff on the curb behind a little garbage can. Then he dived back in the car to wait. He was having trouble swallowing when the sudden image of the squashed candy bar made his stomach lurch. Damned if he'd ever eat a Clark bar again. He put his watch to his ear feeling suddenly adrift in time. Then he watched the second hand drag its way through a minute. His mirror view showed the same car turning the corner behind him and his thoughts began colliding with one another as if zinging in from different parts of his mind. Maybe he should have called Charlie. Warned him. No. Sit tight. But his rap sheet was twice as long as anyone else's. Suppose they called in his license? Still, he ought to be able to con a couple of cops. If you toughed it out you didn't need heat.

Sure enough, they were creeping up on him again. And again he forced himself to look past the rearview mirror, to take in the dimly lit Chicago landscape, to begin counting the parking meters that lined the deserted streets like sentries. He had trouble lighting a cigarette — he couldn't feel his hands.

This time the car moved at normal speed. Were they still watching him? They nosed into his peripheral line of vision, going faster now. Away from him. He sat rigid until he was sure they could no longer see him in their rearview mirror.

He blew out a puff of smoke, his mouth hot. He touched the medal around his neck. You need the luck of St. Dismas in this business, he thought. He thanked God for a patron saint for thieves.

Tony returned to the garbage can and gathered up the guns, walkie-talkies, and Charlie's belongings. He pushed one of the .45s into his belt, where it felt cold. He put the other one in his jacket pocket, then patted the first to make sure the timing device was still safe. He put the walkie-talkies back on the seat and turned one on. Charlie'd been inside for twenty minutes already. What was going on in there? Would he ever get inside? He never did like having the time to figure out how he got there in the first place. He had one rule: what might have been never was.

3

Taylor Street's Alumni: Capone to Marzano

CHICAGO: NO SECOND CITY IN CRIME

Once again the city of Al Capone, Sam Giancana, et al. has taken over first place. Boston's 1950 Brink's robbery now drops to second after this weekend's robbery of $3.9 million from Purolator Security Company, Inc.

— October 22, 1974,
Miami Herald

Chicago is still a patchwork of Europe, a quilt of ethnically separate neighborhoods more segregated than those of almost any other city in the country. In a sense, where you grow up determines what you will be. Tony Marzano lived for most of his early years on Taylor Street, a largely Italian, working-class neighborhood about half a mile west of the Loop. Al Capone, Frank Caruso, and Sam Giancana, in their time, had grown up in the same locality and received their education on the same street corners.

William Anthony Marzano was born in Cicero on January 20, 1943. When Tony was seven, and his sister Therese four, their father was injured in a steel-mill accident, and died of cancer less than a year later. The insurance money — $10,000 in 1950 dollars — would have gone a long way except for the fact that the money had been left in the hands of Tony's paternal grandfather, who invested some of it in the wrong places and loaned the rest to the wrong people, including himself. When Tony was nine, his maternal grandmother died and he left Cicero to join his mother and his younger sister in one of the city's slum-clearance projects on Roosevelt Street.

For the widow and her two children, it was a terrifying place — a black apartment project with only one other white family. Tony seldom dared go outdoors until, within the year, Mrs. Marzano was able to qualify for another apartment on Taylor Street. Tony, at the age of nine, had come to his real home.

Today the area is dominated by the vast, granite campus of the University of Illinois at Chicago Circle, one of Mayor Richard Daley's grandiose building efforts, and the small Italian streets that remain on its skirts seem drained and quiet. But in the 1950s it was like other big-city paisano neighborhoods — Little Italy in New York, the North End in Boston — a tough, noisy, garlicky, fermenting place where you learned civics in front of Whitey's Pizza Palace, business skills in the alleys, and sex education in Peanut Park.

Crap games floated from back stoop to back stoop; street vendors pushed wooden carts with wares of pistachio nuts, olives, lupine seeds, or lemonade. At twilight the older boys, five or six of them, might take a girl off to the bushes in the park. Tony and the younger boys would sit on the curb and describe to one another what they thought was going on in the darkness over there. One morning a stranger (not from the neighborhood) would come out to find his car missing.

Two or three weeks later, it would turn up stripped clean. Knots of young men clogged street corners, girls paraded by, the sounds of radios filtered down from a hundred tenement windows — Taylor Street was always crowded and always moving.

Chicago has two summer climates — there is the one on the lakeshore, where the breeze comes off Lake Michigan to comfort the well-to-do in Streeter's Landing and the Near North Side; and there is another in the steamy hinterland of brick and asphalt. On Taylor Street it would be slightly cooler in the streets than in the narrow wooden houses or the cramped apartments, and everybody lived more or less on the porches and the sidewalks. It was Naples West.

If you could steal a pipe wrench, you could use it to break a cast-iron cap on one of the fire hydrants on Taylor Street. Then, with the help of an angled board, you created a geyser, a shower, and a small river in the gutter.

Eventually a cop would come around to shut off the hydrant, but after he was gone the kids would hit the next one down the street. Others helped the bigger guys loosen hubcaps — working their way up to stickups, store robberies, and home burglaries — but *never on home territory*. This had been drummed into them as kids — "never our own neighbors or our own people." They had learned about the police, too — who didn't really count in this part of town. Everybody knew that the politicians were making sure that the deserving got jobs and probation, and the syndicate was making sure that the undeserving got quick justice and that the exchange system of payoffs worked smoothly.

Tony started hanging around the Wall when he was about eleven. It was four feet high, built of brick, and very good for leaning against while you worked out plans for the next shoplifting job. It was also a good lookout post from which to spot a wino down the street reeling toward some alley where he could be jackrolled. The Wall was grammar school.

When Tony was fourteen the social athletic club in an abandoned storefront became his high school. Going to local dances was a big part of it — for the girls and the music and the fights. That was where you established your status. But where you established your combat record was on the street corners, or at street carnivals — usually sponsored by churches — outside the borders of Taylor Street. Most of the small wars were Italy versus Puerto Rico, and when a dozen Italian boys would come back some night limping and bloody from a Puerto Rican social affair, they could always mobilize fifty to a hundred new recruits, a few cars, blackjacks, and knives to head back with them. Those who couldn't fit into a car took the C.T.A.

Despite the discouragements, ten to fifteen Puerto Rican families moved into and stayed on in the Jane Addams Project on Taylor Street. The Italians had one goal. Move them out. One summer day, when Our Lady of Pompeii took over the entire length of Lytle Street for its annual carnival, somebody passed a remark about greaseballs and somebody else came back with an observation about dagos and that led to one of the most devastating evenings Taylor Street had ever seen. At the height of the battle, several Puerto Ricans in a car came careening into the crowded street and somebody threw a perfect strike with a Molotov cocktail right through their window.

The ambulance and the fire engine arrived too late — a long time after the fireball had died out and the screaming had stopped. Four young men died. The remaining families moved out. It was the first time that Tony, watching from a safe distance, had ever seen anyone killed.

About this time Tony had his first run-in with the law and the courts. After appearing before the same judge twenty-seven times for truancy, he was sentenced to three months in a parental school. On his third day, he was mopping the floor of the cafeteria when a guard came to get him, saying, "You're sprung, the warden got a call." This was also his first taste of Chicago clout — thanks to his aunt who had a friend who knew someone.

In a matter of hours he was back on the streets shoplifting by day and borrowing cars by night, burning the paper off the tinfoil from cigarette packs to make a connection to start cars. He and his friends didn't yet know how to open car trunks, so they used to rip out the back seat to get to the tires. One day he noticed that a yellow '54 Buick belonging to Mike DeStefano, a big syndicate operator, had been sitting on his street for a couple of days. He and an older friend made plans to take it for a ride that night, but the friend got drunk and Tony lost his nerve. The next day the police pried open the trunk and found DeStefano there — murdered gangland style. That was a joy ride Tony was glad he missed. However, more stolen cars resulted in another pickup, and this time he and three friends spent thirty days in the Audy Home while waiting for a court date. When his case came up he was again released to his family because one of his friend's family had contacts.

During this period he committed his first so-called armed robbery. Dino, a friend of his, had a job collecting money from the vending machines in Union Station and he and Tony decided to stage a robbery. Tony and a few more friends from the corner took Dino behind some machines and roughed him up a little — torn shirt, scratched face, just a little blood — nothing too bad, and took off with a bag of change that must have weighed almost twenty-five pounds. It was his first counting job.

They had just finished rolling up the $1500 in coins in a Taylor Street basement when the local juvenile officer stuck his head in the door to say the police were looking for them.

Dino had caved in and ratted on them when the police began their questioning. Tony stashed away about $200 in his mattress and turned himself and the rest of the money in. It hurt, but it got him probation instead of another stay in Audy waiting for a sentence to come down. Again, Chicago clout, in the form of a sympathetic juvenile officer, saved the day.

When Tony was fifteen he dropped out of public school, a nominal withdrawal because he hadn't been around much for the three years past. In the curriculum of the streets, he was now a senior.

When he was seventeen his mother moved the family back to Cicero, but in his heart Tony never went along. Daily he'd sneak a ride on a bus back to Taylor Street, to Whitey's Pizza Palace, where the gang was waiting on the corner. One friend or another sometimes gave him a bed for the night. Occasionally they took time out to catch "The Untouchables" on TV starring Robert Stack as Elliot Ness, who caught everybody but the big guys. For Tony and his friends the video tales of Al Capone and other Prohibition-era gangsters were not an escape into fantasy but a vision of the same streets they'd momentarily left to come inside for some beer and laughs. Invariably there was someone in the neighborhood who had known the gangsters whose impersonators were now shooting it out on a small screen. Someone who had shaken their hands once or who had once ducked into a doorway to avoid real gunfire back in the 1920s. When pressure forced the TV program to use fewer Italian surnames, the Taylor Street gang still recognized old favorites from the past. Then there were the tough guys in the movies, James Cagney, Edward G. Robinson, and Humphrey Bogart, setting a high standard for the kids of Taylor Street. Tony saw the movie about the Brink's robbery, *Six Bridges to Cross* starring Tony Curtis, six times.

During the 1960s Tony discovered the world of scams,

which appealed more to a young man with a distaste for guns and a lot of easygoing charm. He decided he preferred the "construction" business to the risks run by local hoods, such as Roger Touhy, gunned down after twenty-five years in prison, practically in Tony's front yard. (Someone had surmised he was going to write a too-complete autobiography.)

Tony's version of construction included an office, a telephone, and a young receptionist. He would run a few ads, offering to build garages, rooms, bomb shelters, for a very reasonable fee. When the calls came in, Tony would go out and sell the interested home owners on his specialty until they parted with a down payment. If they ever saw any construction work, it was a hole in the back yard dug by a day laborer Tony had sent over. When the finally outraged client complained, the police would find an empty office and a young receptionist who pled that she had been hired by phone and never saw her employer. Sometimes the "remodeling" offer could include a good buy on brick or on storm windows, or on something else once part of a freight consignment that had never quite reached its destination.

Tony had another scam at the airport — moving from ticket counter to ticket counter, buying genuine tickets, with checks on imaginary bank accounts, from American at one end all the way to Braniff at the other. Then he would peddle the tickets at half price. Tony had discovered the ability to stand perfectly still, heart doing a drum roll against his ribs, while airline personnel put their heads together deciding whether to cash his check. When the airlines began to issue their own credit cards with a $200 or $300 limit, Tony and his partner, Gino, could spend all day at an airport making a real haul in tickets and quick-turnover sales.

When the limits were lowered, they invented new identities with temporary bank accounts and got new credit cards, emptying the accounts as often as they "burned out" each card. Ingenuity allowed them to stay ahead of each scam's inevitable detection. One day Tony noticed the new ticket machines at the airport.

"Listen, Gino," he said with the joy of discovery that might have filled the heart of Thomas Alva Edison, "Let's make our own tickets."

"Sure," Gino said, "I got a ball-point." But he finally agreed to try to figure out how they could get hold of either large amounts of blank tickets or — the machine. Only one answer: burglarize a travel agency; steal a machine; make their own plates in the name of a fake travel agency. They could also burglarize another travel agency and steal *its* plate for *their* machine. It worked for eight months and brought in more than $100,000.

They peddled the tickets through bartenders, who found an incredible number of people who liked a travel bargain with their drinks. The operation became so successful others assumed it was operated by the mob and didn't try to horn in. But, as Tony correctly estimated, even the best of schemes must end. Gino didn't agree. Tony pulled out, but Gino continued to supply the bartenders. Eventually the police had 195 angry witnesses whose bargain tickets had been rejected by stung and now wary airlines. The witnesses were shown two photographs — one of Tony and one of Gino. They all picked Gino as the swindler. Toward the end, he had taken to peddling the tickets himself. It's hard, he later told Tony ruefully, to stop making money in your basement.

During this period the banks began mailing out *their* new discovery for coining money: bank charge cards for the person who buys now and, the banks hope, pays much, much later, like 18 percent interest later. For Tony and his friends the banks' generosity was their bonanza. The charge cards reimbursed store owners a maximum of $50 for sales they had inadvertently made to persons with stolen cards, or cards whose owners had exceeded their limit. In the earliest days, even when a careful store owner called the police and named an individual, the police didn't know on what charge to arrest that person. They often resorted to calling the banks, which would send out an investigator.

In the meantime it wasn't difficult for Tony and friends, armed with forty to fifty credit cards garnered from junkies, kids, and mailboxes, to walk out of a store with merchandise equal to $50 a card, and the owner's blessing. He would put in for the $50 (his markup having been almost 100 percent); the credit-card group could then find someone else who would take forty to fifty jackets off their hands for $15 or so each. Matters progressed to a point where groups began to trade cards and customers in order to start all over again. One store made $175,000 from stolen credit cards, their merchandise sales guaranteed by the bank cards. The banks lost $60 million to $70 million in 1966 and 1967 until they learned to parcel out their charge machines more selectively to the stores with less larcenous owners.

Between ingenuities, and spending sprees, Tony worked as a bartender in a friend's bar for some steady cash and legitimate income. Across the street was a clothing store that required a customer to press a buzzer in order to be let in. Regular merchandise was stacked in glass cabinets beneath glass shelves, but the owner was known to be "connected." Larry, the owner, came in the bar sometimes and he learned something about Tony's general background. One day he asked Tony to stop in to see him about a favor.

Tony made it his business to drop in soon after. Doing a favor for a man in the Outfit can only result in good will. After the amenities, Larry said, "My boss likes a certain Tiffany lamp he saw. It seems it costs five thou, which is about five thou more than he wants to spend. Could you get it for me?"

Before Tony could explain that burglary wasn't exactly his line, Larry suddenly reached behind the counter and hauled an enormous set of bolt cutters onto the glass surface. Tony knew it was used to pop open big locks or bolts.

"Christ," Tony said. "I don't need snips. I'll check it out — see what I can do."

"And you can pick out any suit you want and . . ."

"Forget it," Tony said quickly. "And I'll be seeing you."

The next day, Tony and his friend Giovanni, posing as customers, went to case the Rush Street antique store. They didn't like the number of cops regularly cruising the area. A few minutes later, as they stood under the blue glow of the lamp, which was chained and bolted to the ceiling, they began to wonder if the burglary was worth the risk — until the owner remarked that he didn't really care whether he sold the shade because he made extra money renting it out to photography studios.

One week, one small office in Cicero, one new telephone number, one bank account, and a set of crisp business cards later, Tony called and arranged to rent the shade. Then he and Giovanni sat around the office playing cards and drinking beer until the shop called to confirm the studio's number. Another friend went in to put $100 down and to hold the ladder while the owner climbed up and carefully undid the chain from the ceiling.

Tony returned to the clothing shop with the carefully wrapped shade under his arm and was buzzed in.

"How'd you do it?" the owner asked.

"The guy just handed it over," Tony said.

Larry's eyes popped. "He handed it to you?" He insisted on more details, obviously picturing a stickup.

Tony explained.

"That's class," Larry said. Again Larry offered some mer-chandise, but Tony refused. A favor is a favor, he said. Larry nodded.

Business went on as usual — with time off here and there for a little sun. If you were in Tony's trade, you usually took some time off in the winter to warm up in Miami or Fort Lauderdale — with a girl friend rather than your wife. Tony insisted that his friends drive down whenever possible. In 1960 what was then the worst air disaster ever took place when a United DC-8 collided with a TWA Super Constella-tion over New York Harbor. The DC-8 was from Chi-cago — Tony's proof that it wasn't safe to fly out of his city or into any other. He avoided all airplanes until October 1974, when he finally boarded a very small one for a million good reasons.

Tony had not seen anybody from his father's family for most of these years, though the Marzano name was known well enough around Taylor Street — there were thirteen uncles who bore it. But most of the Marzanos lived over in Bridgeport — called the Patch — which was twenty-five blocks away from Taylor. One day in 1973 Tony was read-ing a newspaper and the name suddenly caught his eye. Right there in the *Sun-Times*. A certain Pasquale Charles Marzano had been arrested along with a Wells Fargo secu-rity man, Ralph Marrera, in connection with the theft of $800,000 in gold from a jewelry store. Although not enough evidence was turned up to show beyond a doubt that Pas-quale and his friend and the gold had departed from the store together, Marrera was subsequently released from his job after an inconclusive lie detector test.

Tony wondered if this Pasquale Charles was one of the cousins he used to see years ago racing the streets in a souped-up car on Saturday night. If he was the same, that

Charlie had been fourteen years older than Tony, one of the big guys.

In 1974, burdened by alimony and child support, Tony had to find gainful employment in order to make ends meet. A friend named Johnny owned a small cartage company, so Tony bought a 1970 White diesel truck and began to do hauling.

One Saturday morning when Tony pulled his truck into the lot, Johnny yelled for him to come over to the office. Johnny was just handing a check to a short, stocky man and, when Tony came up, he said, "You guys got the same family name; you related?"

The other driver looked at Tony closely. "What's your first name?"

Tony told him. Mother's name? Tony told him. "You got a sister, pretty bone blonde, name of Therese?" Tony nodded.

The man punched Tony on the arm. "Whadya think of that? My uncle is your grandfather! I'm Charlie."

"I saw you written up in the paper a few months ago."

Charlie ignored that and began to ask a lot of catch-up questions. Then he suddenly stopped and said, "Hey, take a ride with me back to the old neighborhood and we'll go see my father."

Where Charlie took them was the Patch, which borders Chinatown at Thirty-first and Canal. He parked in front of an old building and led the way into a gray-painted entrance hall. Somewhere somebody was browning meat and onions in olive oil and the air was rich as sauce. Radiators clanked. Behind one door kids were arguing and one of them began to cry. All of it was like old times for Tony. He followed along after Charlie to the Marzano door and inside the room.

When Mr. Marzano appeared, Tony thought he was

looking at his own grandfather — there were the same full lips, bald head and caved-in eyes. "So? Danny's son," he said when Charlie introduced them. "Come inna kitchen and have something to drink. This calls for a drink."

Tony and Charlie sat at the oilcloth-covered table while the old man filled three cheese glasses from a straw-encased bottle of Chianti, got out Italian bread and salami, made some sandwiches, and offered one to Tony on the end of a knife.

A long family-events session followed. Tony showed them pictures of his two children. Mr. Marzano went into the marriages, births, and deaths of uncles and aunts and cousins Tony could scarcely recall. Tony explained about his divorce. Mr. Marzano remembered some stories of Tony and Therese as kids.

As Tony and Charlie were leaving, Mr. Marzano, tears in his eyes, gave Tony a big *abbraccio*, and made him promise to come back.

He hadn't mentioned the fact that his eldest brother had done away with all of Tony's mother's money. And Tony hadn't mentioned it either.

After that Tony and Charlie ran into each other a lot. Had breakfast together at the diner. Played a little handball at the Y. Got the kids together, Tony bringing his over to Charlie's house in Berwyn on Sundays, or Charlie bringing his over to Therese's, where Tony now lived.

In August that year somebody ripped off Tony's truck from the cartage company lot. None of his friends could get a line on where it might have ended up. So Tony had $12,000 in insurance money but no job. He began to drink too much coffee in the daytime and too much liquor at night. Charlie would take him along on some of his long hauls now and then and Tony made a little out of that, but not enough to go far. They talked about starting their own trucking place.

One day as they were coming back from a haul and pulling into Johnny's lot, Charlie suddenly asked if Tony was interested in some fast money. Tony skillfully backed the truck into place and turned the ignition off.

"Depends on what I got to do." Tony had heard the question before from most of the guys on the street but usually nothing had come of it.

"Count some money is all." Charlie sat looking at him.

"And I get?"

"Twenty-five, maybe thirty big ones."

"For that much, I can count like an adding machine all day."

Afterward, as he sat at the bar in Faces, Tony thought it over. Half the men Tony knew talked about big scores — most of it bullshit. If there were any truth in it every time somebody said, "I got this big score going down," then every store and bank vault in Chicago would be flapping open. And most of the operations somebody did get started got fucked up halfway through.

But Charlie wasn't that kind of talker. He'd never spoken about any other jobs. Charlie always meant what he said.

Still, it might be his way of saying something might come up some day. Might do you a favor sometime, Tony.

Usually a man stuck with the crew he was used to and didn't bring in outsiders. Now and then a specialist was needed, so the crew took him in. But Tony wasn't a specialist. Anybody can count bills. So he wasn't exactly sure what Charlie was saying or how he stood with Charlie.

But, he remembered, before they had got out of the truck, Charlie had simply nodded and said, "You're in."

In what?

During the next few weeks, although he helped Charlie shop for duffels, garbage bags, and odds and ends, he came no closer to knowing the plan's details. But when Charlie took him to the garage where Tony would help with the counting, Tony shook his head. "I don't know what's going down but this ain't the place," he said. "That alley behind there is full of people, even cops, goin' by. They see a light in a garage at night, for Chrissake, they'll wonder. No. I got a friend with a basement and a garage, not too far from here. Let me show you."

Charlie finally agreed to look over the new location.

"See?" Tony said, showing him around. "We can black out the windows with a couple of layers of crepe paper; put a table down, chairs. Nothin' but privacy. And Frank gets a little rent money."

Charlie looked around, hesitating.

"He's a real good friend," Tony added. "Got a family, kids, everything. We tell him now?" Tony went away and brought Frank back with him.

Charlie said, "But it's gotta stay empty every Sunday night until I say otherwise. In fact, it's gotta stay empty, period. Nobody down here from now on."

Frank and Tony nodded. Now there were two of them who didn't know what was going on.

4

The Method: Men
and Madness

NEW NAMES IN CAST OF BIG CRIME DRAMA

In one short week six individuals, most of them known here-
tofore only on various police blotters, have achieved international renown as the small-time operators whom police now
credit with pulling off the biggest heist in the history of
America.

Capone, Accardo, Battaglia, and Giancana — names so
frequently associated with crime in Chicago — have suddenly
been replaced with the unfamiliar Marrera, Maniatis, Gushi,
DiFonzo, Marzano, and Marzano.

— October 30, 1974,
Chicago Tribune

September 23, 1974. Marrera was already wolfing down
bacon and eggs when Tony and Charlie entered Connie's
Restaurant the Monday after their first dry run. Tony slid
into the booth, first brushing the crumbs away. "Hey
Ralphie," he said.

Ralph's pleasant face creased in a grin.

Charlie was looking around, tapping his fingers on the table. "Where's Barb? I'm starved."

"Don't your wife make breakfast ever, Charlie? I thought that was why we guys stayed married." Tony felt good. Here was their inside man. Excitement zipped through him.

Barb wore a tight red uniform trimmed with white lace. She stood next to Tony, passing out silverware, water, and hot coffee.

"Listen to this, Barb. What does a four-hundred-pound parrot say?" Ralphie was biting his lip for control.

"Make it fast," Barb said, her hand on her hip.

"Polly want a cracker, *nowwwwww.*" Ralphie laughed louder than all of them. "My kid told me that," he said. "Cracked me up."

Ralph Marrera, thirty-one, tall and dark, with an air of Italian geniality, was a solid citizen who owned a parking lot, a Berwyn duplex, a gas station, and an interest in the New Ritz, a fleabag hotel located a block north of the Chicago Police headquarters on South State Street. He must have been an example of incredible frugality if all this real estate derived from his $4.30-an-hour security guard salary.

Ralph wiped up the last of his egg with a small triangle of toast and got up to leave. "See ya," he said.

Later, at the railroad yard, Charlie filled Tony in on Marrera's background and the rest of the operation. "Marrera had a little trouble when he was workin' for Wells Fargo back a ways. So he left them and got a job working the alarm board at Purolator until he was promoted to guarding the vaults. He began volunteering to work Saturday and Sunday nights. Everybody liked that."

Tony wondered if Marrera's going to Purolator had been laid down long ago as the first step, but he didn't ask.

Charlie continued. "So for months Marrera's been opening and closing the vault, setting off the alarm, sometimes two or three times in one night. Each time a signal flashes to

Wells Fargo and one of the guards phones and sends a messenger. 'What the hell's going on?' the guy asks. 'Nothing,' he tells him. If he decides to let the messenger in, all he sees is Ralphie eating a sandwich. Or else he signs a little slip they pass through a door slot. If they try to break in, he's supposed to shoot 'em down. Right? They got no key. I mean, how does he know they're really from Wells Fargo if they're trying to break into his vault? Right? They see his hardware. He gives them a joke to take back. Routine."

"So how does he open the vault?" Tony wondered if Charlie was putting him on. Routine his ass.

Charlie smirked. "He uses the combination." Then he added, seeing the look on Tony's face, "No kidding. Best thing you can have to a vault is the combination. Specially when nobody knows you got it." Four trucks moved away just then and they pulled up in line for their piggyback load.

"So who gives him the combination?" Tony asked.

"Mr. Joseph I. Woods himself. Brother to Nixon's loyal secretary. You heard of Rose Mary? Probably gets him Nixon's old suits to wear."

Charlie explained how a few months back they combed the office of Joseph Woods, former Cook County sheriff and now a senior vice president of Purolator, looking for the vault combination, being super careful to leave no trace of entry and search. Eventually they found the slip of paper tucked into a desk drawer. Ralphie had held the flashlight and read off the numbers as Charlie copied them down. Then they'd put the paper back. The files had looked very interesting, in a Republican sort of way, but there hadn't been time for any real reading.

Tony nodded. That part of the operation made sense.

Then came stage two, according to Charlie: getting Wells Fargo accustomed to blinking alarm lights that eventually were attributed to an electrical short, or intermittent power failure, the only logical explanation.

"Of course, the Wells Fargo guys get teed off. 'When the Christ you gonna fix that thing?' they wanta know. Ralphie points out that ain't his responsibility. And here's the best part. This one time the guard don't come. *He don't come.*" Charlie shook his head, still loving the story.

"So the next Sunday, Ralphie does the same thing. And again Wells Fargo don't come. They give Ralphie a call, just to tell him where to put his wires, but they don't come."

"So Ralphie's all alone in there?"

"No, no." Charlie shifted and moved up a place in line. Stage three went into action about the same time as stage two: getting Ralphie's two fellow guards used to leaving him alone at odd times during the week and on Sunday nights.

"The hardest part for Ralphie," Charlie said, "is getting them out for a sandwich or some Danish, then running over, twirling the dial, opening the vault door, closing it, and getting back in time to answer Wells Fargo. Trying not to breathe heavy over the phone. When he sets the alarm off on Sundays, it's easier 'cause he already sent the other two on their way, or at least the alarm-board watcher. The messenger stays in the garage, or upstairs, for coffee, so he don't see nothin' anyway. It's easy to get him to take in a pornoflick down the street. The girl, her husband don't mind comin' to get her early." Charlie laughed. "So they pocket their four bucks an hour for doin' nothing. Everybody likes to do a little taking on the side." They now noticed that their truck was up next.

Tony was ready. They'd try it again. Sunday. Only now it was real to him. He had a feeling that last Sunday was meant to come up dry.

Early in October Charlie brought Tony along to meet Pete Gushi in his new Worth, Illinois, discount store. Gushi's office, a plywood square set off from the rest of the sales area, looked as though it had been decorated with one item from each of the many store aisles. On a nail hung a picture of an angelic, goiter-eyed boy, with his arm thrown around the neck of a benign Lassie-type dog; a fake Tiffany lamp teetered on a card table; two matching chairs, their seats concave and grimy, rested on two throw rugs with a pile thin as cardboard. Papers, telephone books, catalogues, and garishly covered paperbacks filled steel shelves and covered three gray file cabinets, one locked. Gushi had his feet propped on an office desk that boasted a snow-scene paperweight holding down a John D. MacDonald mystery. As Tony and Charlie entered, Pete remained tilted back in his chair, but he removed his unlit cigarette for a salute.

"Wait'll you hear his stories," Charlie said to Tony by way of introduction.

"Stories? Whadya mean stories. It's my fuckin' life," Pete screeched.

Charlie motioned Tony to one of the chairs. Just as he was about to sit, Pete flung his feet off the desk. "Don't!" he yelled.

Tony jumped.

"We gotta do an errand," Pete said. "Come on."

As he passed one of the clerks on the way out, he paused. "I'm gone for five," he said, giving her a pat on the rump. "She's new," he told Tony and Charlie as they left the store and headed down the sidewalk.

Pete was a big man, more than six feet, with no flab. Behind his thick glasses his eyes seemed to strain, as if he was trying not to miss much; in fact, what he didn't miss, he instigated.

About a block away, he pushed open the doors to a small butcher shop. A man behind the counter was trimming a piece of beef, layers of transparent fat peeling off under his razor-sharp knife. He stopped when they entered.

"Hey, Pete, what's it today?" He wiped his hands on his apron, ready.

"Gimme three steaks, Jimmy," Pete said, peering into the meat cases. "Porterhouse. And cut them new. I don't want anything the flies been chewin' on for two days." Jimmy quickly closed the case he'd just opened and went back to the meat locker.

"Ever see a meat locker?" Pete asked Tony. "Oughta see one once in your life. Looks like the St. Valentine's Day Massacre. Jimmy here'll give you a tour some day. Gimme two pounds sausage, too. And a couple roasts for the old lady."

Jimmy expertly trimmed and wrapped the meat while Pete kept up a running line of chatter. White packages appeared on top of the counter. "That'll be fifty-five sixty-three," Jimmy said. "It's prime beef." He counted out the change. "I'll be coming over to your new store soon. Been meaning to give you some of my business."

"Don't do it," Pete shot back. He leaned toward Jimmy. "Do yourself a favor. Stay the fuck away. My prices are too high. I'll have to beat you on 'em, same as you do me." Then he laughed the same laugh that Tony had come to expect from Charlie's description.

Jimmy just stood behind his counter not knowing whether to laugh or to hide in his meat locker, wondering what kind of business Pete was really in. The corners of his mouth twitched neighborly as Pete gave Charlie a push to leave.

"Got me a new barbecue out back," he said. As soon as they reached his place, he broke open a bag of charcoal, spilled some quick starter on it, and set it blazing. Then he called a stock boy to watch it and to tell him when the fire was ready. As he led Tony and Charlie back toward his office, the ringing wall phone stopped him in his tracks. He turned back and picked up the phone. Tony and Charlie waited by the counter. Two ladies in matching curlers, different head scarves, waited for the clerk to finish filling a bag with their purchases.

Pete spoke around his cigarette into the receiver. "Yeah?" Silence. "Larry, you bastard, where the hell you been? I need your help settin' up this stuff and you're still home fuckin' around. Been three days for Chrissake." A pause. "Stop the goddamn blubbering. Can't understand a fuckin' word." Pete winked at Tony and Charlie, as if making them party to another good story. The two women had stopped talking.

"Christ, can't you keep a wife in line? Listen, she gives you any lip, use an ice pick on the fuckin' broad and stick it to her—you hear?" He hung up and laughed. The two women stared at him, one of them starting to titter. "The dumb shit, he thinks I mean it." Pete laughed again, this time for the women in his audience. "Give 'em anything they want," he said to the clerk, waving at the women as if glad they could appreciate a good joke.

Pete Gushi had been questioned about an unsolved ice-pick murder last spring, then let go. Pete was a smart guy with a lot of connections, according to Charlie. But the question was, Could Charlie control a nut with a thing for ice picks?

Pete settled them back in his office, Tony and Charlie each with a vodka and tonic, Pete with Grand Marnier on ice and the Martell he used as a chaser. He leaned back in his chair, his glasses catching the light, magnifying his eyes. He was still going on about the kid, speaking around his cigarette. "That Larry. He's supposed to be helping me set up this kinda business. You know? But I don't think he's got the nerves to keep selling stuff. Jumps at every little thing."

Pete waved his cigarette. "Just a few weeks ago, he comes

across the street where I'm havin' lunch and looks jumpy as a cat. He hands me forty-five hundred dollars and says, "This is the last time." Can you beat that? The last time. So I told him, 'You can do it one more fuckin' time.' 'Cause he's been bringing in the money pretty good, you know? He really has been sellin' the stuff. And now he says it's the last time."

"Larry's all right," Charlie said. "He's still only a kid. What is he, twenty-eight?"

"I don't know," Gushi said, shaking his head, ashes falling on his chest. "He looks at me like I'm gonna eat him alive. Maniatis may be old, but at least he ain't got the shakes. Speaking of which, Charlie-boy, you use that van yet? Hope you're not just usin' it to cart around your Little League shits." Pete glanced at Tony.

"It'll get used," Charlie said, impassive.

"Take me with you, Charlie. I want to go out in a big way. I'm bored as hell."

Charlie, covering Tony, shrugged. "If I won't take my own blood, you know I'm not takin' anybody."

"Just let me hold a couple guns. Blow somebody away. I need a little excitement." He laughed wildly, gesturing with the cigarette.

"Look. You just take care of the boat, keep DiFonzo on ice, and come Sunday, Monday morning, stay home by the phone. It'll be the easiest fifty grand you ever made. And the safest."

Pete shot forward, slamming the chair legs on the floor. "I'll blow the whole fuckin' block up for free."

"You'll be blowin' up your ass, you and Louie don't come through."

"I got *my* end set. It's you guys. What're you doin' out there — primping like prima donnas? You keep talking, practicing, you'll never do it. Guys lose their nerve, plannin' so much."

"I say it's goin' down, it's goin' down. But I want another little talk with this DiFonzo. Saturday."

"He'll be at my house then," Pete said and stood up. "Let's go look at our fire."

They followed Pete out, Tony remembering that Gushi had found a certain Luigi DiFonzo for them, and as far as Tony knew, was probably going to take another cut from Louie for bringing him in as an expert money launderer. That was his business.

The fire was ready. With a long-handled fork, Pete threw the steaks on the grill. He got out some lawn chairs for Tony and Charlie, the price tags dangling.

"You already told Louie what you want," Pete said. "He'll think up some stuff on his own, too."

"Where'd you get him?" Tony asked.

After a glance at Charlie, Pete said, "He's from Boston. Got no connections here. He was working some deal with silver futures and Count Dante, that crazy hood, tried to muscle in on his operation. You remember the Count. Wears a cape, used to be a hairdresser. Anyway, Louie looks kind of like he oughta be in an ad for shaving lotion or something. And the Count thought he could lay on him. Louie got no protection here, so he comes to me to get the Count off his back. Keep his head from being broke."

Pete shrugged, gesturing with the fork. "So I make a coupla calls, the Count backs off, and Louie is beholden. And he's smart. He knows all about negotiable stock certificates, and silver, and he's washed bills before. I knew he'd come in handy someday. Not a bad guy, just a little fancy. 'Genius' is the straight word from Boston. Fuckin' genius. Known all over up there."

Luigi DiFonzo left a wife, children, and a pile of debts back in Massachusetts. He came to Chicago in 1972 and, after his wife divorced him, married into a wealthy Hinsdale family. He set up two companies selling options to buy commodity futures contracts in silver bullion. Few persons understood this market, and either because of or in spite of that forked over sums from a few hundred to as much as $10,000, enabling DiFonzo to buy a $190,000 home with cash and add to his expensive wardrobe. When newspaper accounts disclosed holes in his scheme, everything went sour. In November of '73 DiFonzo filed for bankruptcy, claiming $2.5 million in debts and only $18,000 in assets. He returned to Boston where, under the name Keith Anderson, he established another options business. Now he was back in Chicago again, making new friends.

"Well, I still like the sound of those Swiss bank accounts," Charlie said, accepting a steak from Pete. "I want to talk to Louie about those, too. The interest and all that."

"Whyn't you get yourself a girl friend, Charlie? You're too serious. Interest." Pete served Tony, as the flames shot up around the last steak. "Anyway, Louie'll know anything you want. Just lay it out for him. Can't be under age, though."

Saturday night, after Charlie and Tony settled themselves with drinks in Pete's living room and watched *All in the Family* at Pete's insistence, Louie arrived. Impeccable in a blue tweed sport jacket and gray wool slacks that broke just above his Gucci loafers, he looked like a young stockbroker on the way up. Tony admired the presentation except for a certain arrogance in Louie's manner — as if the Bostonian believed he was the real thing. Believing in the role was vital to all cons — but only when you were playing it. Not when you were setting up the deal with your crew.

Pete got Louie a drink, Scotch and water, while Charlie questioned Louie some more about Swiss accounts.

Louie was nodding. His steady gaze never left Charlie's face. Charlie talked at Tony as much as he did at Louie.

Tony nodded at intervals, backing Charlie up. This DiFonzo was something else.

"Like I said before, I got maybe a million or so, I don't know for sure, I got some returns coming in. I want the interest. That's what I'm looking for; one of those numbered accounts, no names or nothing, and a regular check, just like social security."

"His fancy lady gets the check and his wife gets the security," Pete said and laughed. Tony took a long drink to avoid laughing at the image of Charlie cheating on his old lady.

Louie ignored them both. He leaned forward, one elbow on his knee. "I've been checking into what you want. Grand Cayman is still better than Switzerland now. All the big banks have moved to Grand Cayman. They're English but they work under the Swiss National Banking Rules. Which the Swiss stopped doing."

"How do you mean?" Tony asked. He liked the sound of that. More sun. Girls on nude beaches. Nude girls.

"The Swiss are starting to give out information now, if the government has either the name or the number. Used to be they had to have the number. Now, if another government has either, the banks will open their books. It's not as secret as before. So everybody's switched to the island. It's really the only way to go." Louie stopped to take a drink. Light glinted on his gold-coin cuff links. "Practically every corner has a bank. All the big people — probably even Nixon from what I've heard — they all have accounts in Grand Cayman now."

Charlie was chewing his lip, watching Louie.

"Really," Louie continued, "it's good. Wouldn't take any time at all, once we get there. I know the lawyer, the bank, the whole thing."

"And I got this guy with a boat," Pete threw in. "Right in

Florida. He'll take us over — fishing, whatever we want."

"You'll drive to Florida with us?" Charlie asked.

Louie spread his arms in an expansive gesture. "I'm at your disposal."

"Can you work without notice?"

"A week ahead helps."

"Can't do it," Charlie said blandly. "Maybe twenty-four, forty-eight hours?"

There was a pause.

"I can do it in twenty-four hours," Louie said.

"And we just carry it over there?" Charlie asked.

"Like I said. Just put it in a suitcase and carry it over there. That's it.

"Be ready when Pete calls you. Keep a bag packed. We'll take a little trip together. Get some sun," Charlie said, sounding satisfied.

Tony thought it sounded reasonable. Louie acted like he knew the ropes. Tony began figuring 12 percent interest on a million dollars. You had to give Charlie credit for not stashing the money in a hole somewhere. Capital. That's where the muscle was. You have $1 million in the bank at 12 percent interest, you could figure on borrowing maybe $10 million. "Rich" wasn't when you had money in the bank; rich was what you could control. He watched Louie smooth his tie, sit up a little straighter, and figured they were thinking the same thing. The only limit a good con man ever had was how much cash he could invest in the setup. With a bundle like a million, or just half of it, he and Charlie could even consider setting up something almost legitimate. Give the syndicate some competition. Flower shops and liquor stores. Hotels.

Tony didn't know then how smalltime flower shops and liquor stores were compared to Pete and Louie's plans. Gushi at one time had had a large and successful Panasonic distributorship in Chicago and the Midwest. Eventually he had sold out at a substantial profit, as he had done with other legitimate businesses. When he and Louie got together, some of their discussions centered on the tax and "cleaning" advantages of commodity trading. Had another deal gone through, Pete's share would have been $400,000. Even Charlie supposedly agreed to give Louie 5 percent more than the 10 percent laundry price if it went for seed money for the commodity operation.

Tony was satisfied as he looked around the room at Pete, Charlie, and Louie, all present and accounted for, and Marrera guarding it all, keeping it safe until the right time. Then it was all gonna pay.

5

Purolator: You Can't Be Too Careful

OTHER INFAMOUS RIPOFFS OF HISTORY

• The $1,551,277 robbery of a postal truck near Plymouth, Mass., in 1962 by a gang whose members posed as police.
• The holdup of a Brink's Express garage in Boston in 1950 by eleven men wearing Halloween masks. They got away with $1,219,218.
• The $2 million robbery of a train near Rondout in suburban Lake County in 1924.

— October 24, 1974,
Chicago Tribune

Purolator. A name originally designed to conjure up an image of efficient oil filters, but now denoting money, enormous amounts of money: picking it up, delivering it, counting it, and storing it in concrete vaults.

When the Purolator Corporation of Piscataway, New Jersey, acquired the Armored Express Company in 1972, they rechristened it Purolator Security, Inc. — a mistake if they wanted instant product identification. The average person still thinks of oil filters. But Purolator already had a name as a courier service and hoped for international expansion. The colors of its trucks and building are red, white, and blue, suggesting the security and wholesomeness of the American flag. The security industry was a good choice, with gross income totaling $64.9 billion in 1974. (In 1979 seventy-five to eighty companies would be struggling to handle an increase of 80 percent: $117.4 billion trundled around in trucks.)

The main business of Purolator Security is ground transportation of large amounts of money, although they offer other services—polygraph testing and advising on security measures. The currency and coin is on wheels every day, traveling from one site to another, sitting at red lights, holed up in traffic jams, stuck in snow. Banks move it out of their vaults the same day it comes in, so they, too, can earn interest on deposits and mortgage and loan payments. But this service is not only for banks and food-store chains, for racetracks and currency exchanges. It is also for the small businessman, restaurant owner, or dry cleaner. The man who exits from his store watching for fast-moving shadows, listening for footsteps behind him, clutching his moneybag under his coat, and hoping he'll make it to his car or bank. Sometimes he will. Sometimes he won't. He can try varying his pattern to confuse the casual observer — the time of deposit, who makes it — but a professional needs only a few days surveillance to determine when deposits are made, and he's not fussy about who makes them because a gun convinces almost anyone. Especially the owner who, sooner or later, calls the armored express service to take over.

The Purolator Security station in Chicago is an unobtrusive building — three packing crates side by side, the middle one two-tiered for offices. The main entrance off Huron Street opens onto cement stairs that lead to a small entry hall where someone asks your name and purpose before a buzzer unlocks the office door. The business offices, where paper — not negotiable — is shuffled, conferences are held, and files multiply, are cheaply paneled and scantily carpeted. A white cabinet, door ajar, in the main reception room, holds extra guns as well as other essential office supplies. "We have guns all over this place," admits a manager, smiling sweetly. A room in back, crowded with tables and a coffee machine, is set aside as an employee lunchroom. The Purolator red, white, and blue aren't in evidence upstairs, where beige and brown establish a neutral atmosphere.

In the supervisor's office, whose walls boast award plaques of crossed guns or a halved revolver attesting to the marksmanship of the Purolator gun teams in competition with other security companies and police departments, sits the official who is responsible for establishing routes and assuring appropriate service for clients. Each armored van is equipped with a two-way radio. Most Purolator vans have three men: a guard, a messenger, and a driver. The first two enter each place of business to pick up the money, which is already in a bag or container marked with the exact amount and indicating which bank is to be its final destination. The bags are usually sealed with two wires passed through a piece of lead, which is then crimped shut. The messenger hands out a receipt for the bag, but does not verify the amount; he drops off any currency that has been requested for the day's business operation. The drops and pickups are completed within five minutes to lessen the risk of robbery.

The supervisor's worst headache is Chicago winters. He must make the crucial decision to allow the trucks to continue on their routes or to call them in and then deal with angry clients who feel like sitting ducks. If the trucks are brought in, Purolator notifies its customers immediately so they can make other arrangements. (During one of Chicago's biggest snowstorms of the century, a large bank had piled its day's receipts — $13 million — on a counter waiting for the pickup by another security firm. Its timed vault had already been closed for the night and wouldn't open again until morning. Minutes melted away like snowflakes, and beads of perspiration gathered as the bank official waited for the armored truck to come. The distraught manager lay down on top of the canvas sacks and metal lockers of money as the snow reached a record three feet — but the truck did not arrive that night.)

At the end of the supervisor's long room is a stairway going down to a small area that leads to the dispatcher's office and the vault room. In this area seven narrow, locked booths, which look like those in the listening room in a record shop, line one wall. At right angles to them are the doorways to the huge garages, their walls painted blue at the base and white the rest of the way up to the ceiling. Bright fluorescent lights augment the illumination afforded by a few high windows.

One of the garages has maintenance equipment and a gas pump. Purolator does its own maintenance to avoid the possibility of a planned breakdown set up by a machanic in an outside shop. The red, white, and blue trucks come in varying sizes, some equipped with hydraulic lifts in back for loading and unloading dollies of money onto green and gray carts. Some vans are drab olive green for anonymity.

The transfer of money in and out of Purolator follows a definite procedure. All the bags are brought back to Purolator's garages and unloaded onto dollies. Doors into the vault area are all controlled by inside buttons and buzzers. The messenger, when buzzed in, drags his bags into the area in front of the narrow booths that separate him, and others, from the actual sorting room and vaults. He steps into one of the little rooms, with the bags of money, and the door locks behind him. In front of him is a second locked door with a window that opens into the sorting room. About twenty employees control the locking mechanism and receive the money. They give the messenger a receipt and drag the money in after they have locked him out again. They do not count any money in any container. The lead seals remain untouched. The vault employee registers the bank for which each bag is destined, then heaves the bag into a tanker (metal footlocker) marked for a particular bank. An invoice records receipt of money *said* to be in the bag and now in the vault. At the end of each day the tanker is closed, sealed with a similar lead seal, and the entire receptacle delivered to the proper bank the next morning. The bank verifies the amount of money actually in each canvas sack, and credits the proper amount to the proper account. Purolator itself sorts and wraps coins for only a few of its customers. An elevator to the basement carries canvas sacks of coins, some of which may be tagged with a sheet of paper marked $25,000. Later the sacks are brought up again, wrapped and sorted, from the counting room.

Purolator's security system was carefully planned. The walls of Purolator's vault room are two feet thick, complying with the standard set by the insurance company. TV scanners, some apparent, some hidden by a light fixture or heating duct, constantly patrol the area.

By far the most important ingredient in Purolator's system, however, is the alarm inside the vault. In 1974 Purolator was using the oldest and most common ultrasonic type, a sophisticated sound-discrimination system that emits low-frequency sound waves. Every night the timing mechanism in the doors is set and the vault is locked. After that, if the sound waves are interrupted by any noises — footsteps or other — within the vault, an alarm sets off a buzzer and lights a light at the same time on the alarm board at Wells Fargo. (Wells Fargo provides the same security for its clients, including Purolator, as Purolator does for its own customers.) Wells Fargo, getting the alarm signal on its wires, immediately calls the client and the police, and sends a messenger to investigate. One of the major flaws in the system is its propensity for false alarms — which can be triggered by something as slight as an atmospheric change. Thus the police are not always called right away.

In the late 1970s a new alarm system for space protection replaced most of the old methods. The new one is also based on ultrasonic sound discrimination, but it works on motion detection, or the Doppler effect. It emits high-frequency waves, inaudible to human ears, and relies on the "push" and "pull" of sound waves by a moving body to trip the alarm. It is not the sound of the dropped hundred-dollar bill hitting the floor, but rather the *movement* of the C-note that triggers the alarm as it pushes or pulls sound waves away or toward the detector. And brings human hands to the rescue.

As a further form of protection, companies such as Purolator must send a new guard's fingerprints to a state agency to verify that he has no prison record — a state requirement because guards carry guns. However, it can take eight to twelve months to process the information, and the turnover in guards can be as frequent as once a month. Thus the time lapse effectively delays any preventive action on the part of the security company.

Still, at a casual glance, Purolator is a veritable fortress, bristling with alarms, security checks, and technology. Every contingency had been allowed for — except for Ralphie, hired on the recommendation of a superior who used to work for Wells Fargo when Ralphie was employed there.

6

Money to Burn

If a hall of fame for notable thieves is ever established, the burglars who looted the vault of Purolator Security here over the weekend will rank close to the top.

— October 23, 1974,
Chicago Tribune

Charlie's voice shattered the silence. "It's O.K."

Tony jumped, knocking ashes onto his pants. Charlie had been inside almost thirty minutes. Christ. A little sooner and they might have had two extra partners going into that vault. At least they'd have been wandering around, knowing they were on to something, but not sure what. Charlie should have thought of that.

Tony started the car and drove around to Clark Street to park outside the Hotel Wacker on the corner of Clark and Huron. He waited a few minutes to see if he'd been noticed, then got out of the car. This was going to be the longest walk of his life. The sidewalk squares stretched ahead, cracked and crumbling. The city crew hadn't hit this spot — the alderman probably didn't squawk enough or have enough clout. He passed the shoddy hotel marquee jutting over the wide sidewalk like an unfinished bridge; he passed the entrance to the Purolator offices and the front garage doors. Knowing that the few Purolator vans parked on the street were empty somehow made them look smaller. He walked up to the corner of La Salle, glanced around, then hurried back to the front of the building. Finally he was in the home stretch. He kicked hard on the overhead door and in a few seconds ducked under the huge door as it began to rise. He was in.

The door clanged shut behind him, taking the last bit of evening light with it. He blinked and waited for his eyes to process the negative of trucks and the dim, high ceiling of the room.

"Over through here." Charlie's voice added depth to the garage and Tony saw his head between some trucks, outlined by a light coming from the door frame. Fifteen or twenty trucks stood parked in rows. The green van was snuggled between two trucks up on jacks. As Tony crossed the cement floor spotted with puddles of congealed oil, bits of gravel among the oil leaks crunched underfoot. The smell of gasoline and exhaust hung in the air.

He kept following Charlie. A heavy door stood propped open by a dolly cart. Tony went through this door into the vault room.

"In here," Charlie said. There, in the back of the room, loomed the two huge vaults of Purolator Security, impossible for anyone to enter but the most dedicated electronics genius with all the time in the world and tons of TNT.

Tony approached the vaults uneasily. They looked more like the mausoleums in the cemeteries on the outskirts of Chicago than the shiny, compact deposit box rooms behind fancy iron bars that banks like to display for the edification of customers.

These weren't bank vaults; these were bomb shelters,

tombs, the guardians of dead treasure. One door stood partially open with a flashlight on the floor at the entrance. The door looked to be a foot thick, suggesting the maze of hidden wiring embedded in it — the alarm system that Marrera had set off just before.

Charlie emerged carrying his miner's flashlight, which he set down at the doorway, pointing the strong beam toward the inside of the vault. "In here. It's all ready."

Tony picked up the flashlight and played it around inside the vault. "Will you get a load of this?" he said and stared at the piles of canvas bags and metal footlockers looming around him, almost touching the fifteen-foot ceiling. Little lead seals hung from crimped wire closures, ensuring that none but the proper receiver would open the containers stuffed with money. A little wire-cutting gadget — snips — hung from Charlie's belt.

"Come on," Charlie said, and Tony helped him pull the big vault door closed. Now they were locked inside, with the gasoline bags that Charlie had already placed, the duffels, the tankers, the canvas bags, and, thank God, Tony thought, a walkie-talkie.

"Take these," Charlie said, handing Tony a pair of surgical gloves identical to the ones he wore. Tony returned the flashlight to its post on a shelf and pulled the gloves on. Then he fished out the second gun and handed it to Charlie, who slid it into his belt.

"Now the cash," Charlie grunted, kicking at a huge silver tanker destined for the First National Bank. "This is it. We want the bags just brought in. It's all the stuff on the floor."

Canvas bags of various sizes also lay slumped around the center of the vault as if thrown there by guards in a hurry to get home and to forget that millions of dollars slipped through their fingers every night.

"Take the cash out of the bags I cut open and put it in

ours," Charlie said, indicating the duffels he had brought from the van.

Labels printed themselves like deposit slips on Tony's mind. Hawthorne racetrack. National Tea. Merchandise National Bank. Jewel Foods. All unmarked bills. Untraceable. Ready cash for whatever the world had on sale. And everything was for sale. The bags' muted colors, dark green, khaki, brown, spotted the floor like jungle cover, while the silver gleam of a tanker seemed like the fuselage of a downed plane.

Tony grabbed the container nearest him and pulled it open. He breathed in his first, unforgettable smell of pounds and pounds of used, circulated money. Money that had been in back pockets of racetrack junkies, the sweaty hands of children, the bras of thousands of black cleaning women too scared to carry purses on streets prowled by predators.

He shook his head as if to clear it of the sour-sweet smell of money, of paper with a rag content so high you could wash and wear it. He began stuffing his first duffel, lifting the heavy bundles of packed bills and pushing them down, like a grocery boy packing food. He felt as if he were shoplifting in a supermarket that stocked only money and he felt sick that he couldn't take it all.

The red lockers glowed in the flashlight's beam and the room seemed full of flames. Tony peeled off his leather jacket and promised Charlie that he'd cut his throat if he forgot and left it behind. His hands, snaking in and out of bags and duffels, looked, in the surgical gloves, as if they belonged to a mad scientist.

"How we going to cram it all in?" Tony muttered. The bulk of the bundles of wrapped money made them fit awkwardly inside the army duffels. Somehow he had expected huge piles of hundred-bill packages. Flexible enough to fill the corners of their bags. Not these cement blocks.

Suddenly Marrera's voice cracked from the box on the floor. "Guy's still watching his movie. Called in from the popcorn counter to give a blow-by-blow description."

"Tell him to jam it," Charlie said.

Tony interrupted his packing to press the button on the box. Time was running out, getting close to the limits they'd given themselves. The unwritten rule. Every score has to end. Even if something gets left behind. "Fuck off," Tony said into the box. Then he returned to his work and moved faster. Bad enough they had to leave the rest of the money. He imagined the other guard reclining in the shabby rows of seats, huddled over his walkie-talkie, unnoticed by the other scattered occupants, silently breathing in their fantasies. Doing is better.

An hour later the air was thick with perspiration. Tony and Charlie were breathing hard. Tony's shirt was wet. His hands, inside the surgical gloves, stung as if they'd been dipped in a salt solution. His ears were ringing over the grunts he and Charlie emitted into the silent room. He hoped to God no one had come from Wells Fargo, or Marrera would have to wait before opening the door so the guards would see nothing but vans and the blank face of the steel vault door. He would hate to be shut up in this steel box a minute longer than necessary, even with a billion dollars for a pillow.

"This crime stuff ain't all it's cracked up to be," Tony gasped. He zipped another bag shut and looked around. That must have been the last one. Charlie, too, had just finished loading his. "We better start packing up."

Each bundle of money had been a foot thick and now the crammed bags seemed to weigh a ton. They half-lifted, half-pulled the duffels out of the vault, past the droopy bags of gasoline. Tony put his arms and shoulders through the thick straps and staggered out of the vault room into the garage, right behind Charlie, who was hoisting two of them on his back. Charlie heaved his in first, pushed them to the back, and motioned for Tony to do the same. Tony could feel his gun pressing into his belly as he strained to lift his bags a foot up to the steel floor of the van. He had forgotten Charlie's incredible strength that made the lifting look easy.

When they had shoved the last one in, Charlie slammed the doors shut and locked them. They returned to the vault for the flashlights and a last look to see if they had left anything behind, besides another million or so. The gasoline bags were all strung together through their tops by a waxed cotton wick that trailed along the floor. Tony shrugged into his jacket, pulled the timing device from his pocket as Charlie went on ahead. He carefully followed the directions, but he didn't have to reset the time. With the stuff burned up, and all containers refastened, no one would get an exact count of how much money was missing, or know for sure if there even had been a burglary. They planned it as a case for the fire department and the insurance companies — not the police. And in no way for the FBI.

He took one last look. The bags, with a greenish cast, stood out against the red money lockers as if Christmas had come two months early. He stepped out of the vault and closed the door, leaning back against it.

He continued on to the van. Now he thought his legs were trembling, or shrinking. He felt exhausted but high. Or as if a high were waiting just inside his throat, behind his eyes. A high or a scream. He took in the bleak cement walls, the silent hulks of vans. Christ, there must be nothing worse than guard duty, especially at night, when there's no one coming in or out to shoot the bull with, he thought. No wonder Marrera had no trouble getting the others to leave him alone.

Charlie climbed into the van and peeled off his gloves. He

rolled the window down and pulled the cab door shut. Then he hit the box button for the last time. "O.K. We're ready to move," he said into the box.

"*Move*," Marrera echoed back through the box.

Tony stepped back. The huge doors groaned open. Charlie leaned his head out of the window, adjusted his cap.

"Let's get the fuck out of here," he said.

7

Undercover

In spite of all the government's technology, it still takes the stool pigeon on the street to crack a case.

— J.D.

If there is a maxim on which police and criminals almost universally agree, it is one to the effect that no major crime is ever solved without an informant. The latest detection equipment, the most painstaking footwork, and the most sophisticated dedication often fail unless there is an informant to whisper the who, what, when, and where of the underworld.

There are two kinds of informers — the familiar stool pigeon and the undercover agent. The stool pigeon is often a kind of fringe underworld character whose information may be dubious, thirdhand, or peripheral. A much better source, of course, is the actual participant in a crime, but — according to Ramon Stratton, a retired FBI agent with an outstanding record of service — this kind of informant is rarer than the movies would have us believe. During his long career Stratton spent a lot of time trying to "turn" many criminals, but his percentage of success, he says, was very low.

The other kind of informant is the undercover agent, an actual employee of a law-enforcement agency. He lives a borrowed life as realistically as he can, and he moves as close to the sources of crime as possible. He is similar to that well-known figure in espionage fact and fiction, the agent-in-place, or the mole.

Such became the role of Larry Callahan in 1974 when he was caught in a fencing operation and "turned" into an informer for the Illinois Legislative Investigating Commission (ILIC). His assignment was to report the methods used for moving about $5 million worth of stolen merchandise through discount houses every year. In his day-to-day existence, Larry's job was to stock a discount store in Worth, Illinois, from the owner's sources of supply — and to fence quietly whatever merchandise was too hot for open sale.

The store was owned by one Peter Gushi. As proprietor, he especially drew the interest of the authorities because he had served a sentence for interstate transportation of stolen property some years before. He was also reputed to be an enforcer for the mob — a notion that kept Larry Callahan in a cold sweat much of the time.

In the usual practice of this kind of surveillance, there is often another agent nearby, an agent of superior rank or, in some cases, even the head of an investigative division. He is usually the one with the broom in his hands — or the one who is always getting sent out for sandwiches and coffee. In Russian embassies he would be the obscure clerk who occupies the windowless office in the basement. He is a second pair of eyes and ears, a supervisor for the operation, and in need, a back-up man. The Illinois Bureau of Investigation (IBI) loaned the ILIC, and Larry, just such a partner as his control.

It was in early September of Larry's first year of operation when he began to pick up some very interesting fragments of information. Pete Gushi, Larry reported to his control, was having a number of meetings — and a recent meeting included some faces Larry hadn't seen before. Very soon thereafter, Gushi got into a bragging mood one day and told Larry that he was into one of the biggest scores in history — maybe two million, maybe three — and Pete Gushi was going to be right there in the middle of it. Larry thought it might be just some of Pete's usual bullshit, but his control felt they had to act on the assumption that it might be true.

He set up arrangements for a secret meeting with State's Attorney Bernard Carey and members of his Chicago office as well as Assistant State's Attorney Nick Ivarone of the prosecutor's Special Investigation Unit. By the time they met, Larry had some more fascinating items to add.

On September 12, he said, Gushi had met and talked with a man named Pasquale Charles Marzano. The next day Gushi had taken Larry with him to a meeting with an associate of his called Elmer Silva at a Holiday Inn in Chicago. During the course of the conversation, Larry recalled, Gushi referred to Marzano and said that he and Marzano had talked about renting a boat in Miami from a certain Jack Garden. Then Gushi had asked Silva if he knew the other guy he and Marzano were dealing with. Yes, Silva knew him all right; sure he knew Louie DiFonzo.

Names; bits and pieces. But the hard news came just before Pete and Larry parted. Pete was riding a high of big dreams. "Larry," he said, "get this. I'm sick and tired of being so goddamn poor all my life, and so now I'm gonna be either one of the richest guys or one of the deadest guys you ever see." He'd added that the big score he had in mind would probably go down on a Sunday, probably Sunday the 29th.

The prosecutor's men immediately obtained the full coop-

eration of the IBI. Because the location of the coming heist
was unknown — it could be Miami or any part of the
country — the FBI was given the particulars. And for the
same reason, by a queer kind of reverse logic, the IBI and
the prosecutor's men omitted notifying the Chicago Police.
That oversight was to have some interesting results.

The IBI superintendent assigned to direct the case, Wayne
Kerstetter, began with the idea of a huge score. If such a
large amount of money would be involved, he reasoned, the
unknown crew would probably have to deal with a sophisticated alarm system somewhere — the kind of alarm system
a modern bank would have. And an FBI file showed that
Charlie Marzano was very likely a good hand at dealing
with complicated burglar alarms. He had been one of the
suspects in the still unsolved robbery of $800,000 in gold
from the premises of a jewelry manufacturer in Evanston the
year before. On February 11 of that year Chicago Police
Department burglary investigators had entered Marzano's
house with a search warrant. Among the things they took
away with them was a huge array of alarm-circumventing
devices and manuals of burglary alarms. They had arrested
Marzano. But the case had been thrown out on the grounds
that the warrant had authorized a search for gold only —
and no gold had been turned up.

Now, although the actual target remained unknown, the
IBI and the FBI deployed their available manpower in keeping all the suspects under surveillance. But Larry Callahan
was still the key man. In late September he reported that
Charles Marzano had asked him to get a new driver's license under the name of Charles Rossa. Before Larry
turned it over, however, one of the agents on the case had
photographed it.

On September 27 Larry reported the purchase of a van.
That morning he had heard Gushi talking with James An-

drew Maniatis, known as Jimmy the Greek, who had something of a long reputation as an "associate of criminals." Gushi wanted Jimmy to buy a green van in his own name. The van was going to be used for something risky, but, Gushi assured him, if anything did go wrong, Jimmy could simply say he'd sold the van to Gushi just after he'd bought it.

That afternoon Jimmy turned up at Hawkinson Ford in Oak Lawn, Illinois, and bought a 1974 Ford Econoline van, Vehicle Identification Number E25GHV14352. The only odd thing about the purchase was that the buyer refused to show the salesclerk his driver's license. But he did read the data from it aloud. The car was duly registered in the name of Jim Maniatis, 7235 West 110th Place, Worth, Illinois, as an IBI agent discovered the next day.

So far, so good. The government agents now knew some of the people who would be involved. They had exact knowledge of at least one of the cars to be used. But the target was still a mystery.

September 29 came and went peacefully. There was no enormous score reported. Word filtered back from Larry that everything had been delayed because the van as yet had no license plates.

On October 2 Maniatis applied at the Chicago Motor Vehicle West Side Facility and received truck license 51508B. The IBI and FBI went on red alert.

On October 7 Maniatis returned to the facility to complain that he had found only one license plate in his envelope. He knew that it was unlawful to drive with only one license plate. He was issued new plates and license number 516747B.

But the truck still didn't appear on the street.

The surveillance continued through the weekends of October 6 and 13, but they passed without incident. The agencies involved were beginning to lose patience. For nearly six weeks they had tied up a lot of manpower that was urgently needed elsewhere: the state's attorney's investigators, the sheriff's deputies, and the IBI and FBI agents. And all they had thus far were quotes from a well-known gasbag named Pete Gushi and the proof of purchase of a green Ford van. And their costs were mounting. In mid-October, the big-score surveillance was called off.

But the ILIC continued its original watch, carefully reporting that Peter James Gushi was seen late on Saturday night, October 19, driving a black-over-blue Lincoln Continental Mark IV with 1974 Illinois license KJ5192.

But without full surveillance nobody could tell where Gushi was headed. And nobody would know that the green van would finally take to the streets the next evening.

Another thing the FBI and IBI didn't know was a small item buried in the Chicago Police Department files. The dossier on Marzano noted that he was an associate of a certain Ralph Marrera. In fact, the two of them had been implicated in the Evanston robbery. At that time Marrera had been employed by Wells Fargo, the security company. Wells Fargo had given Marrera a lie detector test about his part in the Evanston job, which proved inconclusive. He and Wells Fargo then parted company. Perhaps someone in the IBI might then have thought to check out the present employment of Charlie Marzano's old buddy and sometimes breakfast companion. But only the Chicago Police had the vital clue — and they hadn't been called in.

After the big score went down, the Chicago Police pointed this out.

8

The Crooks Are in the Counting House

October 20, 1974. 9:20 P.M. The garage door opened as the van sputtered into movement, emerged from between the Purolator trucks, and rolled out into the alley. Tony saluted the TV monitor and its watcher; then he followed the path of the van down the alley and around Erie Street to Clark and his parked car. He placed one of the talkies on the seat next to him and started the car. It was thirty-two degrees, a cold night for October in Chicago, and the only people on the streets were those few who had good reason for being out. For Tony and Charlie the easiest part was done.

Tony passed Charlie and the next stage of the plan began.

Two separate routes to the same place — a small, lower-middle-class suburb of Chicago.

Tony turned the heat to high, wishing he had real gloves, not the sticky surgical things in his pocket. He didn't like being alone, Charlie off in the night taking the van for a ride, Marrera sitting on a sort of time bomb. Most scores you had someone to keep you talking, keep you from thinking. Anyway, it was Ralphie had to take the heat now. He almost laughed aloud at his own thoughts. Those gasoline bags bursting into fire bombs weren't the heat he meant. Most guys killed the inside man, the main link, because the pressure on him's the worst. Marrera knew that. Must have thought of it, up there with his shotgun across his lap, wired to Wells Fargo and a porno flick. But he'd been in with Charlie before. Well, he was set now, all right. You have to take some chances in this life or you get nowhere. End up a nine-to-fiver.

Tony didn't have to check house numbers to find the little two-story frame house with peeling paint and geraniums already dying in the wintry weather. The garage, too, looked about ready to be carried off to the dump. He parked a few feet past the sidewalk leading to the front door, then walked back, up the steps, and knocked. His hands hurt. On the second knock his knuckles hit air. A thin young woman stepped back from the open door and motioned him in. "It got cold out there," she said. Her lipstick was newly applied, making her small, pinched face look drawn and pasty.

"Yeah," Tony said. He walked past her to check the kitchen. "Frank gone?"

"Playing cards. Like you said."

"Good. We'll be using the basement the rest of the night. The kids?"

"In bed."

Tony nodded, and returned to the dining room, where he

put his gun, walkie-talkie, and Charlie's sweater and I.D. on the table. Doris followed him. "Charlie'll be here soon," Tony said.

"Frank said to tell you it'd be a real late game."

"He's making more money here tonight," Tony said.

Doris twitched the corners of her mouth, but she was too tense to laugh. Sounds of a cops-and-robbers show drifted down from the second floor.

Tony paced to the stairway, looked up, walked back to the dining room where Doris still stood, staring at the items on the table. Charlie should be here by now. Where in hell was he?

"I'll be outside," Tony said. He retraced his steps through the living room and down the front sidewalk. He couldn't figure what was keeping Charlie. He'd be driving like a schoolteacher but he should be here by now anyway. He paced up and down the sidewalk. Should he get the car — go out and look for him? Go back over Charlie's route?

An elderly couple, out walking their dog, stopped to encourage it to pee on somebody else's lawn.

"Evening," the lady said.

Tony nodded coldly and turned away. Christ. Did they recognize him from visiting here before? He knew some of Doris and Frank's neighbors. Relax, he told himself. No crime to be visiting friends anyway. But fifteen minutes had already passed. Could Charlie have got picked up? Or in an accident? Forget how to get here? They should've stayed together. They could lose it all now.

A blue Impala pulled up and the driver stuck his head out of the window. "Hey, Tony?"

Tony whirled. Of all the fucking luck. The guy next door. Tony shrugged and bent his head to light a cigarette.

"How ya been?"

Tony turned as if he didn't hear the question and walked a few feet away from the house. Would the guy give up? Go on inside. Charlie should be here any minute. He could almost picture the guy asking if he could give them a hand with the luggage. Tony looked at his watch. Now it was almost twenty minutes. He was afraid to look around.

"Well, see ya," he heard behind him. Again he pretended not to hear. Finally some doors slammed. He turned. The guy was nowhere in sight and Doris was poking her head out.

"Hey, Tony," she called, waving for him to come in. "That thing on the table is talking."

"Damn!" He'd forgotten the walkie-talkie. Tony took the front steps two at a time and brushed past her to the dining room table, where Charlie's voice was singing out Sinatra's line "I did it my way."

"I'm here," Tony said. Then he pressed the button and had to say it again.

"Christ." The relief in Charlie's voice was plain. "I'm just coming off the Eisenhower. Be there in five minutes."

Tony clicked off, stuck the gun back in his belt. "We'll be in the basement," he said to Doris. "Stay upstairs and make sure the kids don't decide to sleepwalk. Lock the front door, back one, too, after I leave. The basement open?"

"No." She shook her head.

"I'll do it. Go on up." Tony waited until she had locked the doors; then he turned off the downstairs lights and hurried down into the basement and out the back way into the alley. Some kid had left his tricycle in front of the garage. Tony wheeled it around to nearby bushes.

Chicago and adjacent suburbs are known for their alleys, bisecting each city block like narrow lines on a grid. Huge garbage trucks plow their way through, scattering kids playing dodge ball or kick-the-can, or roll-the-drunk. Each garage had its own pile of debris like an offering. Two of

these had old refrigerators, their doors conscientiously missing; a few had cars, not quite abandoned, stepladders, and
rows of garbage cans with lids.

Headlights rounded the corner. The van was coming
home to papa. Tony began dragging the two frame doors
open as Charlie pulled up, his window open. "They up?"

"Frank's out playing cards. She's keeping the kids in bed.
They're not looking to know nothing." He stepped to the
side. "Pull it in."

"It don't look big enough." Charlie eyed the garage,
pushing his cap back on his head.

"Just drive. We'll enlarge it if we have to."

He leaped back as the truck lurched forward, missing him
by inches. The brake lights went on and Charlie slowed
down to half an inch an hour.

"Move it," Tony called in a hoarse whisper. "You think I
want to direct traffic out here till the neighbors send for the
funny wagon?"

"I can't see the fuckin' back wall," Charlie whispered
back.

"You don't have to see it. You got to *feel* it. *Hit the damn
thing.*"

The truck moved forward and finally nudged the back
wall of the garage with a small thump. Charlie stopped and
again put on the brakes.

"Your behind's sticking out. Move it. You think this
garage got doors like fuckin' bay windows?" Tony pushed
on the van as if he could compress it with his hands.

Charlie stage-whispered out the cab, "We're goin' to
wreck their garage, you asshole. Why didn't you measure
it?"

"We'll buy them a new garage. It'd be doin' them a favor.
Just poke that wood a little. We only need an inch or so.
You want, I'll do it."

The roof seemed to sag toward the van as the tail finally

disappeared beyond the doorway. Mercifully, the brake lights went out. To Tony they had looked like searchlights, bright enough to blind a pilot flying overhead.

There was no one in sight as they slid the van doors open and lugged the duffels of money across the small yard and down the four cement steps into the basement. The black crepe paper was still in place, and the folding tables were set up. Tony figured fifteen grand wasn't a bad fee for the family to ignore a little night activity on the premises. Frank out at cards was even better. Ignorance was the best excuse.

Tony heaved the last duffel bag onto the floor and slammed the basement door. "Now I know why people have checking accounts," he said. Then they stared at the bundles heaped around them. The room was a strange sight with army duffel bags piled near the door and five or six suitcases tilted around as if a load of campers had been misdirected from Camp Minniehaha. Three tin folding tables stood in the center with a bare bulb dangling over them.

"Whadya figure we got?" Tony gasped.

"First lock the door," Charlie said, all business. Then he looked around with the air of an accountant. "Let's see," he said, opening the nearest duffel and pulling out one of the blocks of bills. "Must be at least a hundred thousand here in this bag." He looked as if he were mentally pressing buttons on a calculator. "The whole count could go over a couple million, maybe three," he said judiciously.

"Can't be," Tony said, taking another bag and turning it upside down. He deposited a two-foot-square block of cash tied with string on the table. "All hundreds and fifties," he said. "Christ. You're right. I think we got half a million in this here block alone."

Charlie methodically continued to pile stacks of money on the table. "Probably three million, or more," he said, as if it were a burden to consider.

"You know what, Charlie?" Tony said, peeling off his jacket. "Nothing's ever going to bother me again. There's something about money, you know? There ain't nothin' can make you feel that good."

For the first time, Charlie smiled, and the creases in his cheeks looked like dimples. "Yeah," he said. "I know what you mean."

Tony got another duffel for himself and dumped blocks of tens and twenties on the table. Then he took his seat across from Charlie, who was pulling on a pair of surgical gloves.

"Better put yours on," Charlie said. "You'll get all cut up otherwise."

Tony reluctantly retrieved his from his jacket. "Feels like a fuckin' rubber," he muttered.

Charlie held up a razor and proceeded to instruct Tony on the removal of the money wrappers embedded tightly between the larger blocks. A quick slash and a Hawthorne racetrack wrapper parted. Then Charlie poked his fingers between the bills and pulled the sliced piece of paper out. Tony nodded. Wrappers could be traced, unlike the much-circulated bills. And they had to pull each one out by hand, because if they opened the whole brick they'd have bills flying all over the place and would have to count from scratch.

With a movement similar to Charlie's, Tony slit another wrapper and pulled it out. Each one accounted for anywhere from $10,000 to $20,000. He had to pull a few rubber bands off in order to reach down and get hold of the narrow pieces of paper. His fingers began to ache.

An hour later Charlie had his jacket and cap off and his sleeves rolled up. A small hill of wrappers surrounded him. "We got to haul these away," he said, pointing to the mound. "Put 'em all in an empty duffel." He began first to fill a suitcase with what looked to Tony like $400,000. Tony didn't inquire about the exact amount or its destination. This was still Charlie's game.

"Think you could get some coffee?" Charlie squinted past the bulb.

"Coffee? You so bored you're fallin' asleep?"

"Or Kool-Aid. Or both."

Tony peeled off his gloves and wiped his hands on a stack of money. At the top of the stairs he knocked on the closed door, then cautiously pushed it open and peered around it. The muffled sounds of the TV still struggled down from the second story. He located some instant coffee and put water on. An open can of powdered Kool-Aid waited on the sink, as requested. He poured some into a pitcher, added ice and water, and waited for the kettle to boil. Here I am, he thought. Millions of dollars under my feet while I make like a busboy at Faces.

The basement felt steamy as he gingerly descended the rickety steps balancing a tray with a thermos of coffee, a pitcher of Kool-Aid, and two cups. Not the time to break his neck. Gets sticky explaining things to ambulance guys. "We get four bucks an hour to count money for the bank. They can't get anyone else on Sunday nights." That'd go over all right.

Charlie was packing another suitcase and he whirled around like a guilty husband when Tony set the coffee tray down with a thud. "Couple hundred thousand in here," Charlie said. "One bag gets picked up here at the house. One in the lot."

Tony nodded, impassive.

Charlie poured some Kool-Aid into a cup, took a deep swig, then dumped another duffel near his chair.

Tony tried a sip and shuddered. He poured it back into the pitcher and tried the coffee instead. "Beggars can't be choosers, huh Charlie?" He grinned.

Charlie was poking between the bills for the elusive wrappers. Tony settled himself again across from him, without the gloves this time. One fingerprint among millions can't prove anything.

"See this, Charlie?" he said suddenly, making a neat pile of about $50,000 in front of him. "Wid this I'm gonna buy a Rolls Royce." Then he stacked another pile. "And with this here I'm gonna get a Lincoln and a yellow Corvette." He corralled another pile. "Then this for clothes to look right on the streets. And this hunnert thousand, this for a year of taking girls out for rings, and trips — to cabaret 'em."

"Thing is, I know you're not kidding," Charlie said dolefully.

"What're you gonna do with yours?" Tony asked.

"Me, I'm going to buy some property. Maybe a beef-and-sausage stand. And you can run it for me, Tony."

"Me?" Tony grabbed a handful of loose bills and threw them to the ceiling. "You crazy or something? Me with a million dollars and *you want me to run a sausage stand?*"

"Why not. You gotta think of the future." Charlie seemed aggrieved that Tony found fault with the suggestion.

Tony shook his head at his cousin. "Charlie, millionaires don't sit around countin' sausages for their future. I buy anything, it'd be a disco. Probably Faces."

Now it was Charlie's turn to head-shake. "Put your rubbers on and stop talking so wild."

"I don't need the gloves." He stacked the bills for a few minutes. "You know, I never figured counting money would be so boring. My back's killin' me."

He moved away from the table. Felt like he'd just played ten too many games of racquetball. And the smoke was getting to his eyes. He rubbed them, luxuriating in the pressure and the deep blackness. When he opened them the scene before him seemed unreal. As if a recent dream had deposited him on a stage where the only props were piles and piles of money. "The king was in the counting house" — the old nursery rhyme. He was the king, counting all the money. And suddenly it all seemed right. His cousin Charlie, peering into a pile of bills like a witch into a crystal ball. It was going to be good. He'd get off the street. It was too hard these days, not like in Jesse James's time. Everything had gotten complicated.

He was about to return to his chair when he heard footsteps on the stairs. Charlie's face turned white just before a voice called, "It's me. Frank."

"Christ," Charlie said.

Tony smiled as Frank entered their section of the basement.

"What is all this money?" Frank said, his greeting smile turning scared. "Counterfeit?"

"Nope," Tony said. "Real."

"I never saw this much in my whole life."

"About three or four million," Tony said.

"Can't be." And there was no mistaking the fear in his face.

Tony realized his friend had visualized some normal haul. Maybe a little jewelry. Or a couple of bags of cash. After all, he had just seen them a few hours ago when they came back for one last check on things. The fear asked the worst question: what did they do to bring in this kind of money? Kill? No way had Tony indicated that something this big was going on.

Frank practically ran out of the room and back up the stairs. From then on they heard him pacing back and forth. Even heard faint sounds from a radio. Tony knew that Frank wanted out — wanted no part of it.

Charlie looked up. "Two bags to go," he said, "and that duffel's almost full of the little wrappers, can you believe it?"

"I'm starting to, Charlie," Tony said, and emptied the last

duffel. "Christ," he amended. "Just tens and twenties. Lousy fifty thousand of them." He shook his head in disdain. "And fives for Chrissake. What're we supposed to do with fives?"

A siren split the basement air like a shot.

"Fuck," Charlie said, leaping from his chair. "It can't be us."

Tony froze, each hand holding almost $10,000. He looked around helplessly as if wanting to buy at least one thing before it all caved in. Had Frank made a call?

The wail came toward them like some mechanical bloodhound; they could feel it sniffing from block to block. Just as Charlie was peeling back some crepe paper, it reached the height of its crescendo and veered away.

It was moving away from them. It wasn't coming for them. It was gone.

"They wouldn't have had the fuckin' siren going anyway," Tony said, dropping the two piles of money on the table. He felt sick from the sip of Kool-Aid he'd had. "Shit, I lost count; now I'll have to start all over again."

9

Meanwhile, Back at Purolator

Investigators believe an electronics expert silenced the alarm on the heavy vault door . . . then circumvented two other alarms inside the vault.

— October 24, 1974,
Chicago Tribune

Sunday, October 20, 1974. In less than twenty-four hours on Chicago's Near North Side, two bombs went off. The first bomb exloded at 2:30 A.M. Sunday, in the rear of a three-story building at 14 East Chestnut Street. Police, fire, and ambulance forces rushed to the building, which was owned by Cook County Board President George W. Dunne. He was home alone in his second-floor apartment, asleep in bed at the time. He said he heard "a sort of swishing noise rather than a detonation." The blast blew out the windows and doors in Dunne's building, and shattered a concrete stairwell, where the bomb apparently had been placed. It cracked plaster walls as well, and smashed windows in nearby buildings on Chestnut and State streets. A resident of the John Hancock Center, about three blocks away, called the *Sun-Times* to say her sixty-sixth floor apartment had been shaken but had sustained no damage. "It was just like dynamite going off," she said. The police suspected a battery-timed device attached to dynamite or a plastic explosive.

"I sure don't think it's anything political," Dunne said, unable to come up with a possible motive.

Later an anonymous caller to the *Sun-Times* insisted he had set off an explosive device at the Continental Engraving Company, a small firm on the third floor of the Chestnut Street building, but the owners couldn't think of any reason someone would want to sabotage their company. Nor could Loyola University, which rented the first floor for its Institute of Urban Studies, shed any light on the deed.

A weary police officer speculated that one of Chicago's less adept criminals may have been aiming elsewhere and missed.

"Hit the wrong building?" he was asked.

"Maybe the wrong block," he replied.

About twenty-two hours later, on Monday morning at 12:15, a second bomb blew out the front windows of the Harem Leisure Spa, a nude massage parlor (first described in the *Sun-Times* as a "nudist manicure shop") at 839 North La Salle. It, too, broke windows half a block away. The same John Hancock resident called again to report shock, but no damage. But another apartment dweller on La Salle said, "I almost fell out of bed. Oh, brother. There was a great big flash and it sounded like a big shooting party. I took a nerve pill because I couldn't sleep and I was just relaxing when —Wow!"

That explosion was heard as far north as Armitage and Sedgewick, about a mile away. It also blew a hole in the wall and knocked out all the windows in a four-story dormitory building of the Moody Bible Institute across the street from the massage parlor. Again no one was injured, except two students who stepped on some broken glass.

Monday, October 21. 1:12 A.M. Not even an hour later, and before all the debris could be cleared from the streets, a light began flickering in the office of Wells Fargo, activated by heat sensors in a vault at Purolator Security, Inc. At the same time an alarm, set off electronically, sounded at the fire station half a mile away at Dearborn and Illinois.

The bedeviled residents of the North Side neighborhood once more awoke (if they were still asleep) to sirens, as the usual fire trucks and patrol car careened through the streets to the new scene of disruption. (Not until January 1, 1979, did area police automatically respond in numbers to a fire.) They all converged on the nondescript brick building where nothing at all seemed to be happening. Second Battalion Chief Edwin Nelson and two firemen approached the plain entrance and pounded on the door while other firemen prepared their hoses for possible entry.

The door was finally opened by the lone guard on duty, Ralph Marrera. He barred their entry. Shotgun at his side, and speaking softly, he insisted that only the chief, and two men, could enter — no more, for "security reasons."

Nelson peered past Marrera's shoulder but could not see any signs of a fire. Exhausted by the earlier call to the massage parlor, Nelson agreed and told the remaining men to wait for further orders but to stay on the alert.

"What set off the alarm?" one of the men asked.

Marrera said he didn't know of any fire or that any alarm had gone off.

The firemen began their search in the basement, then returned to the first-floor garage and moved slowly through the entryway to the money-exchange rooms into the vault room beyond where Marrera again awaited them. A bare wisp of smoke seemed to hover around the heavy vault door.

"Someone leave a cigarette in there?" a fireman asked.

Marrera shrugged.

Then the fireman pointed to the clock with its cord disappearing inside the vault.

"Smell that?"

They all sniffed at the odor of burnt rubber, or an electric cord that has shorted out. "Might be that," one of the others said.

"How do you open this door?" Chief Nelson called over his shoulder.

"You can't," the guard replied. He explained that only a few officials of the company had the combination.

Chief Nelson eyed the heavy door. "Better get someone down here," he ordered.

Marrera summoned Pat Hopkins, night supervisor responsible for vault operations. He arrived ten minutes later clutching a small white card with the vault combination written on it. The pressure of the waiting fire trucks, police, and Chief Nelson's scrutiny made him fumble. Three times he tried to open the vault unsuccessfully.

"Call Mr. Hardt," he told Marrera.

Russell Hardt, regional vice president and branch manager, rushed over. By the time he got there, Lieutenant Edward Nickels, commander of the Damen Avenue General Assignment Unit, and his men had arrived. They, too, waited while Hopkins read the combination aloud to Hardt, who didn't have his with him. Hardt twirled the dials. On his first try the tumblers clicked into place. With a minimum of pull, the solid vault door slowly swung out into the room. As Hardt turned aside, he noticed Marrera in back of him peering into the vault. Before Hardt could tell him to move away, a wave of dense black smoke poured out of the vault right into Marrera's face.

Everyone fell back coughing.

"Arson," a fireman said immediately. "I'd know that smell anywhere." He later explained that it wasn't the smell of gasoline, but the smell of material burned with gasoline that has the most distinctive odor.

Chief Nelson instructed his men to don masks, have their hand extinguishers ready, and "check the inside of the vault. Hurry." He had already called for the bomb squad, which arrived just as the other firemen were bringing in blowers to get the smoke out of the vault and permit the others to enter and assess the damage.

As the smoke thinned, Hardt watched in growing horror. The vault walls were completely black; charred bags and blocks of currency were jumbled all over the floor, and here and there he caught the glint of coins.

"My God. Look at that," one fireman said. "They tried to burn up money!"

When the air was partially clean again, a pungent smell of gasoline was traced to eight unburned plastic bags that still held a gallon and a half of gasoline each. Only two of ten bags had erupted. The vault contents had suffered a short, intense blaze that had charred some stacks of bills and some footlockers, and melted what may have been a time-delay fuse that lay in the ashes on the floor as a strange, hard piece of debris.

Russell Hardt put in the first of his calls to the FBI.

Soon the two-story brick building was surrounded by police cars, investigators, and employees reporting for the day's work. The bomb and arson squad, headed by Lieutenant Edward Neville, carefully began to remove the remaining bags of gasoline from the vault. Other empty money containers were then discovered, as well as several more tightly bound bundles of currency, their edges scorched, but still usable at any grocery store or racetrack. Trying to burn them was like trying to start a fire with a telephone book. The final assessment of fire damage was relatively small. Apparently, when the first bags had ignited they had flared up and sucked all the available oxygen before it could be replaced, in quantities sufficient to sustain the blaze, from the ventilator in the ceiling of the 25-by-25-by-15-foot vault. The thieves seemed to have overlooked a relevant law of physics — without oxygen, flames die, and so died their foolproof plan.

Marrera stood around echoing the disbelief of those involved in the cleanup and maintained that he didn't know a thing about either a fire or a burglary.

Further speculation continued as the vault was dusted for fingerprints and scrapings were picked up and sent to the crime lab for analysis. It was clear to experts present that a specialist in deactivating complicated burglar alarm systems had circumvented the system hooked up to the Wells Fargo security board because it was undamaged — just as the specialist must have had the combination to the vault, for it, too, was intact. They suspected the robbery was thirty hours old, the money removed immediately after the final deposits of Saturday. A check of the vans showed that none was missing.

Meanwhile, Russell Hardt told Marrera to summon all extra vault personnel to keep an eye on the police and firemen and to set up a section of the first-floor money rooms to begin counting the remaining stacks of money. They had to determine how much was gone and from whom. He assured everyone that he expected to have a decent total by Tuesday. In reality, Purolator officials couldn't begin to guess the amount missing until some of their clients' footlockers and tankers were delivered and opened and their contents checked.

Another call went to the FBI, who explained again that bombs and burglaries were not their business. "Try the Alcohol, Tobacco and Firearms Bureau," they suggested.

To the policemen and investigators at work in and around the vault, there seemed to be a lot of money left as employees used the low, four-wheeled dollies to cart hundreds of thousands of dollars into the small currency room to be counted. White tags bearing totals up to and over $50,000 hung from the charred canvas bags like price tags.

"Did you ever think there was this much money in here?" one investigator exclaimed.

"I never knew there was this much money, period" was the reply.

The third call to the FBI turned out to be the charm. Six hours after Chicago Police Lieutenant Nickels began gathering details, such as the fact that two Purolator employees had left their posts earlier that Sunday, the FBI arrived.

Some policemen were known to consider the federal men glory hunters, who arrived after the hard work was done. Russell Hardt couldn't assess the justice of the accusation. But he did know one thing. As much as he admired Lieutenant Nickels's hard work around the clock, he wanted the case to go to the FBI. Especially after the final count showed $4.3 million missing — and $44 million left behind.

10

Monday Morning Blues

Police said the thieves left behind at least another $21 million because they didn't have the time or manpower to complete the job.

— October 25, 1974,
Chicago Sun-Times

About 3:00 A.M. on Monday, October 21, when they were almost finished, Charlie said, "O.K. Make the call."

Tony rose and stretched. His back was killing him. Then he staggered upstairs, again listening before entering the kitchen. Doris and the kids were still on the second floor. Frank was still pacing the living room.

Tony spread out a crumpled piece of paper in front of him. It took a while for his eyes to focus on the numbers. He was tired of numbers. He rested the receiver on his shoulder and dialed the exchange of a western suburb. About an hour away, he figured. A man answered on the first ring, ready, as he had been every Monday morning for the past five weeks.

"Yeah?"

"Frenchy?"

"Yeah."

"Come on over," Tony said, and hung up. He thought he could smell money on his fingers. The sweet smell of success. That's what a money smell really was. Old or new. He thumped downstairs.

Charlie looked up. "Frenchy answer?"

"So he said."

Charlie nodded.

Tony could almost hear a click, as if some vital machine part or gear had slipped firmly into place. "You're a planner, you know that, Charlie?"

"We ain't finished yet. I want all this other stuff put away before he comes. He gets the duffel of paper, remember, and that big suitcase there with the two hundred thou. Tell him what you're givin' him. No mistake."

Tony began packing a third suitcase, stacking the piles of bills in neatly, first one layer, then another. "Around a million, right?"

Charlie looked up absently. "Yeah, one million plus. You might need another little case. When you pack that up it goes in your trunk with the three talkies and the forty-fives. All I want in the van is that two million two in the duffels and the other four hundred thou in those two cases there."

"And the hundred thou? My car or the van?" Tony said.

"In the van. You follow me when I make the drops."

They continued packing in silence until all the money was redistributed among the suitcases and duffels, except the cash that they stuffed in their pockets. They figured about a thousand or so would carry them, in smaller bills and a few hundreds. They could always open a case for more. Suddenly an image of the stacks of fives crossed Tony's mind. He had a feeling he counted them double. He shrugged. So the count should've been $2500, not $5000. Big deal.

They began dragging the duffels up the basement stairs,

across the back yard, and into the garage. The grass gleamed wet in the darkness where the duffels left streaks on the lawn. Charlie stowed them in the van while Tony went back for the cases to put in his car trunk.

He felt exposed in the night air, walking down the sidewalk with suitcases in each hand. He wondered if Doris and Frank were watching at the window.

Tony fitted the suitcases in the trunk, and locked it. Then he went back for the talkies and the pieces. He squeezed them in the trunk and put the .45s on the floor in back with two talkies. The third box he placed next to the driver's seat. He hated leaving the car, even for the half-hour wait they still had. My Ford never had it so good, he thought.

It was almost four. They were all sitting in the dining room, Tony with his chair pulled up to the window to keep an eye out for Frenchy. Charlie had the radio on and he, Doris, and Frank were half-talking, half-listening to the news and snatches of song. Frank had lost about $30 that night.

"Just couldn't concentrate, you know." He was drumming his fingers on the table. One of his thumbnails was blue from being smashed in a car door at the garage where he worked. He had a tic at the corner of his eye that Tony couldn't recall noticing before.

A few minutes later a car drove up and parked behind Tony's Ford. His stomach lurched for a second until he realized it was their pickup. He carried the duffel and a suitcase outside where the guy waited by his open car trunk. Frenchy moved forward to take the money from Tony, who said, "Hold it. It's two hundred thou in this case. Got that? Put it away. Don't call us. Don't do nothin' till you hear from us — even five years — you don't do nothin'." Then he handed over the suitcase and Frenchy laid it gently in the trunk. Threw a red blanket over it.

"And this here," Tony said, hefting the duffel. "On your way back you gotta do something. This is full of four million money wrappers and some thousand checks. You burn it until it's all burned up. Till nothing's left. Understand? Nothing."

Frenchy nodded, placed it, too, under the blanket, and slammed the trunk. Tony jumped. "Christ, you wanta call a neighborhood meeting?"

"I'm getting out of here now." Frenchy ducked back in his car. Tony tensed, expecting a squeal of tires, but the guy was careful. A nice smooth takeoff like any experienced burglar.

He returned to the small dining room where Charlie was listening intently to the radio. Frank was walking around the table. He held up his hand for quiet as Tony entered. The announcer was excited about a couple of explosions. At first Tony thought they were referring to Purolator, but then he caught "massage parlor on La Salle," and "George Dunne's house."

"Shit," he breathed.

He watched Charlie for some sign of what was going on. Of all nights. After what they'd done at Purolator they could really catch some heat — another beef on them if they got caught. Especially if someone got hurt. Charlie didn't look bothered at all.

"You have anything to do with that?" Tony asked.

Charlie didn't look up from the radio, just laughed and put on that smirk of his. Frank looked sick.

Tony couldn't figure it. Had Charlie planned it? Was someone else helping out? Were those bombs supposed to take the heat off Purolator? — make it seem all one thing? But they'd be in worse trouble if it was all the same, with George Dunne such a big muckamuck in the machine. Hell, Charlie knew that. He just liked to keep everybody guessing. Looked just like that's what they'd be doing.

When the report was over, with a lot of theorizing by the police because there was a massage parlor and a big-name politician involved, Charlie said, "Now we go." He turned to Frank. "There's something on the table for you in the basement. Make up for your poker loss. Thanks for everything."

Tony shook Frank's hand, gave him a punch on the arm. "You did all right," he said. "Poker's a good game, keeps you out of trouble, huh Doris?" Doris laughed and started gathering up the coffee cups from the table. She wore a faded pink robe. There were dark circles under her eyes.

"Take it easy," Frank said. "Call if you need anything." His voice shook. With relief — or fear that they *would* call, Tony wondered.

"Wait a minute," Charlie said, looking suddenly struck. "I got to make one call."

They watched while he went into the kitchen, heard him dial, wait, then say, "As long as you're up, let's us have breakfast."

Then he called to Tony and they filed out the back way. "Keep your box on and I'll direct you," Charlie ordered. "Just follow me and stay close behind."

He climbed into the van as Tony opened the garage doors wide. The rear lights blinked on and the van started to back out toward the street. Tony headed for his car. Frank could shut the doors later.

Charlie passed Tony's car as he was climbing into it. He slowed down to let Tony ease in behind, and then with nearly $4 million between them, they drove off into the darkness. No thoughts of sleep.

It was nearly 4:30 A.M. Tony had no idea where Charlie was going. He followed the directions coming over the box: "left ahead; right at the stop sign." Whatever Charlie said, he stayed close, Charlie only crossing on newly green lights, so no gap opened between them, and no car could slip between.

Suddenly, after twenty minutes of driving, Charlie said, "O.K. You're gonna park here," and Tony pulled automatically into the spot just vacated by the van. He watched Charlie turn into an alley. Tony looked around. It was a nice enough neighborhood. Then he heard the screech of a garage door lifting and winced. Christ. The heat could come around a corner any minute and see Charlie dragging stuff into the garage. Only it would look like he was robbing the place. Not too many people throw a few million in a garage and take off. Little gambling debt, officer.

A car passed their street a block away, Charlie shoulda doused his headlights. Suppose a guy's looking out his window. The fuckin' houses were so close together, only a gangway to walk between. If you sneezed the next family'd say Gesundheit. Shit. Every time he thought their worrying was over, it was something new. When you're sitting on a million bucks and two pieces of hardware, it just don't feel good on a dark street — not even knowing the name of the street.

He lit a cigarette, then saw Charlie backing out of the alley. His voice came over: "Follow me."

Tony took a deep drag as he pulled in behind the van. Wouldn't have killed Charlie to give him some idea of where they were going.

Again Charlie called out rights and lefts until Tony realized they were pulling up to the tollway. Did he have any change on him? He felt frantically in his pockets and came up with a handful of silver. Two hundreds fell out onto the seat.

South. They were heading south. He knew they were eventually going to Denny's Restaurant at 111th, but Charlie still had another drop somewhere. Then Charlie's voice came through. "Pull over at the oasis — on the side."

The van swung to the right and Tony followed, heading for the far edge where a car was parked alone. As Charlie pulled next to it, his window and the man's car door opened almost simultaneously. No words. The man reached his black-gloved hand up to Charlie, who handed him a small suitcase. He never looked at Charlie, or toward Tony, just closed his door and pulled off, without looking in the case, either. Must've been the hundred g's, Tony figured. Then Charlie's voice: "O.K. Now follow me all the way in."

Tony glanced at his watch. A little before five. Very smooth, he thought. He wondered about the explosions, but he didn't want to turn on the radio and miss any of Charlie's directions.

As they entered the restaurant parking lot ten minutes later, Charlie broadcast his last message. "Park over there." He was pointing to the middle of the south side of the lot. Two other cars were parked on the east side, near the huge Denny's sign. Charlie pulled into a space on the north side, directly across from Tony. No other cars or customers were in sight. Just them, out looking at the stars. He turned off his motor and peered out the window. So what the fuck was going on now?

11

Tell Me the Way to Go Home

VAULT ROBBERY A PLOT FOR "MISSION: IMPOSSIBLE"
Authorities believe an operation of this magnitude had to be set up well in advance, with foolproof arrangements to dispose of such a large amount of cash without arousing undue suspicion, probably through international fences. Police think the loot was aboard a plane bound for parts unknown within an hour of the heist — before the fire bombs went off — and even the legmen who stole it don't know where it is right now.

— October 27, 1974,
Chicago Tribune

The meeting at Denny's Restaurant parking lot had much in common with a one-ring circus — something was missing. Namely, a guy willing to stop by for the $400,000 cooling in Charlie's van. The last drop.

As Tony looked around at the various cars, he could see, even in the dark, that the guy wasn't there. Now what? Charlie's orders had been explicit. Each car must park in a different section of the lot so as not to draw attention. But

Louie DiFonzo was out of his black Lincoln and draped over Pete Gushi's window. He caught Tony's watching silhouette and waved. Dumb fuck. Someone oughta let him know he's in on a *real* score.

The door of Charlie's van slammed shut. Tell 'em, Charlie. He watched as Charlie stalked over to Pete's car, throwing his arms around. They all seemed to talk at once, with occasional phrases reaching Tony through the morning air. Two minutes, three minutes passed. He got out of his car and walked over to them.

Just as he reached Pete's car, Charlie turned and shouted, "Get the hell back to your car. All of you. You think this is a fuckin' convention?"

"So what the hell's going on?" Tony didn't move.

"Look." Charlie turned back to Gushi and DiFonzo. "We don't want to attract any attention, I told you. Suppose some customers come? Or cops?"

"At 5:00 A.M.?"

"Denny's is open all night. Anyone could come."

"Except the guy who's supposed to."

"Let me handle that. Get on back."

Tony and Louie returned to their cars. Again the feeling of fear hollowed out Tony's stomach. Wide open parking lot. Empty streets. He looked back and saw Pete and his wife, who was still in curlers, getting out of their car. Charlie, who had started toward his van, turned and motioned them to stay put. But Mrs. Gushi wasn't having any of his orders and gave Pete a slight nudge as he started backing up. "Get the fuck back in the car," Charlie yelled.

Mrs. Gushi did. But Pete suddenly darted into the restaurant, his coat flapping behind him. Charlie looked as if he might have a heart attack. With Pete's crazy drinking habits, who knew what attention he'd attract? He never seemed too drunk, but nobody was sure they'd ever seen him sober.

Charlie then caught Tony staring and gestured for him to get back in his own car. Tony pulled the door open and backed onto the seat with his legs extended outside onto the concrete. He didn't feel like sitting.

Five minutes passed before Pete finally emerged from the restaurant. Charlie gave him the finger but Pete just grinned. Tony tensed, waiting for the crazy laugh, but Pete saved it for his wife in the car.

Tony remembered a story a friend had told him about the crazy bastard. The guy said that whenever he and Pete were going to check out a score or something, Pete knew they were supposed to leave between four and five in the morning, but still — every single time — Pete would be asleep and come stumbling to his door like it was all a surprise. So one time, when he got to Pete's house and was ready to knock, the door suddenly opens and there's Pete, all shaved, clean, and smiling in his robe. "Come on in," he says, "and I'll finish dressing." Then he suddenly puts some marching music on the record player. Real loud.

"Whadya think you're doing?" the friend asked. "You'll wake the neighborhood. And your family's up there sleepin'."

"Never mind," Pete yells over the music and heads up the stairs toward the bedrooms. "It's a glorious, beautiful morning," he shouts. "Everybody get up. It's a beautiful day." And then, sure enough, in a few minutes Pete returns, dragging his wife, pushing the kids before him. He then makes them march around the living room, stumbling from sleep, in time to the music, while he beats the air with an imaginary baton. He keeps it up maybe five minutes before he lets them go back upstairs. Then he and Pete laughed themselves sick.

Tony could imagine the woman in her wrinkled nightgown and bare feet, the kids in pajamas, marching in crazy circles. He shook his head. It didn't seem funny to him. And waiting here didn't either.

He glanced at his watch by the light in the glove compartment. Getting close to six. A few cars were beginning to travel the streets, their headlights seeming bright as searchlights to him. He wasn't sitting here all morning.

He walked across to Charlie's van and leaned against the door. "Look, we sit here any longer and you'll be sitting here alone. You call that bastard and tell him he ain't here soon we'll be putting the money in the men's room. Paper's paper."

Charlie studied his watch, then looked in his rearview mirror. "Shit. He proably ain't showing. O.K. Move. I'm going to pull the van over to Pete's car."

"What for?"

"Get rid of the case. His wife can drive it home and hold it."

Tony stared as Charlie started up the motor; then he backed up and followed him. Charlie pulled out a suitcase and a large attaché case. Pete had already opened the trunk of his Plymouth and removed a two-suiter traveling bag. Then Charlie deposited his cargo.

Mrs. Gushi climbed out. "What am I supposed to do with that?" she squealed. "Stick it in the cookie jar? The kids'll be up any minute." She stood shivering in the predawn air, trying to keep a scarf over her curlers as if her dignity lay in a covered head when her nightgown stopped short of her bare, veined ankles.

"Tell her," Charlie said coldly.

Pete turned to his wife. "Like you said, stick it. I'm going fishing."

Her jaw clamped shut.

"Tell her to take this money home and put it away for me," Charlie said. Louie had joined them now.

She climbed back in the car, behind the wheel. Pete poked his head through the window. "You hear Charlie?"

She nodded, looking straight ahead, and he handed her the keys.

"Then do it."

She started the engine and backed up with a squeal of tires, her expression like that of an underpaid and abused whore.

"O.K. Pete, you ride with Tony. Let's get over to the store and leave the van. It's empty now. We're all set."

Tony and Charlie moved away. Louie was patting his pockets. "Listen," he called. "My car's running and the key is still in it. I guess I locked the key inside." They all looked toward his car.

"I don't fuckin' believe it," Charlie yelled. "We're already running behind time."

Louie just looked at him.

"Go in Denny's and get a coat hanger for Chrissake," Charlie said.

As Louie left, Tony said, "Is this what we need a genius with a fuckin' one-eighty IQ for?"

"We need him for the money," Charlie said, "the dumb fuckin' shit."

Louie returned with a black wire hanger and tried to snake it through the window. His carefully draped, longish hair kept flopping in his eyes as he poked the hanger, elbows out, the cuffs of his cashmere sport jacket a discreet distance from his thin wrists.

"Give it to me," Charlie growled at him. "Now all we need is some cop snooping around asking to see your owner's registration, and then taking an interest in a bunch of grown men standing around with their fingers up their asses."

"Some genius," Tony muttered, as Charlie, with a few expert twists, caught the handle and pulled it up sharply.

"Hey, thanks. You've had a little more practice than I've had." Louie opened the door.

Charlie looked tempted to use the same hanger on Louie, but threw it in his back seat instead. "O.K. Let's get out of here. Louie, you follow right behind me. Pete, you go with Tony, and keep behind Louie. A nice little fuckin' parade." They all nodded and Charlie climbed into the van.

Pete and Tony walked back to Tony's car. "I'll show the way," Pete said, getting in next to him. "We're only a couple of miles from here."

The three remaining vehicles began backing out just as an early customer's car straggled into the lot, the driver foggy with sleep, needing a jolt of morning coffee.

Tony saw Charlie exit, and then Louie pulled right behind him. They were about forty feet away going straight on 111th Street.

As Tony followed after them, Pete said, "I know a faster way to the store. Turn at the next right."

"Look. Let's just follow them, Pete. O.K.? We'll all stay together."

"I know this fuckin' neighborhood," Pete insisted. "So just turn right at the next corner."

Tony turned right, too tired to argue. Suddenly his eyes widened. "Pete. This is the fuckin' tollway!"

Pete swiveled his head. "You know? You're right." He laughed.

"I hope you don't die laughing," Tony said through clenched teeth. "I got some money and things in here."

"Huh?" Pete was checking the signs.

"I said," Tony continued, "I got over a million dollars in the trunk."

"A million what?" Pete laughed hysterically. "And we're going the wrong way. We're going north on Two-ninety-four."

"North?" Tony yelled. "What the fuck you mean *north?*"

Pete laughed harder, tears forming at the corner of his eyes. He wiped behind his glasses. "I mean we're going away from Hundred-'leventh Street. You shunta turned there. I meant the next corner-corner, not the fuckin' ramp."

"So where the hell do we get off?" Tony yelled. His jaw hurt.

"Maybe Seventy-fifth, Seventy-ninth." Pete pushed his glasses back up his nose. "We ain't lost, you know."

"Lost! It ain't lost I'm thinkin' about." Tony wanted to hit him in the mouth. "I'm thinking about Charlie waiting in your lot, and what's riding in my car."

"Over a million." Pete whistled. Then he noticed the walkie-talkie and picked it up. "Call 'em on this."

Tony grabbed it away from him and threw it in the back seat. "You're gonna broadcast bringing home the bacon, you dumb shit. That thing picks up about a mile. Thanks to you we're about thirty miles away from them by now. And no exit signs. You get us off here fast. Now where?"

"I told you. Around Seventy-fifth."

"Where's that?"

"Coming up soon. 'Bout a half hour from the store."

"Half hour? You know what Charlie's gonna be thinking, with you directing me and a million dollars just a lousy fifteen blocks?" Never mind the .45s in back, he thought. In the beginning, Pete was involved only to the extent of the $50,000 he was to get for arranging for the boat to get them out of Miami. Now he'd just sent his wife off with $400,000 to hide in her petunias, and who knew what went on behind that laugh of his? Pete was called a lot of things, but "dope" wasn't one of them.

"There's the exit," Tony said. "Which way. Should I make a right or left?"

"Left." Pete's glasses glistened.

Tony made the turn at the end of the ramp, then frowned. "Hey, we're going west, further away."

"Yeah, I just seen that. There's Roberts Road up ahead. Make a left and we'll go back south. Take too long to get back on the tollway."

"Shit." Tony's knuckles whitened on the wheel. The urge to push Pete's face in fought with the need to stay on the road. It was still pitch black. He squinted into the early morning darkness. "We're out in the goddamn country. Those are fuckin' cornfields." Blackness stretched before him and behind; his headlights seemed to create the road. He hadn't gone more than a mile when he suddenly jerked backward, as if struck by the light that appeared in his rearview mirror. It was revolving and about ten blocks away.

"Pete," he choked. "There's a squad car on us. Now what'll we do?"

"Maybe they can give us directions." Pete laughed hysterically until he turned around. "Christ."

"Yeah, it's the man. And we got a million dollars, three walkie-talkies, and two forty-fives under the seat. Now what?"

"Don't know. Don't know," Pete said.

"Should we try to outrun them? But there's nowhere to turn off till Hundred-'leventh, is there? Take the stop? Show our licenses? If we outrun them, we gotta straight-away run. No streets."

"Hell, we can shoot it out we have to." Pete reached around for one of the .45s.

Tony had slowed to thirty-five as soon as the lights appeared. Now they were creeping up. Not fast, like a chase, just a steady move up on them. His heart was pounding. If they shot it out, they could get a murder beef if anything else went wrong. Bomb explosions were bad enough. You had to think "if." You don't cover yourself, ain't no lawyer can fill in the holes later.

Pete was lining up his shot.

"Put it back," Tony yelled. "We don't need no murder

rap." Maybe Charlie was right about Pete being good if you're in trouble. Maybe because it's Pete gets you into it. "Don't do nothing."

The lights were getting closer but they weren't coming up that fast. If he was going to make a run for it, he'd have to do it now. But the heat could call in, have cops waiting for them at the first turnoff. Then the shit would fly. Their guns would be ready. "We better take the stop," he said.

The light was almost on them now, flashing like disco strobes. He could feel them behind his eyes, his head throbbing in a kind of crazy rhythm with the stabs of red. He slowed down. Practicing: anything wrong officer? problems? a steady voice, a steady look right in the cop's eyes, slight frown, concerned-citizen look. Keep the hands dry.

"I'm taking the stop," he said again. Pete didn't answer. He sat frozen, eyes, glasses, staring straight ahead. "So take it. You want me to vote?" he said finally.

The light was immediately behind them now. Tony could see it was a double — jabbing the air in red spurts. He pushed gently on the brakes, felt the car bump off the road, hit gravel. He fought the steering wheel's turn to the right. Finally got it straightened.

The double light swerved around them. Tony felt ready for anything. Loudspeaker, shots.

It passed them wide, pulling a wrecked Buick.

"It's a fuckin' truck! A tow truck." They spoke together. Tony braked to a stop, flexed his fingers, hands, one at a time, and tried to breathe through the ache in his throat.

"I gotta piss," Pete said. "Surprise."

"It's gonna wait," Tony said, pulling back on the road. "Just lean on it with the forty-five."

"That's Hundred-'leventh up there," Pete said, leaning forward. "Turn east. You're on top of it." He laughed.

"Think you can figure a turn more than twenty seconds

ahead?" Tony said, wrenching the wheel. He added a weak laugh. "You're nuts. Nuts."

Pete twirled the gun on his finger. "We'd a made it," he said.

"Tell it to Charlie."

It was about 6:30 when they finally pulled into the parking lot behind Pete's store. Charlie and Louie were standing outside. Tony stopped the car and let his arms relax away from the wheel.

Pete opened his window. "Wait'll you hear this one."

Tony knew that only relief kept Charlie from choking him with his bare hands, just like when his kid was missing a few hours. You want to kill the kid, except you're so fuckin' glad to see him.

Charlie screamed into Pete's face, "Stuff it." Then to Tony, "Let's just get the fuckin' hell outa here."

12

Stratton's Strategy

I once met and talked about a case with Erle Stanley Gardner years ago and he told me to speak my piece.

— Ramon Stratton

"The FBI gets called in for everything," said Ramon Stratton, the agent who coordinated investigation of all bank robberies and burglaries in the United States. "Those TV shows did it." Thus, when the FBI office in the Federal (Dirksen) Building was frantically notified on October 21, 1974, at 2:00 A.M., about the possibility of a bomb explosion at Purolator's vault, the caller was patiently and routinely referred to AFT (the Bureau of Alcohol, Tobacco and Firearms), a department of the Treasury.

At 3:00 A.M. a Purolator official called again. This time he reported an estimated theft of more than $100,000 — isn't that FBI territory? The FBI could understand the increased concern, but again explained that they didn't have any jurisdiction in such a case.

At 5:00 A.M. the FBI received another call from Purolator. Circumstances had changed; an official reported they were certain some of the missing money belonged to Chicago banks — and with this the magic word had been spoken. Richard G. Held, special agent in charge of the Chicago office, called in his nationally known bank robbery coordinator, Ramon Stratton, who would direct the case and report to Kenneth Grant, official head of the bank robbery squad. Stratton immediately sent out calls to the robber squad to come in for assignments. At 6:50 A.M. he phoned Russell Hardt and told him he and his men were on their way.

By 7:00 A.M. Stratton and eight agents had joined the Purolator officials, firemen, and Chicago police on the premises of Purolator. The smell of smoke greeted each new arrival — agent and employee — a pungent reminder that the unthinkable had happened.

Stratton asked for Hardt immediately as he headed for the vault room to survey the scene of the crime. The vault still showed the effects of the violent but brief blaze, as police and Purolator employees sought to establish a sense of order in the midst of charred bills and gutted tankers. Stratton noted the presence of Lieutenant Nickels, who was talking with his men.

Hardt appeared to welcome Stratton with relief. He immediately reported what had happened so far — the fire alarm going off, his being summoned to open the vault, the suspicion of arson, then theft.

"Who was on duty during the fire and theft?" Stratton asked.

"Our building guard, Marrera."

"Ralph Marrera?" Stratton nudged Hardt. "There's the guy."

"You know something about him?" Hardt asked, incredulous.

"I sure do," Stratton said.

"Well, I told him to stay here. I told everybody to just stay put. Lieutenant Nickels has already started to question some of them. He's been here all night. And I called in last Saturday's night shift to check the count and keep an eye on outsiders."

"Good," Stratton told him. He knew that, far from being insulted, the firemen and police always preferred this sort of protection. That way they couldn't be accused of anything later. He got out his notebook. "And tell Marrera I want to see him as soon as I complete my inspection."

Before doing anything else, however, Stratton phoned his good friend Deputy Chief William Hanhardt. "I want to check out a name," he said without preamble. "Marrera."

"Marzano," Hanhardt said. "Charlie."

That was the match Stratton thought he remembered.

"Marrera works here at Purolator," Stratton told Hanhardt.

"Uh-oh," Hanhardt responded.

Then Stratton asked his friend to check with his lieutenants to see if they had heard any buzzings in the streets. Once again he was grateful for the cooperation he had learned to count on from the police officer he considered one of the best in the country.

Marrera. Stratton remembered that Marrera had worked for Wells Fargo during the gold theft of the Tiara Jewel Company in Evanston. At that time Stratton had concurred with Hanhardt that Marzano and Marrera had probably defeated the alarm system. But they didn't have enough evidence for a court case. The FBI had been called in because the gold theft could have involved interstate transportation of stolen goods and therefore come under FBI jurisdiction. (Stratton's squad was not involved in the cooperative surveillance with the ILIC and IBI, or he would have made the connection for them earlier. Purolator's Joseph Woods later blasted Stratton for not telling him about Marrera when the company first hired him. But Stratton had merely noted the fact in a file begun at the time of the gold robbery. If Purolator had called the FBI to check Marrera out, they would have received the information on file. Now, because of recent rulings, the FBI is no longer allowed to keep general files on persons but must request a file from the police only when it relates to a specific case.)

Next Stratton sought out Lieutenant Nickels, who was assigned the case because the Chicago Police Department first sent word from downtown that the robbery was classified as a theft. Stratton later put in a request for the police department's burglary people. (The designation of "theft" declared the robbery to be strictly an "inside job" like an embezzlement. "Burglary" acknowledged the fact of outside aid.) Although the department later reclassified the crime as a burglary, Stratton was informed that the case would remain in the original hands.

Nickels agreed with Stratton that there had to be an inside man, but indicated he could not spare the time to recount what he had learned during the past hours. At this point Stratton felt the first of many regrets that Hanhardt had just been transferred to a different section and wouldn't be in charge of the case. Many local police were known to treat the FBI with the attitude "Don't call us and we won't call you." He knew that some police detectives hoard information hoping to break the case themselves, and a few even don't share it with the rest of their force.

He shrugged and pushed his way through the more than fifty lawmen milling around, trying to stay out of the way of Purolator's employees and still watch what was going on — and, in the case of Nickels's men, proceeding with earlier assignments and interrogations. (Stratton was startled to hear one of the policemen, who was eyeing the black personnel who had been called in to help count the money, conclude: "The niggers did it." He didn't regret not receiving that piece of information personally.)

Stratton wanted to clarify Purolator's current procedures

and study its physical layout, but first he assigned his arriving agents to interview personally every Purolator employee. Forty of his men were at Purolator by 8:00 A.M. They knew he wanted every detail: who was on duty; who they saw as they arrived and left the building, inside *and* outside; who was supposed to be at work and who was not; who was late, even one minute; and who was on time. Records and timecards would be collected to corroborate the employees' testimony and provide the agents with addresses and phone numbers to check.

The agents would pile detail upon detail for Stratton, knowing the way he worked. Later, with intense concentration, which Stratton labeled "the name of the game," he would pull the facts together to create a single clear interpretation — an interpretation to aid the U.S. attorneys in leading a jury toward the only possible conclusion.

With his men already assigned, Stratton then moved methodically through the two-story building, jotting down notes and more questions to be answered. He immediately learned that the vault's time locks were secured at 9:26 P.M. Saturday by two employees. One, called a vault coordinator, is supposed to watch while the second, a vaultman, locks the safe. Next, three people were supposed to be on duty every twenty-four-hour period: the person who watched the alarm board, which controlled the security alarms for other buildings Purolator protects (just as their counterpart and competitor, Wells Fargo, was watching out for them); a messenger with a walkie-talkie, who is dispatched by the alarm-board person to investigate when an emergency seems minor, or when verification by someone on the premises is required; and the vault guard, armed with a shotgun and stationed at the vault, whose sole charge is the vaults and their contents.

Stratton knew from the first, as had Lieutenant Nickels,

that the job required an inside man — especially when no signs were found of forced entry to the building or the vault. This knowledge helped, because an inside man makes the job easier for everybody — cops and robbers.

One problem was, How did all that money make an exit with the three employees present? Were they all involved? Logic dictated that the vault was opened by someone who knew the combination, and the money carried away in a vehicle. But Stratton forced himself briefly to consider another possible method of theft resting on an assumption that the money never got into the vault. An employee could kick a small portion into one of the narrow locked rooms where the money transfer is made, and later cart it out, either by emptying its contents into another case or, if it was small enough, by carrying it on his person. But the vault working area is so small and crowded with employees and messengers delivering money that the chance of getting away with even a few thousand was slim. The sheer bulk of the missing funds was sufficient to rule that method out.

Yet the question remained: Had the vault been opened again Saturday night, October 19, or October 20, or never? Had thirty hours, or three, elapsed before discovery?

The agent Stratton had sent to interview the Wells Fargo board watcher called from there to say he was getting nowhere. The young Indian boy on duty at the time of the burglary insisted that, although the vault alarm wiring had been faulty for weeks, going off for no reason, on this particular Sunday night the vault definitely had not been opened — no alarm had flickered or buzzed on the Wells Fargo board until the fire alarm went off, an hour after he had been replaced.

"Tell the police he's lying," Stratton said. He knew the puzzle piece he was looking for. "Have them put him on the lie box and send me the results." There was too much red tape involved for the FBI to do it. First they would have to send the attorney general in Washington a synopsis of the case and explain why the individual was suspected of being involved in the case as well as what they hoped to gain from a polygraph examination of said individual. It was easier to have the Chicago Police do it. Stratton assumed he would hear within the hour if the man was found to be lying. He didn't — until six weeks later.

At 10:00 A.M. Stratton and Nickels agreed that Marrera had to be the inside man. Stratton sent for him. Minutes passed as he paced outside the small room set aside for him, preparing questions, going over the facts he already knew. Finally Russell Hardt came to tell Stratton that Marrera had slipped away some time between 8:30 and 9:00 — he'd vanished as easily as the money he'd been guarding. Phone calls to his home had brought the response that he wasn't there either. Would Stratton join Hardt in his office?

Hardt shut the door behind Stratton and asked him if the question of jurisdiction had been decided yet.

Stratton admitted that he and Nickels had been batting it around a bit.

Hardt, a tall and solidly built man, similar in stature to Stratton, then made his plea. He wanted the FBI to take jurisdiction. "It seems likely that interstate transportation will be involved," he said, and Stratton nodded. "Well then, as I see it, the FBI could go into other states, without red tape that could tie up local police. Even go into other countries."

Again Stratton agreed.

"Then, I think that a case could also be made for Purolator holding bank money because the money we pick up is headed for banks. That makes it really a bank robbery, doesn't it?"

"That's the way my mind's been going," Stratton said.

They left the office together. "Should we tell Lieutenant Nickels how we feel?" Hardt asked.

"It's really up to the state and federal attorneys," Stratton said shaking his head. "And if Marrera calls in, don't tell him anything's wrong. Just ask him to stop in and see you first before he comes in to work."

Meanwhile the banks were reporting back in terse phone calls that their tankers of money were not adding up. In fact, the First National had received a tanker filled with a plastic bag of gasoline, while the seal outside had, to all appearances, never been broken. A harassed Purolator officer recorded the calls as the missing amount slowly built up to a substantial figure. Staff continued counting the money left behind.

Other pieces of information began to form their own pattern, aided by Stratton's well-known "total recall." A mental note tugged at the back of his mind. As he handed out more assignments, he suddenly called over one of his agents who had been working with the Illinois Legislative Investigating Commission a short while ago and had been telling him about a case and the surveillances of suspects planning some big score.

"That surveillance case you mentioned, with a Charlie Marzano and a Pete Gushi. Is Marrera one of the other names?" Stratton asked him.

"I think so, but I'll check. I probably won't be able to get the information right away."

"Keep checking," Stratton told him. "I want to know soon as possible."

Stratton didn't leave the building for lunch. Instead he grabbed a sandwich at the desk Purolator set aside for him. He already knew the case was not going to be a question of "who," but a matter of "with whom," "how," and "when." Therefore it was vital to fill in every particle of time, and identify every person. He called this "locking in the time of the burglary." A good investigator builds a mosaic of "pieces." Even if one or two are missing, he can still discern their outline, and know what he is looking for. One piece was the sheer bulk and weight of the money, which would dictate its interlocking partners: a vehicle to hold the money and carry it away; people to load the vehicle; time for loading; time to get into the vault; time to place the gas-filled bags there; time to get out. There had to be a fat time gap to allow for all that action. Which brought the question back to who was on duty when the money disappeared.

Marrera.

He had come in at 6:00 P.M. Sunday after being on duty only sixteen hours earlier. The vault was locked by 9:34 Saturday night. The fire was a little after 1:00 A.M. Monday. Who greeted the firemen?

Marrera.

Who was guarding the vault?

Marrera.

The vault had to be opened to put money in and get money out. The door opened only by combination. If it was opened illegally a signal showed at Wells Fargo. Who knew the combination?

"Not I," Marrera had said.

During the course of the day, forty people were discovered to have the combination of Purolator's vault, and each was entitled to have it. Two of them had it taped to the inside of their lockers in the building. To Stratton's shock, the company informed him that the combination had not been changed for more than a year. Most corporations and banks change their combinations every three to six months because, according to Stratton, if a company doesn't change the combination regularly, it leaves open the possibility of "someone going sour on them." Most large banks, however, have timers, and their vaults cannot be opened until the preset time. Joseph Woods pointed out that the huge vault had to be available at all hours for servicing its customers, so a time lock was not feasible. (Two weeks later Woods told the media that a time-lock device had been installed on the vault and "a more thorough system for investigating potential employees" had been adopted.)

By 1:00 P.M. Monday the ILIC called Stratton and confirmed that Ralph Marrera had indeed met for frequent breakfasts with Charles Marzano—the man they had had under surveillance for a future grand-scale heist.

Stratton summoned four of his agents. "Find Marrera and bring him in. And if he won't come in voluntarily" — Stratton underlined his words — "then put him under arrest. I've got enough information to write up a complaint sheet and make it stick."

By 2:00 P.M. the missing-money count was in: $4 million was gone. Purolator people had been working frantically all morning to deliver the remaining tankers and bags of money to clients in order to more quickly get reports back to determine the exact amount stolen. The count given to the newspapers that day was $3.9 million — or approximately 700 pounds of cash. According to Joseph Woods, "You don't carry this amount of money around in your wallet. And if you start to spend it in large amounts someone is sure to notice." He purposely neglected to report that the thieves had left behind $44 million, because Purolator didn't want the public to know what large amounts of cash they sometimes kept around. "They'd need a train to haul that away," Stratton said later.

While the Chicago man in the street, when interviewed by Bill Kurtis for Channel 2, cheered the robbers on to success, the newspapers speculated wildly about what you would do when stuck with half a ton of money. They suggested that the thieves must have had an outlet even before the theft, that the money could have been distributed to mob emissaries throughout the country to be swallowed up and washed in legitimate businesses. If hidden in a house or garage, there is always the chance of fire or theft. And burying money causes other problems — someone else might stumble over it, or mildew might set in if it isn't packed in airtight containers. They didn't speculate on how many and what kind of airtight containers. But on one point there was no doubt: a criminal mastermind had engineered the entire caper.

As befitted what was finally recognized as the largest cash haul in United States history, the Commercial Union Insurance Company offered a reward of $175,000, the highest reward ever offered, for information leading to full recovery of the currency taken in the robbery.

"This will bring every creep out of the woodwork," predicted Stratton. One creep was all he needed.

Speculation in Monday's late newspaper editions concluded that by now the money was probably out of the country — only hours after the robbery put aboard a plane bound for parts unknown — Angola, for instance; that the thieves undoubtedly had a foolproof plan involving international travel and fencing connections worthy of the Chicago tradition: the Taylor Street Alumni.

13

On the Road

Investigators said two false alarms of "robberies" at the Purolator headquarters were received by police in recent months.
Investigators now view these as "dry runs" by the thieves to
test how long it would take police to arrive.

— October 24, 1974,
Chicago Sun-Times

Monday, October 21, 6:45 A.M. Once more the two cars
set out, Louie and Charlie in Louie's rented Lincoln Continental, and Tony's Ford bringing up the rear with Tony,
Pete, a walkie-talkie, pistols, and a million dollars plus.

Before they had gone five miles, Charlie rolled down his
window and signaled them to follow into a gas station.
Tony pulled up to an air pump a few yards away and waited
while the attendant came out to service the Lincoln.

Suddenly, Pete got a schoolboy smile on his face; he
grabbed the walkie-talkie, pressed the button, and began to
speak in his version of an announcer's voice: "Calling the
car filling up. We have a message for you — " The station
attendant straightened up and stared around for the source
of the voice.

Charlie came whipping out of his car and opened the door on Pete's side. "You dumb fuck, you think that's some kinda toy? Put it away and don't touch it no more!"

Pete laughed his cracked laugh. "Just testing, Charlie. Just testing."

"You'd like to test a forty-five in your mouth, shithead?" Then Charlie pulled the door all the way open. "You get in with Louie," he said.

"Charlie's afraid I'll wear the battery out," Pete said to Tony. He spat into his Kleenex.

"We got a million bucks plus guns in this car and you start giving imitations of Walter Cronkite to the pump jockey. Get out."

When he'd gone, Charlie slid in beside Tony and muttered, "Shit-for-brains is better off in the crash car, anyway."

They were almost in Indiana, the flatness of the land seeming to flatten their thoughts, when Tony said, "I don't think we got a crash car, if you know what I mean."

Charlie, who had been dozing, sat upright. "What's that?"

"Louie keeps fallin' behind. I lost sight of him. Say the police set up a roadblock and we get stopped. Can you see Louie rammin' that Lincoln into a police car? Pete neither. They see us stopped and they'd breeze by just as though they never heard of us."

"Maybe so," said Charlie thoughtfully. He craned out his window to look behind them. "Slow down and let him catch up."

Tony slowed to forty miles an hour. In about five minutes Charlie said, "I see them. Go slow and head into the next turnoff where there's a coffee shop or something."

But there was no sign of a turnoff and so Charlie turned the radio on. They caught the last part of a news broadcast about the mysterious bombings in Chicago. No mention of a robbery.

A few minutes later, they saw a sign advertising a diner and they turned off the highway.

"You know, I think you're right," Charlie said. "We switch the suitcases to the Lincoln and this is the crash car then. I'll ride with Louie."

"And me with that goofy ape again," Tony said and groaned.

They all went into the diner and sat down at a booth. There were two men in overalls at the counter, drinking coffee. A sad-faced woman with a hairnet and a too-short skirt came from the kitchen and handed them menus.

"One Seagram's and a chaser," Pete said loudly.

Charlie frowned at him. "This is breakfast."

"That's what I always have for breakfast," Pete said.

Tony turned to the waitress. "Great sense of humor, huh? He means that he wants a glass of orange juice."

Tony, Louie, and Charlie all ordered ham and eggs and toast.

"Gimme a bowl of chili," Pete said. "And bring the ketchup."

When the waitress had left, Charlie said, "Now about that boat in Florida — "

"Jeesus, the boat," Pete said. "I gotta check on that. Gimme about three dollars in change for the phone."

While they were pooling their loose change on the table, the two men in overalls swung around on their stools to watch.

"I thought it was all set," Charlie said.

"Nothin's ever all set," Pete said. He began to gather up the change.

Charlie looked over at the phone on the wall and extracted a quarter from the pile before Peter set off. As soon as Pete had started to use the phone, Charlie put the quarter in the juke box and turned it as loud as he could. Pete began to bellow into the phone and the two men at the counter swiveled around to gawk at him.

"Jesus, we oughta be on TV," Tony muttered.

Pete returned to the table just as the waitress brought the food. "Guy says there's a storm or somethin' — and he can't take us," Pete said, sitting down.

"Whadya mean he can't take us? A deal's a deal. A storm don't last forever."

"No go," said Pete. "He just won't take us."

"Well, so we drive to Florida and hope somethin' will turn up when we get there," Charlie said. "How long does it take? Two, three days?" They argued awhile about what they ought to do when they got there.

Finally Louie said, "I got an idea. There's a private jet service in Ohio. We charter a plane and they fly us down — no fuss and we get there in time for dinner."

"Which means leaving the cars behind."

"So we have to leave them behind sometime."

Louie got some more change from the waitress and Charlie turned the juke box on again.

Louie came back to the booth. "It's O.K."

"Wait a minute," Charlie said. "Who are they and what did you tell them?"

"They're Executive Jet Service. It's going to cost us forty-six hundred bucks in cash. I said we're fishermen on our way down for a vacation."

"What name you give them?"

"James Morini."

"Hey, nothin' doin'," Tony said. "Nobody gets me into one of them flyin' coffins."

"It's a Lear jet," Louie said. "A big plane—two engines. You'll see."

On their way to the cars, Charlie announced the switch. They hauled the money out of Tony's trunk, with the pistols, and stowed it in Louie's. Then Charlie and Louie got into the Lincoln and led off.

Tony and Pete followed, with Pete doing the driving so Tony could rest. They rode in silence for some time. Then Pete said, "Soon's we get out of Indiana, watch out for the first little package store in Ohio. I'm gonna make a stop."

"Shit you are," Tony said, sitting up. "No drinks till we get to where we're going."

"A guy's got to have some kind of a hobby," Pete said. He hummed to himself, and coughed into a Kleenex. Then he said, "Indians and drinkin' reminds me of the time I coulda had a real big score, with the blessings of the U.S. Government Indian Fucking Affairs Agency — "

"Shit, the government keeps tabs on that, too? I mean what goes on in the wigwam after lights out?"

"Anyway," Pete plowed on, "this government official and me, we got it all set to give a grant to these Indians and so we flew down to someplace in Arizona, with the papers, see, to meet this chief and his son — "

"They gotta fill out a form after they do it? They have to wait for you to bring them the papers?"

"And I bought some whiskey and we went out to some cabin or other and there's this chief, a big guy but about a hundred years old, in stinkin' clothes. And I mean drunk. Him and his son both — "

"I seen it on TV already," Tony said. "He wants you to sell him some guns so he can burn down the wagon train."

"Shuddup. Meanwhile, we're all drinkin' and drinkin' and the G-man gets these survey maps spread out on the floor and is telling the Indian how we'll help him sell the land for a profit so's he'd never have to work another day in his life — "

"How many days had he worked so far? I thought you said he spent his time drinkin'?"

"It'd be news to me, I mean him workin'. Anyway, we're all drunk and Sittin' Bull takes offense at somethin' I said — don't ask me why — and then we start punchin' each other out — "

"I don't want to hear about it, unless it ends up with you like Custer."

"I'm tryin to tell you a story, fuckhead. So, the next day Ross, the G-man, gets the bright idea that maybe the chief shouldn't stink so much if we want him to go back to Washington with us. So we go to this crossroads general store, you know, cracker barrels and kerosene and all that shit, and there's a rack of clothes in the back, and onna rack a white sharkskin suit, for thirty-eight-fifty, that musta been inna store since the Civil War, and that fuckin' chief loves it — "

Tony had slumped in his seat and closed his eyes and was giving dramatic, drawn-out snores.

"Hey, Tony," Pete said in a hurt voice. "That ain't the end. Doncha wanta hear how we go out to this place drinkin'; and the chief and me start to Indian-wrestle, and how I throw a bowl of chili into his — "

Tony snored on, like a lonesome train whistle. Pete hawked and spat into another Kleenex and dropped it in Tony's lap.

A little after ten, Tony woke with a jerk when Pete snapped the radio on. He caught the news report after it had started.

". . . of the Purolator Security Company, an armored-car service that transports and holds large amounts of cash for other firms. Police estimate that something over three million dollars is missing. Illinois Bureau of Investigation agents and police are continuing to probe the case and the the FBI has been called in. No arrests have been made as yet. According to Charles Siragusa, director of the Illinois Legislative Investigating Committee, earlier bombings of a nearby massage parlor and politician George Dunne's house may have been diversions to direct attention away while the biggest American burglary in history was taking place. . . ." Tony flipped the radio off.

Tony didn't like it. Charlie hadn't mentioned any bombings as a diversion for the score. And the FBI getting into the act wasn't good.

"What's he talking about?" Pete asked.

"Seems like somebody got into Purolator."

Pete was frowning and licking his lips. "For three million he said?"

"Yeah, he said."

"Jeesus — I'm gonna take that turnoff. I need a drink."

"You crazy? Stay on the road. I mean it."

"The IBI, the FBI, the police, and probably the whole fuckin' army. Shit, I didn't know —"

"And you still don't know. And keep up with Charlie, willya?"

Pete drove leaning forward and his forehead was sweat-shiny in the light from the dashboard. "You guys bomb them places?"

"Yeah, but it's only a Halloween trick. And then we was walking by Purolator and somebody was throwin' away packages of old cash."

"I don't like my wife gettin' mixed up in this one."

"You're gonna get mixed if you don't keep up with Charlie."

The car leaped forward. Pete hawked a wad of phlegm into a Kleenex and dropped it on the floor. "I could drink about a pint of Seagram's."

"You can drink some cough syrup next stop."

Tony had known Pete for a little more than a month. But he'd heard that Pete was a standup guy, a loan shark, a dope peddler, maybe even a killer. He had mob connections, for sure. But he wasn't acting tough now. In fact he looked very shaky. He'd done his part with the van, but he'd fucked up on the boat. Maybe the guy and the boat never existed. What did they need with this nut?

But Charlie was the rockhead — a standup guy, a real bull — but a rockhead. Once he decided to put somebody in a slot, you stayed there, whatever happened. But still, he ought to warn Charlie about this Pete. The way he was pissing his pants now.

After a spell of silence during which Pete managed to keep the tail of the Lincoln in view, he finally said, "Where we goin', you know?"

"Ohio."

"I know Ohio. But where, what town?"

"If Louie said, I didn't catch it. So stay for Godsake close enough so we know when we get there." He fiddled with the radio and got some music. "I ain't in no hurry to get on no box kite."

"The stewardess gives us a drink and turns on the stereo and you think you're back at Faces. Nothin' to it. Gimme a new box of Kleenex."

"Can you drive without spittin'? When I get back, I'll have to have the car scrubbed out. Maybe get a new one, though. A Corvette."

At about three o'clock they reached the outskirts of a city. The turn signal on the Lincoln flashed and they followed it into a gas station. They saw Louie get out and go into a phone booth outside the station.

Tony went over to inquire and Charlie informed him that Louie was calling the air charter company. "Just so they got the plane all warmed up for us," he said.

"Pete heard the news broadcast. Now he knows. And I think he's kinda spooked."

"O.K., O.K.," Charlie said. "He'll get over it."

They squealed back onto the highway. Suddenly, as a traffic light was changing and the Lincoln was slowing down, Pete gunned his engine and passed it. He accelerated and passed four or five cars in the right-hand lane.

"What in the Christ?" Tony asked.

Pete didn't answer. He put a hard right on the wheel and they skidded into a parking lot in front of a state liquor store. He got out and jogged into the store.

Tony looked back and saw the Lincoln bogged down in the traffic. Not much risk they'd get too far ahead. Anyway, there was a sign by the roadside that read AIRPORT.

Pete came out, clutching a bottle-shaped brown paper bag. Tony slid behind the wheel and made him get in the other side.

"I did it for you, Tony," Pete said happily. "I hate to see you scared shitless about gettin' on that plane, so I got you a little encouragement."

"Yeah, thanks, but don't expect me to help you if Charlie tears your throat out with his bare hands."

There was a chugging sound for an answer.

At last, Louie turned onto the long road that approached the airport and, one turnoff to the right, they saw the sign for Executive Jet Service.

14

And Awaaay We Go

On the theory the money was flown out of town, possibly to Mexico, from where it could be transferred to a numbered Swiss account, FBI agents and others are checking records of flights from area airports.

A suspect in the case, Charles Marzano, forty-two, an expert at silencing alarm systems, reportedly is a pilot. A number of top Chicago hoodlums have access to or own planes, investigators said.

— October 25, 1974,
Chicago Tribune

The lot alongside the Executive Jet building wasn't crowded, but Tony parked his car near the Lincoln. There was an old limousine next to him, but it looked more as if it had been abandoned than as if it awaited passengers. In fact, the whole place seemed surprisingly shabby for an expensive charter service — a littered parking lot, a nondescript office, and a stretch of woven-wire fencing.

Louie insisted his car trunk be completely emptied, including the small leather gun case and all the walkie-talkies. They all joined in, hauling the mass of suitcases over to a place beside the office door. The pistols and walkie-talkies went into Tony's car trunk. That made him uneasy, but now there was no time or place to dump them safely.

Tony and Louie went inside to get the paperwork done. In the low-ceilinged room two men were sitting — one who seemed to be the manager and one who, from the looks of his uniform jacket, could be a pilot. They were at a double desk, talking and drinking Pepsi. The manager looked up and said, "Hello. You Mr. Morini's party?"

As the manager laid a sheaf of papers out on the counter, Louie did the talking and asked the questions. Seven flying hours to Grand Cayman? O.K. Forty-six hundred dollars? Well, it wasn't loose change, but he guessed it was worth it. Beat standing in line at ticket counters. Yeah, sure, he had credit cards and an I.D. Louie was sitting down at the desk and opening his wallet. He was talking too much and trying too hard to be an obliging customer. Tony went outside.

"The jerk is in there giving them his whole biography," he said to Charlie. "I.D., license, address, everything. The goddamn charter papers look like a book."

Charlie glared at him. "He leaves a trail like a bulldozer in the mud. What kinda I.D. you say?"

"I didn't say. I'm guessing, but I think he must have one in the phony name."

Louie appeared at the door and motioned Tony inside again. "They need your car keys."

Tony turned to the manager. "No way. Look, we're paying you cash so why'd you need any collateral?"

The man smiled. "I didn't mean collateral, sir, I mean, if you leave your car in our lot, you have to leave the key. Sometimes we have to move cars from one parking spot to another. But if that doesn't suit you, there's a lot about five miles down the road where you can keep your keys and park for as long as two days." He gave a short laugh. "They

got a way of moving your car without a key." He was holding Louie's brass key ring in his hand.

"Well, I guess," Tony said, and handed the ignition key
over, reluctantly.

"We'll give you a mileage check if you want." He tied
a tab to Tony's key ring.

"Forget it," Tony said. "I ain't worried."

Louie had finished signing the papers, and now he
counted out $4600 in hundred-dollar bills. The manager
gave him a receipt.

"We're ready if you are," the pilot said and opened the
door.

He led the way out onto the apron, and there was the
plane — a hulk against the lighter gray of the hangar. To
Tony it looked like a toy. It wasn't normal size. There
weren't any mechanics clustering around and checking it for
leaks or whatever they check it for. And the pilots looked
like kids just out of college. Tony's stomach took a roll.

"Into the wild blue yonder," Louie said with an expansive
gesture. "C'mon, men, let's get our fishing gear aboard."
Him and his fat mouth, Tony thought.

The two men from Executive Jet followed them back to
where Charlie was still guarding the bags, but he waved
them off when they offered to help load. "No, thanks," he
said sourly. "Whyn't you check the gas tank or the brake
fluid or whatever?"

And so the four of them made a laborious procession to
the plane — Charlie bowlegged with the weight of three
bags, Louie with an overnighter and a hanging case, Tony
and Pete clutching the rest. A high-class bunch of sportsmen
on vacation — Tony was glad that there was nobody else
around. They looked like the Four Stooges heading for Mud
Lake.

Charlie did let the pilot stow the bags away, and then
three of them were climbing up the rollaway steps. All ex-

cept Tony. He stood at the bottom and said, "I ain't flying in that thing. I'll drive down and meet you there."

Charlie turned around. "You get the fuck inside, Tony." He sounded very sore.

"Coupla drinks and you'll love it," Pete said.

Tony shook his head. If that plane could lift six people and maybe a quarter of a ton of money, he was the next police chief of Chicago.

One of the pilots took Tony by the elbow and said soothingly, "It's one of the most reliable planes in service, sir. It's a standard-size executive jet — why, just like the one Hugh Hefner and all his bunnies fly in. And the weather is fine."

Tony reluctantly allowed himself to be urged into the plane. He felt a little reassured at the steady throb of the engines and the sight of Louie and Pete already seated and pouring drinks into glasses. One of the pilots gave them a pitcher with some ice in it and Louie poured Tony a hefty Scotch.

"Wipe off your tears and join the picnic," Pete said. "Kerist, I spent half my life in the air between Chicago and Vegas."

Somebody had pulled the stairs away and the plane was taxiing down to the end of the runway. Then it was making its sprint to take off. Tony looked outside and saw the ground beginning to recede as the plane rose steadily into the cloudless late-afternoon sky. He began to feel a little more secure. He watched the wide spread of the city drop away. The thing was really flying, like a real airplane. He relaxed and looked over at the other three.

Pete's hands were shaking so badly that the liquor was spilling out of his glass. His neck was stretched out and he glared at the door to the cockpit like an alarmed bull.

"You ain't gettin' into the spirit of the picnic, Pete," Tony said. "You're sloppin' your liquor on your nice new pants. What will the rest of the Sunday school think?"

"Fuckyew," Pete said. "It's the goddamn noise; I ain't used to it."

"I'll tell the stewardess to turn on the music," Tony said. He finished his drink, unsnapped his seat belt, and strolled casually to the pilot's cabin.

He knelt behind the pilot's seat. "Mind if I watch?" he asked. He was looking over the dials and gauges for some little red light that might show a malfunction, like the one on the oil gauge in his car.

The copilot took his headset off and turned around and smiled. "Nothing to it, is there?" He reached down for a thermos and poured himself a cup of coffee.

"Shouldn't you keep looking out the window?" Tony asked.

"*They* are watching for us," the pilot said and, with his elbow, pointed at the array of instruments on the panel. He began explaining the function of each dial — wind resistance, air speed, altitude, horizon, fuel supply. The words settled reassuringly in Tony's head, along with the Scotch. These guys really did know what they were doing. He'd have to go back and explain it all to Charlie and Louie, and Pete. Give them some idea of what went into flying one of these jets. The sky stretched out like a blue road, with an occasional wisp of cloud, like cigarette smoke rushing by.

As Tony walked back, he could hear that Pete had recovered. Pete was saying something about getting busted.

"I said, shut up," Charlie said.

Pete seemed well sloshed. His seat belt dangled now and his paunch lay in his lap like a pillow. He was waving his glass. "I said, 'If we get busted, anyways it's the biggest.' Biggest of all!"

"Tony, sit next to him and keep him shut up before one of those pilots hears him," Charlie said.

"No secrets between friends," Pete said.

"You got no secrets and pretty soon you got no friends," Charlie said.

Tony turned and went back to the cockpit to see if the pilots had, by any chance, caught any of that — but they seemed not to have. Tony wondered if Louie knew what Pete was talking about. Charlie had laid down the rules about not listening to the radio or looking at newspapers and, so far, Louie had acted right — as if he knew there was something he was better off not knowing. Tony stared out the window at the darkening sky. Louie had been told nothing that he didn't need to know. His job was to put the money away in a nice safe bank vault on Grand Cayman. Tony smiled sourly. A nice, safe bank vault when they'd just extracted the money from what everybody thought was a nice safe vault. Maybe Charlie had a lousy idea. But 12 percent interest on the million was going to be good income.

Just to distract them from Pete's loud voice, still coming indistinctly from the cabin, Tony began to chat with the pilots. "You guys in the war?" he asked.

"What war?" asked the copilot.

"What's the last war? The one in Vietnam, I guess."

"Sure. We did a couple of missions in Nam."

"Rough?"

"Well, the R and R part of it was O.K."

"What's R and R?"

"Rest and recreation."

Tony wasn't getting anywhere, and he couldn't think of any more questions.

Suddenly the copilot began to stand up. "Where you goin'? What's the matter?" Tony asked.

"We'll have to stop in Miami to refuel. If we keep on to Cayman, we'll have to check in with Castro, since we're flying his way. I better see what Mr. Morini wants to do. It means going through customs in Miami."

"You keep this thing pointed right," Tony said hastily. "I'll go check with him for you." He made his way unsteadily back to the passenger compartment.

"Hey, Charlie," he said. "The news is we gotta refuel in Miami, and they say that means we go through customs. You wanta go through with the crew — not to mention the customs officers — gettin' a look inside them bags?"

"Yeah, maybe we better get off in Miami," Charlie said in a low voice.

Louie said, "I'll talk to — "

"Siddown," Charlie said.

"After they see what's in the bags, they get a bright idea about hijacking the load," Tony said.

"It's 'skyjacking.' What you mean is skyjacking," Pete said in a slurred voice.

"Stick that glass in your mouth or I will for you," Charlie said. He turned to Louie. "We stop and that'll give you time to call your Cayman people. Also, I'm not so sure if going through all the way with these guys is such a good idea. Tony, go tell 'em."

Back in the cockpit again, Tony was almost beginning to feel like one of the crew. "Hey," he said. "We had a change in plans. Important business in Miami before we go down to the islands."

"Anything you say," said the copilot. We'll be there in about twenty minutes."

"Where's the airport in Miami? Far from the town?"

"Right by the ocean. Close as you'll ever get to it without getting wet."

Tony shivered. "That ain't funny. Listen, I'll give you a bonus if you make a nice, slow landing. No funny stunts like in the war." Tony was remembering shots of planes bouncing and skidding along runways in old war movies. He was also remembering his car back at the airport with two guns for cargo.

"We planned something like that just for fun," said the copilot. "But we'll follow your instructions, sir." He leaned over to the pilot. "Please use both wheels, Bill. And no figure eights." Then he was on the radio, talking with the Miami control tower. He motioned for Tony to go back to his seat.

As they made the landing approach, Tony watched the ocean grow bigger than the sky. They seemed to slant in from the left and then they seemed to be skimming over all the water in the world, reaching for that little strip of concrete somewhere beyond. Then, before he knew it, there was a thump and a change in the engine roar and they were rolling along the ground, green Florida ground on either side.

Pete, almost cut in half by the seat belt, was looking sick again. Louie was smoothing his jacket and adjusting his tie. Charlie was looking out the window as if trying to spot a squad car, the pulse jumping in the side of his forehead.

As they rolled to a stop, Tony went forward and presented each pilot with a hundred-dollar bill. "Nice goin'," he said.

"Just a part of our service, sir," said the copilot. "But for a tip like that, we'd be willing to go up and come down again."

"I had my quota," Tony said. "Just get somebody to bring out the goddamn stairs."

The pilots wanted to help with the luggage again. Tony saw that Pete was still green and hardly making it from his seat, so he let them.

Charlie, bent under the weight of two suitcases, slowed Tony down and asked, "You give them a tip?"

"Yeah. I figure they earned it."

"How much?"

"Hunnert apiece. It's a bargain, Charlie."

"You *balordo*. A couple more bargains like that and you'll be back runnin' a fruit stand. And no fruit."

Tony thought it was too bad that Charlie would never think big league. The biggest score in history — bigger than Brink's — and this guy was still squeezing his nickels.

15

Stratton: Man and Mode

WOMAN IN PUROLATOR CASE — STORY OF
A NIGHTMARE

"The way I look at it, my life wouldn't have been worth two cents if I'd been there when the action started.

"I was pretty tired and asked Ralph if he would mind if I went home early. This wasn't the first time I skipped out early. I would say there were at least five other times, too."

Sylvia said the monitor wasn't really unattended because "Ralph was there and he knew what the procedure was."

"They [the thieves] would have killed me to shut me up. For all that money, wouldn't you?"

— Sylvia J., October 29, 1974,
Chicago Tribune

Monday, October 21. 5:00 P.M. "We got Marrera." That was one of Stratton's agents. "We're at his home."

"Is he willing to come down to headquarters and talk to me?" Stratton asked.

There was a pause. "He says 'sure.' "

"Bring him in."

"With traffic, might not get there till six-thirty, seven."

"I'll be waiting," Stratton assured them.

Still at Purolator, he picked up the phone and called Leonard Harrelson. Harrelson was head of the Keeler Polygraph Institute and Stratton considered him the best in the business. Luckily, Harrelson was still at his desk and he answered.

Would Harrelson run a suspect on the lie box tonight, sometime before 7:00 P.M.? Stratton asked. He didn't yet have Bureau authorization, he explained, but he'd try to get some from Purolator.

Harrelson agreed.

It took a few more phone calls to locate a Purolator official at his home and get his permission. As he called, Stratton was jotting down the questions he wanted Ralph Marrera asked.

Through previous interviews with Purolator employees and bits and pieces of clues, Stratton had patiently reconstructed a partial scenario of what must have happened on Sunday night. It was no more than a small part of the story but, he thought, one good way of getting into it.

There had been three Purolator employees on duty that evening — Ralph; Sylvia J., whose job was to watch the "fireboard," the console where any alarms automatically registered; and Johnny, the messenger. The woman had arrived at the Purolator headquarters on time, and had spent a little while talking with Ralphie. He was good company and fun to have around. He even volunteered for Saturday and Sunday night duty, which were the least popular nights among the security guards.

Ralphie had remarked on how dull things were — that was Sunday night for you — and had said that she might as well leave early if she felt like it. He'd keep an eye on the alarms for her, as he had done before. She'd thought about it for a minute, and then she'd agreed. If she left a bit before eight, her husband could pick her up. After all, there were still two men around to keep an eye on things.

After she'd left, Ralphie got into a conversation with the messenger about movies. Then they talked about porno movies — especially the hot flick that was playing at the theater just down the street. Neither of them had had a chance to see it. Ralphie said that he hated to miss it, but, well, there was no reason they both had to lose out. Why didn't the messenger take a breather and a look at the show?

After all, it wasn't as if Johnny would be out of touch, Ralphie pointed out. He could take his box — the walkie-talkie — along with him and check in from time to time, just as he did now when he went upstairs for coffee. Ralphie would let him know if he was needed back at Purolator, or on a run to one of the customers. And so the messenger had gone off, leaving Ralphie alone from eight to midnight.

There were two more odds and ends in the tale Stratton was trying to put together.

When the runner got back, Ralphie had complained that the vault area was stuffy and had opened the door that led to the garage, "to get some air in here." Stratton wondered if Ralphie, at that time, might have been worried that the vault would blow up when the gasoline-sack bombs ignited.

One more small thing. A three-inch pile of metal debris, fused solid by heat, had been found on the floor of the vault. It could be some kind of a trigger device, and Stratton had sent it to the lab for spectroanalysis.

With Ramon Stratton in charge of the investigation, the FBI had put one of its best and brightest into the field. He was tenacious and dedicated and, as Sanford J. Ungar, Washington editor of the *Atlantic Monthly,* described him in his book about the FBI, *An Uncensored Look Behind the Walls,* Stratton could be "abrasive." (Stratton once abrasively pointed out that Ungar promised him an autographed copy and he never got it.)

As a thirteen-year-old, already on his own in rural Oregon, Stratton had read J. Edgar Hoover's book *Persons in Hiding;* he had wanted to be an FBI man ever since. After an army stint as an M.P., he took a minor civil service job and worked his way to a law degree from the Northwestern Law Division of Lewis and Clark College. Very soon after, he was admitted to the ranks of the FBI.

His first assignment was more like a Canadian Mounty's than a G-man's, however. Based in Juneau, Alaska, he had a territory that stretched over 86,000 miles. With hard work and increasing expertise, he made a name for himself, and eventually he was given an unprecedented promotion to the rank of GS-14 — a rank otherwise reserved for administrators and supervisors.

Then came his fall from grace. Stratton had become an expert — among other accomplishments — in instructing ·police classes in search and seizure. One day, during such teaching, he happend to tell a mildly off-color joke — off-color to the extent that he used the word *ass.* Somebody in the Juneau FBI office reported this offense by letter to J. Edgar Hoover.

Presumably, Mr. Hoover was horrified. In any case, the result was that Stratton was transferred at once to New York as a field agent and his GS-14 rating was in jeopardy. Eventually he was allowed to retain his rating — but for Stratton, who hated big cities, New York, and then Chicago, were punishment enough. He spent thirteen years in Chicago before retirement, polishing his reputation as a specialist in bank robberies and becoming familiar to cops and criminals alike as a very tough man — but a straight and fair one at the same time. If he so desired, Stratton could fill a book with his cases. Probably Stratton's favorite story concerns a long-time underworld figure known as The Hawk. In one of Stratton's cases brought to trial, the gentleman, now rather elderly, was called upon to testify. In order to prove his connection with the accused, The Hawk was asked repeatedly if that was indeed his nickname.

"Never," he said. "I have never been called that."

Repeated questionings could not budge the old man. "I never heard that name before," he insisted. "I don't even know anybody by that name."

Finally, the federal attorney gave up and told the man to step down. A bailiff rushed forward to help the elderly man, took his elbow, and said, "Be careful. There's a step here. Don't slip."

The old man drew himself up to full stature and intoned before the entire court, *"The Hawk never slips!"*

Now Stratton was in the midst of the biggest burglary case of his career, the largest ever pulled off in the United States to that date, and second only to England's Great Train Robbery. And he was convinced that Ralph Marrera was going to help him solve it — if he could lean on Ralphie hard enough.

He returned to the FBI offices, which occupy the ninth and tenth floors of the Dirksen Building. The only entrance to those offices is from the ninth-floor elevators into the reception room. All doors have alarms and security is tight. The ninth floor contains the chief clerk's office, pending and closed files, the offices of top administration officials and secretaries, and three squad areas. Each squad area has several plain desks and a small room for the supervisor's office. The tenth floor, where Stratton headed, has the steno pool in one corner; the remainder of the floor is divided into sections for agents' desks, and little rooms for each squad's supervisor. The bank robbery squad was along the middle of the north wall.

By the time the four FBI men arrived with Ralphie, Stratton was waiting at his desk, uncluttered except for the few sheets of paper with his notes. Stratton himself asked just one question — would Ralph willingly take a lie detector test?

"Sure," said Ralphie.

He was hustled into the supervisor's room where Harrelson and his polygraph equipment were waiting.

Ten minutes later Harrelson came out of the small room to the waiting Stratton. "He's lying in his teeth," Harrelson said. "He's in it up to his ears." Now it was Stratton's turn to take over.

He questioned Marrera most of that night and for long sessions over the next two days. Eventually, the questions and answers boiled down to a script with a few main points.

STRATTON: How did you open the safe, Ralphie?

MARRERA: I didn't have the combination; I couldn't do it.

STRATTON: You opened the vault. You opened the door and let a friend come in with a truck; then you set off those gasoline bombs, didn't you?

MARRERA: No. While I was on duty, the vault was locked. I don't know what was in it.

STRATTON: You sent the other guards away, didn't you?

MARRERA: They always like to leave a little early. I just sat there until the firemen came. And I wouldn't let them in, either.

STRATTON: You set the fire.

MARRERA: What's the use of talking to you? You don't believe me anyway.

STRATTON: I believe you, Ralph. Only I disbelieve you when you say you didn't do it. I know you did.

MARRERA: I'm a millionaire — why would I do it?

STRATTON: You got to be a millionaire afterward. You weren't before. Are you afraid of your partner? We'll protect you as a witness.

MARRERA: I got no partners.

Stratton finally wearied and turned him over to the waiting Chicago Police detectives who wanted their turn at questioning an agreed-upon prime suspect.

On Tuesday Assistant State's Attorney Nick Ivarone decided without Stratton's concurrence to bring Marrera before the Cook County grand jury, to make him testify under oath.

On Wednesday Marrera was again brought to Stratton's office, this time accompanied by his lawyer. After she left, they began to go through the Q. and A. script again, one they had both learned by heart. They faced each other all day long, neither varying his position. Early in the evening, after having been printed and photographed, Marrera rose from his chair. "I can't take it any more. I'm never going to talk to you again!" he yelled, and bolted out the door.

The two FBI guards outside were taken by surprise. They pounded after him, but somehow Ralph managed to get out of the building and to lose them outside by ducking in and out of stores. The look Stratton leveled at his men surpassed his quiet expletive. Now, both Ralphie and the money were missing.

16

Fools and Their Money

Imagine, our own Second City, the true-life scene of the biggest, most bizarre, most bungled, most unbelievably successful heist in the annals of American crime.

— October 31, 1974,
Chicago Tribune

At the Miami airport, the four men stood among their array of assorted suitcases and waited at the curb. "We gotta get a cab," Charlie said, but there was no cab in sight. Louie went inside to find somebody who could help, and a few minutes later two cabs pulled up alongside them.

The drivers got out to help with the luggage, but Charlie said stubbornly, "We're just taking one."

"You guys like to sit on top of each other?" the first cabbie said. "I ain't going to fit you and the suitcases inside."

"One cab," said Charlie. "You got a trunk ain't you?" Pete slid into the front seat and the other three got into the back.

"Where to?" the driver asked in a disgusted voice.

"Miami," Charlie said, putting down his window.

"No kiddin'? It's a big town. Could you maybe figure out some point where you want to land in it?"

There was a pause. The last specific places in their plan had been Denny's Restaurant lot and the rendezvous at Pete's.

Nobody had thought about what happened when they got to Florida. Pete finally conjured up a name. "Go to the Colonnade," he growled.

Florida at night is a place of electric colors — bright greens of the palm trees that line the highway into the city, the glare of neon signs, the palette of colored shirts and dresses on the streets, the gaudy lights of the big hotels that line the beach like huge Monopoly pieces. They passed those ostentatious inns whose names are meant to recall — for those who have never been there — the charms of France: the Fountainebleau, Eden Roc, the Doral.

The Colonnade had a plainer name, but it looked just about as fancy to Tony. The cab entered the circular driveway and pulled up before the doors. A doorman hurried up to help them. "Tell 'im to keep the fuck away from them bags," Charlie said. He was digging out his wallet to pay the driver.

Charlie paid and they got out. Then Tony looked back and saw the driver looking grimly at a fifty-cent tip — and Tony quickly stuffed a five into his hand. They waved the doorman away and struggled with the dead weight of the suitcases — four figures wobbling into the elegant lobby.

Halfway across the wide expanse to the desk, Charlie began to sense something strange about the place. Strolling around the posh cavern were a lot of middle-aged men in well-tailored suits. Most of them had young cool-looking girls on their arms. Familiar faces were swimming past Charlie's vision.

"Wait a minute!" Charlie said. He put his suitcases down and turned to Pete. "So what made you pick the Colonnade, asshole?" he asked. "Look, there's Slim Gariti and he's on his way over."

Tony noted some men at the counter — a guy he knew only as Danny, with half his crew.

"It's a fucking Chicago convention," Charlie growled. "C'mon!" He began trundling his two cumbersome bags toward the door.

A face sometimes shown in the *Tribune* or the *Sun-Times* appeared on the other side of the glass. "Holy shit," Charlie said. He bumbled through the door and made for the street corner to catch a cab. The others staggered along in a trail behind him.

In October and November, the armed robbers, burglars, and jewel thieves who have had a successful year gather their girl friends — or even their wives and kids — and take a plane for Florida and a holiday in the sun. It is a well-earned break before the busy Christmas season, when they have to suffer the snow and cold of Chicago again. But business is business, and the Christmas season is the best time for shoplifting. Pickpockets thrive then. For those higher on the larceny scale, there are mansions on the Gold Coast or in Kenilworth whose inhabitants are on cruises in the Caribbean. Tony and company had arrived in the wrong week.

Charlie yelled in the cab window. "Open the trunk. Yes, we're all going to get in this one cab. And, no, I don't know where to. You just drive — somewhere not too fancy and not too far away. Like a family motel."

The cabbie drove in silence for a while. Finally, he said, "How about the Airport Tower Hotel? It's convenient."

"Try it," Charlie said.

The soaring façades of Miami Beach diminished behind them. The storefronts now were squat and crowded together. The motels they passed had pastel stucco buildings with parking areas of cracked concrete and small swimming pools surrounded by fake grass and wire fence. The rent was dropping fast.

The cabbie suddenly made a fast U-turn and pulled into a motel driveway behind a camper. They got out. The cabbie accepted Charlie's 10 percent tip in silence.

"Good thinking," Tony said. "Now he'll never remember us."

It was about 8:30. Charlie led the suitcase parade into another lobby — this one in somewhat woebegone Spanish style, with potted palms, a crying baby, and a kid on a tricycle wheeling in circles. Charlie told Louie to check them in at the desk. He signed himself Keith Anderson of Jersey City, New Jersey.

"We can find the way," Charlie said to the bellhop. "Gimme the keys — and here's two bucks. Get yourself lost."

Up two flights of stairs and through a maze of corridors, they finally found rooms 37 and 39.

"This ain't the Ritz," Tony said as he heaved one of the suitcases onto a bed.

"Charlie thinks the Ritz is a cracker," Pete said.

In a few minutes Charlie came and made them transfer the suitcases to his and Louie's room. "Now siddown on the beds," he said, "and we gotta have a conference. First rule is, you don't make no phone calls. Don't buy no newspapers. Don't talk to nobody. Second rule is, when you get hungry, you call room service. Everybody stay in their rooms till we check out. Runnin' around this zoo lookin' for you guys ain't in my plans."

"Fuckin' unreal," Pete said after he and Tony had gone back to their room. He was pacing up and down.

Tony stared at him and knew that he couldn't make it through even a day or two stuck in the room with this animal. He picked up the phone and called Charlie. "We gotta get out of the room — just go down for dinner, Charlie." There was an argument from the other end, but Tony finally won. He promised to come back up right after dinner.

Tony and Pete walked around the motel, looking into shabby conference rooms, at the swimming pool where four or five kids were throwing rubber balls at one another, and finally into the dining room. It was all brown Naugahyde and plywood paneling. A family of six sat at a round table by the door. Little brother sat in a highchair building mounds of mashed potatoes wherever he could reach; sister topped each mound with green peas from her plate.

"Somehow, I ain't so hungry as I thought," Tony said.

Across the red-carpeted corridor, there was music, and there they found the bar. Artificial candles sparkled on each table. Four or five men were setting up music stands and getting out instruments. They were dressed in glittery white tuxedos.

As they sat down at the bar, the bartender laid down the sports section and said, "That Namath. Best passer in the game and he goes on TV in pantyhose. You seen his legs in them things?"

"Better'n my wife's," said Pete. "Give me Grand Marnier on ice and a shot of Martell for a chaser." Tony took a vodka and tonic.

"We got company," Tony said. Louie was peering in at the doorway, hands in his jacket pockets.

"He got the wrong place — no hairdressers in here," Pete said, squinting.

"Charlie's going to feel lonesome, all by himself with those bags. He's gonna start talking to them," Tony said.

"Be quiet and take a sniff. I think I smell a French whorehouse approaching." He turned around and, in mock surprise, said, "Jeez, it's Louie! Did you fall through the perfume counter in Woolworth's?"

"Cut it," Louie said stiffly. "Come back to the room if you aren't going to eat. Charlie doesn't want you getting drunk."

"I never get drunk," Tony said and chug-a-lugged his vodka and tonic.

"There are a lot of ears around," Louie said in a low, angry voice.

"If you're goin' to stink the place up, you might as well sit down and drink while you do it." Pete slapped the stool next to him, but Louie turned and moved away. "Well, fuck 'im," Pete said.

The band had swung into its first number and Tony and Pete were beginning to relax. A short man with a delicate walk, wearing wire-rimmed glasses, came up and sat next to Tony at the bar. Just then another man — wearing a plastic badge that read MANAGER—came up and leaned over to speak to the man in glasses.

"They were late again. And that's three times this week. Are you running an amateur hour or something?" He was leaning into the little man's face. "Once more and they'll be playing on the sidewalk."

"Aw, c'mon. They were practicing," the little man said.

"Leave 'im alone," Tony said. "I like this music — it's a good group. And those tuxedos with sequins all over are cool." The band had finished now. The manager went away, shaking his head.

Louie — in a different shirt and jacket — had reappeared and was motioning them to a table. Tony ordered another round of drinks before they ambled over to Louie.

"You back again, Notre Dame?" Pete asked, and they sat down.

"You guys — " Louie stopped as the little man in glasses sidled up to their table.

"You don't mind if I buy you guys a drink? I heard you say you like my group."

"Come back some other time. We're in conference," Gushi growled. The man shrugged his shoulders and moved back to the bar.

"Hey, he don't mean it like he sounds," Tony called after him. And to Pete he said, "Whadya say that for? He probably thinks we don't like him."

"Let him go," Louie said. He kept wiping his forehead with a silk handkerchief from his breast pocket. "You guys, we'd better get back to Charlie." He pushed his chair back slightly.

"I'm hungry. I'm going to order a sandwich. Charlie wouldn't want me to faint from hunger, would he?" Pete asked.

"Hey, maybe we should talk to him about buying the band," Tony said, still looking after the little man. "Call him back, see what he has to say." He beckoned toward the man.

Their voices were getting louder and they sprawled in their seats — except for Louie. Tony and Pete got more expansive with every drink. Tony filled two ashtrays.

After another number that featured a drum solo impossible to talk over, the little man came over to their table and sent a waitress for another round. "Where you guys from?" he asked.

Nobody answered the question. Tony peered at him a little unsteadily.

"By the way, my name's Jimmy," the little man continued.

There was a loud pop just then, like a gunshot. Pete stood up quickly, tipping his chair over, as a champagne cork bounced on their table. He sat down again.

"Jimmy, whyn't the fuck you go away and come back in maybe fifteen minutes?" Pete asked.

"O.K., O.K.," said Jimmy, a little offended. He gathered

up his drink and cigarettes and went over to the bar again. Another round of drinks came to the table and Pete sent the check over to Jimmy.

"You must be the only guy who ever gave his group a good word," he said to Tony. The band had come back after a twenty-minute break. They had changed into black satin jump suits. The music seemed louder now. Parents, who had got their kids settled in front of the room TV sets, were beginning to filter in from the lobby and the place was filling up. There were men who looked like traveling salesmen and a few single women, locals, who seemed to be looking for action.

"Listen," Tony said, "If this guy is on the level and he owns them — well, it's a ten-piece band and it isn't bad. Why don't we buy them and take them back to Chicago?" Tony was in a warm, vodka-flavored mood. It seemed to him that men as rich as they were ought to be making deals, planning for the future. "When I buy Faces, I'm going to put some live music in."

"Jesus, Tony, what would Charlie say if you turned up with ten musicians and their instruments?" Louie said. "I don't think he'd be too happy." He was drinking with them now.

"Call the guy back to the table," Tony said. Pete made a gesture and finally got Jimmy's attention. He came over again and sat down.

"So you own this group," Tony said, leaning across the table. "How much you got invested in them?"

"Maybe six thousand, maybe a little more," Jimmy said cautiously. "They're a top rock group down here and pretty soon they'll be known all over."

"They play a little louder and they can't help it," Pete said. He suddenly turned to the table behind him and said to nobody in particular, "Shut up an listen!" A middle-aged tourist couple, who had been sitting quietly, nodded vigorously. Pete glowered at them.

"Louie," Tony said, licking his lips. "Louie, tell Jimmy here we want to buy his group off him." He turned to Jimmy. "Louie here represents our organization in business matters and I need a top band for my nightclub. Shake hands with the man, Louie." Louie had a little trouble, but he managed to extend a wobbly arm.

"Night Flight. It's a good name. All they need is a lead singer. Somebody with a big name. Like Janis or Sinatra, I mean," Jimmy offered.

"I don't like Sinatra," Pete said. He leaned forward and the candlelight glittered on his glasses. "Sinatra is out."

"Well, yes, I know what you mean," Jimmy said. "I was just giving a couple of names for example. I agree with you — Sinatra is over the hill."

Pete shook his head heavily. "Sinatra ain't over the hill. He's still better'n all these new fuckoffs. I just don't like him is all. The deal's off if you want to sell us Sinatra."

"I'll give you eight, nine thousand without Sinatra," Tony said. "Louie, you talk."

Louie cleared his throat. "Well, Tony here has made you a fair offer for — " He looked around the room as if he'd lost something.

"Well, nine thousand sounds closer to — "

"One hunnert percent cash," Tony said. "Here, we'll sign this napkin." He smoothed out a damp napkin with an unsteady hand. "Louie, you write it out."

"Paragraph one. Sinatra stays the fuck out of this deal," Pete said.

Louie was trying to get his pen to write on the napkin. Tony struggled to pull a big roll of bills out of his pocket.

"Listen," Jimmy said. "They don't want to be sold. We've been through some times together."

"We'll pay whatever you want," Tony said. "Louie, show him some money. How much you got? Pete?"

Louie fumbled and produced some bills. "Maybe twenty g's."

Tony drew four scraggly lines on the napkin and wrote his name over the top one. He passed it around and Pete signed. Then Louie leaned over and wrote his name unsteadily. When they looked up, Jimmy was gone. He was not at the bar; he had disappeared from the room. Louie waved the napkin, "But we got his signature."

"What does it say?" Pete asked.

"It says J. P. Morgan," Tony said.

"Didn't I hear of the name somewhere?"

"Fuck I know. Hey, he forgot his money." Tony and Louie were stuffing bills back into their pockets.

When they finally rumbled back to Charlie's room at 3:30 in the morning, Charlie was still sitting up, watching the TV with the sound off. The suitcases were piled on one bed.

"You drunken assholes," he said. "Don't talk to me. Just get to bed." Pete had fallen onto the other bed snoring with a kind of blubbering sound. "And get that baboon out of here."

Tony steered Pete toward the door. "Charlie just don't know how to enjoy himself," he said.

17

Tuesday Troubles

Police think the loot was aboard a plane bound for parts unknown within an hour of the heist — before the fire bombs went off — and even the legmen who stole it don't know where it is right now.

— October 27, 1974,
Chicago Tribune

After forty-eight hours awake, Tony needed sleep beyond normal sleep. He pulled the pillow out from beneath the spread and flopped on the bed, waiting for oblivion. He was dimly aware of Pete spitting and coughing while he got ready for bed. The light that Tony wished he'd turned off glinted from Pete's thick glasses every time he moved. Finally the springs in the next bed gave a lurch and Tony, disgusted, got up and turned off the light himself. Traffic still moved outside as if it weren't four in the morning.

Tony was just on the edge of unconsciousness when a wild shout brought him upright. He clutched at the bedspread wondering why it was under him, not over him. He stared around the room looking for cops.

Nothing. Then another half-moan, half-shout tore out of

Pete, freezing Tony again. He leaned cautiously toward the other bed and, in the dim light straining under the windows, saw Pete writhing beneath the blanket. Christ, the bastard was having a nightmare. Tony stretched and kicked Pete's bed. He finally had to get up and shake his shoulder until Pete shuddered awake.

"What — what — "

"You was having a nightmare. Damn near gave me one."

"Probably just snorin'," Pete mumbled, his face shiny with sweat.

"Snoring, shit," Tony said. He pulled his shoes off and slid under the spread. He guessed Pete had done plenty to have nightmares over. Rumors about killings as well as all the other stuff. Yeah, an ice pick should give the bastard nightmares. Tony tried to get rid of the adrenalin that Pete's shout had sent through his body. His legs were twitching as he turned on his side — facing Pete across the distance between their beds. He concentrated on the thought of the piles of money being stuffed into duffels — the stacks he and Charlie had counted. Dollar bills were floating through his head when another shout from Pete brought him upright.

"Goddammit," he shouted, and Pete rolled over mumbling something. Probably his prayers.

During the next two hours Tony dragged himself out of bed five times to shake Pete loose from the terrors that infested his sleep. In between sleeping bouts, Pete paced the room, the spaces between the beds, the area near the window, hacking and spitting as he moved. His blue silk robe flashed in the dim light. When Pete would lie down, Tony tensed, waiting for the screams. If they didn't come right away, he'd drift into half-sleep like the second driver on a long haul in bad weather.

At 6:00 A.M., Tony couldn't stand the seesaw anymore.

His head was killing him — still balanced between too much to drink and the beginning of a hangover.

"Let's go down to the coffee shop," he told a now wide-awake Pete. "Get some toast. We ain't gonna get any sleep up here."

Pete's red-rimmed eyes blinked agreement behind his glasses.

Tony wondered if last night was a regular pattern for him. He had heard that Pete tried to hang himself once with a bedsheet in Leavenworth, where he was serving a term for hijacking.

Some said that he had another case pending that could add on ten more years. He wanted to help his lawyer get that sentence made to run concurrently by showing that he couldn't take that much time in jail. And it worked. Other word was that being confined was *really* driving him nuts. He didn't do too well in motel rooms either. Tony wished Charlie would get rid of the guy before he went off his nut and got them into real trouble.

At the door of the coffee shop, Pete disappeared suddenly, saying he had to make a call. The words didn't register with Tony until Pete was out of sight. He waited a few minutes, then decided he'd better take a swing around the deserted lobby. He passed a bank of phones and two cleaning carts.

No Pete.

His circuit brought Tony back to the coffee shop and he shrugged. Charlie would have to deal with him. He'd played keeper for a psycho for the last time. He settled himself at the long counter. The place was practically empty except for a couple of golfing nuts. The waitress didn't look much more awake than he felt. He was relieved — bright cheerfulness would have hurt his eyes this morning. "Toast," he said. He wasn't up to eggs just yet. He moved a crusty ketchup bottle down two stools.

He was finishing his third cup of coffee and was consider-
ing the idea of food when Louie appeared and perched on
the next stool.

"Where's Pete?" Louis asked, pushing Tony's water glass
toward his toast.

"He said he was going to make a phone call."

Louie fidgeted, turning on the stool. "Maybe we better
tell Charlie."

"Better tell him this is Pete's second call. At least. He
called last night from the bar."

"What!" Louie's stool stopped moving.

"Called his wife. Something about the money. He was
probably checkin' to find out if anything is going around.
You know — like the clap," Tony said as the waitress
brought more coffee.

Louie waited till she left to bring his. "Charlie said no
phone calls. No newspapers. Nothing."

"Yeah, yeah," Tony didn't want to hear it from Louie.
"I'll check the room. You stay here in case he comes back."

Their room was just as they had left it, Pete's robe slung
over a chair and his overnight case open on the bed.

Tony knocked on Charlie's door and when Charlie let
him in explained that Pete was missing, and making a call or
two.

Charlie began hollering. "What the fuck's he doing making calls? I told you guys — "

Tony cut him short. "*We guys* ain't making calls. Pete is.
And he's in bad shape, if you ask me." Tony slumped onto
the bed.

"Couldn't you stop him?" Charlie was buttoning his shirt
in quick short jabs, his hair still wet from the shower. Tony
had a sudden vision of Charlie first dragging all the bags of
money into the bathroom with him.

"Hey, Charlie. You ain't got the right handle on this guy

Pete. When he ain't spittin' he's having nightmares. Or drinking. Or phoning his wife from his tree. He called her last night, too. Probably missed her hair curlers and his once-a-month fuck."

"I said — " Charlie began.

"Bullshit," Tony said. He stretched out on the bed as Charlie finally clamped his mouth shut. Tony didn't need to take no shit about Pete. Louie's smells were spread out on the dresser — three bottles — along with an array of hair-brushes, combs, and bottles of after shave. His clothes hung neatly near the entrance of the room — even last night's shirt. How did he see to do it? Tony wondered.

Charlie sank into a chair and pulled on his shoes and socks. They waited in silence, Tony with his eyes closed, until a key in the lock focused their attention.

Tony's watch read 7:30.

"I can't find him," Louie said, his face white.

"Christ," Charlie stood up and paced the small space between bed and window. "Couldya take another look around, huh?" he said to Louie, who had picked up a comb.

"Try the bar," Tony called. The door slammed shut. "So now what? What're you going to do about Pete?" He could see the blood pumping through Charlie's temple.

Suddenly a frantic knocking at the door took Charlie back across the room to unlatch the chain. Pete burst through holding a newspaper and shaking like an old man. He held it up for them to see, but it was dipping up and down so badly no one could read anything.

Charlie grabbed the paper from him. "What the hell did you think the papers would say? You been in the news before."

"But my wife says there's an alert out to pick you up. Something about an expired driver's license. We're sitting on a million bucks and they're after your license. They gotta be kidding. And look at those headlines — the score is all over the fucking place." Pete's glasses were sliding down the sweat on his nose.

"Get back to your room and pack up your stuff," Charlie said, jerking his thumb toward the room next door. "Go on," he shouted.

Pete stepped into the hall as if it were wired.

"What're you going to do about him? 'Cause you gotta do something," Tony said.

"Sending him home," Charlie said. "Then we gotta figure what to do. Where's the best place to take the money?"

"You'll get picked up if we go back home," Tony said. "With the warrant out on your license."

"And we don't got any fake I.D.s to get us over to the island. If we have to give our names we might get picked up that way too. Especially if we try to get another private plane to shuffle this money around."

Tony's stomach lurched at the thought of another small plane ride.

"Maybe we better send the money over with Louie."

"Yeah, but would it get there?"

"How the fuck do I know? But what else we going to do? We can head out right after him. Go commercial. Meet him there. Pete trusts him — he brought him in."

"Do you think Louie'd go?" Tony asked.

"Don't know. He has a stake in this too, you know."

Pete returned just then with his small bag stuffed. "You wanna go home?" Charlie asked him.

Pete nodded. "Yeah, yeah. I think I better." He looked like a man just given parole when he expected a ten-year hitch. He pointed at the newspaper still in Charlie's lap. Charlie folded it over and threw it at him in disgust.

Tony could see only the headline LINK BOMBINGS AND 3.8 MILLION THEFT as Pete sat on the edge of the bed. His mouth went dry. He swung his feet to the floor. "Maybe we should wait a couple of days before deciding anything. Especially with that warrant thing. Something smells about that."

Charlie pointed to the suitcases. "Every day we wait, we lose the interest. We gotta get started — " He paused. "We better send Louie ahead."

"Whadya mean send Louie?" Pete's glasses left the paper fast.

"To Grand Cayman. With the money." Charlie started folding clothes.

"What if he keeps going?" Pete screeched. He tossed Tony the newspaper. Tony ignored it as it fell to the floor.

"What do you mean, what if he keeps going?" Charlie whirled around as he spoke.

"Just what I said. What if he keeps going? You only know the man three months." Pete's voice was rising.

Charlie pounded his fist on the dresser. "Hey, you're the one brought him in on this deal. Now we find you don't trust the guy."

"Trust." Pete said it like a foreign word.

"Louie," Charlie said, advancing on Pete and towering over him. "Trust Louie."

"Oh, he's all right," Pete said, looking around to Tony. "I just thought we'd all be together like."

"Like now," Charlie said. "Except you're taking off for home. Leaving us with *your* friend Louie. You wanna go south with us instead of north?"

"I'm going home," Pete said, standing up. "Louie's O.K. I tell ya he's O.K."

"Louie's the only one knows anything." Charlie glared at Pete, that steak barbecue forgotten. "How to set up the accounts — the corporations. He's got the contacts. Lawyers, banks. He wants to screw us he can do it under our noses. And he don't have to worry about anybody chasing him." Charlie looked to Tony for confirmation. "He's gotta carry the stuff over unless you got a better idea."

Tony shrugged. He didn't like the idea any more than he liked Louie, but it made sense. If Charlie was on the wire for a pickup, chances are they included a cousin. Nobody would be looking for Louie — and he looked legit. Tony said as much and Charlie grunted as they heard a quick knock. The door swung against the chain and stopped. Charlie moved to open it as Louie passed him holding his key like a ticket to enter.

"Where you been?" Charlie demanded.

"Waiting for him to show." Louie jerked his head toward Pete. "How long you been here?"

"He's going home," Charlie answered for Pete. "But we think we better get the money out of here and over to Grand Cayman where it can do some good."

"Sooner the better," Louie agreed. Pete looked sour but they all ignored him as they made plans.

"The money goes with you," Charlie said to Louie, his voice harsh. Louie kept nodding.

Pretty cool, Tony thought, watching the exchange — Charlie's instructions, Louie's nods. They had known Pete longer and better, but that didn't prove his sanity. It would be a disaster to send him anywhere now, even with cab fare. If he didn't drink it first, he'd shake till it fell out of his pockets.

"You'll use the name Martin," Charlie was saying to Louie. "Go to the Holiday Inn. We'll meet you there." A steely note vibrated in Charlie's voice and Tony was sure Louie had caught it. He trusted Louie to figure out you don't mess with Charlie.

Louie wrote down the hotel phone number and his Grand Cayman lawyer's number for Charlie, who in turn gave them to Pete — "In case you need to, you'll be able to get hold of us."

Pete stuffed the numbers in his wallet along with some bills. Charlie instructed him to return to Chicago via New York. "And don't call your wife from here anymore. Wait till New York. You hear?" Pete nodded, not a joke left in his head.

"I better get ready," Louie said, gathering up his clothes.

"You call the jet rental," Charlie told him. "Don't go commercial. You'd be pounds over the weight limit."

"How you gonna get through customs?" Pete asked.

Louie winked. "Not to worry. I know how."

"Just do your job like we said. Get your stuff together." Charlie looked around the room at Louie's bottles and things. "Don't leave nothing behind." They watched in growing disbelief as Louie first wet his hair down and then began to blow it dry. He held the dryer in one hand and a small brush in the other while he rearranged and shaped his hair. His eyes never left the dresser mirror.

"Come on, come on," Charlie said once, but even he was too fascinated to push Louie harder. The whir of the dryer made Tony sleepy. He felt himself drop off. When he woke with a start five minutes later, Louie was still drying and brushing. Charlie was pacing behind him. Tony finally realized Louie was fluffing his hair over a particular area — he had a bald or almost bald spot that he was covering like a coconut. Tony ran his hand through his own thick curly hair. If he had that problem maybe he'd give it two minutes with a dryer — but ten? He hoped Louie's brain wasn't being fried.

Charlie now insisted they stuff Louie's hanging bag with cash. Louie protested and said something about wrinkled suits but stopped as Charlie straightened up and looked at him hard. When they had finished the bag was so full they couldn't fold it over. Then Charlie counted out $25,000 in hundred-dollar bills and handed it to Louie for "expenses."

"Anyone call a cab yet?" Louie asked.

"There was three of them," Tony said, "but they couldn't wait."

"We'll get one downstairs," Charlie said, picking up a bag. "One for Louie and one for us. We'll go to Lauderdale. Miami's got too many eyes."

Louie climbed into the first waiting cab and they pushed the suitcases in back until he was surrounded. As the cabbie walked around the car to the front, Charlie turned white. Louie was unzipping one of the cases and then rummaging around through the contents. He pulled out a bill, saw them watching, and waved. "Didn't have nothing to pay the fare with," he said through the window. He already had his sunglasses on.

"Creep," Charlie said as the cab pulled away.

And one more to go, Tony thought as they went back to collect Pete.

18

Whose Money, Whose Case?

The $4.3 million Purolator theft had one salutary effect. It probably ushered in a new era of cooperation between the FBI and the Chicago Police Department, which heretofore dealt with each other at arm's length . . .

— November 3, 1974,
Chicago Sun-Times

Back in Chicago, another drama concerning the Purolator case was being played out: whose case was it and who would prosecute? While the local and state law-enforcement agencies gathered facts and data, interviewed Purolator employees and officials, and sifted through files, Ramon Stratton, too, was busy gathering evidence to make an airtight case: for the FBI's jurisdiction as well as for the prosecution. When he had first assigned his agents to interview every Purolator person, he had begun the locking-in process. Moving nearly a ton of money takes time and space. But his major concern was, Whose money?

In order to justify prosecution by the FBI one of the following interpretations would be necessary: proof that *bank* money was stolen; proof that money was stolen from premises partly used as a bank or in part as a bank; proof that stolen money was transported across state lines; or proof of a conspiracy to commit one of the above three.

Stratton began with the first known "money" fact: In one sense, Purolator "acted as a bank" for Jewel Tea Company. That is, the money was *not* en route to a bank, nor pre-counted and bagged, as was the case with other clients. Purolator picked up each evening's receipts from Jewel stores, counted them, recorded them, and the next morning brought to each Jewel manager the amount requested in various denominations needed to begin the day. When an excess of funds piled up, Purolator wrote a deposit slip and that amount was transferred to the Jewel account at the bank. Thus, Stratton concluded, it could be said that Purolator "banked" Jewel's money. At least this interpretation, he felt, gave the FBI the initial authority to act as investigators and prosecutors. (Ultimately this section of the complaint would be deleted, at the government's request, because the phrase "act in part as a bank" was determined to refer to a small shopping-center building that might house a bank, an insurance company, and other businesses on the premises.)

Other information was needed to buttress the "bank money" proof, however. Simply receiving a locked and sealed tanker with only a plastic bag of gasoline inside, as was delivered to the First National Bank the day of the robbery, does not prove that money — bank or otherwise — had been in it. Ultimately the cornerstone of Stratton's strategy seemed to lie with the Hawthorne racetrack's money and Purolator's procedure for handling it. Stratton knew that he needed to dot every available *i* for juries that often confused "reasonable doubt" with "eyewitness proof." Therefore, the timing of the transportation of the racetrack money was crucial for jurisdiction and prosecution alike.

Saturday, October 19, 1974, was the last day of the racing

season, and Purolator officials had been told to keep the vault open until that money was brought in. They had had to wait until Hawthorne people counted it, packed it into blocks, stuffed it in their own silver chests, and — because there was an overflow from an unusually large day's receipts — finally into canvas bags. (Each footlocker held a little over $500,000, so more than two were needed to handle the more than $1.5 million from bettors anxious to take advantage of the last day.) At least twelve people at the racetrack timed the truck out. Another group at Purolator timed it in *fourteen minutes later*. (Stratton's men drove the exact route themselves a number of times and each time they reported it took them more than twenty minutes. "Someone must have had a special Saturday night date that barred slowing down for red lights, pedestrians, or corners, with over a million dollars acting as ballast," Stratton finally concluded. Upon the arrival of the money, the waiting Purolator people wrote out a receipt, threw the chest and bags into the vault on top of all the other bags and tankers, and locked the vault door.

Beside the signed receipts, which showed when the money was clocked in at Purolator, the next time recorded was the closing and locking of the vault, at 9:34 P.M., about an hour later. It was decided that the Purolator people were in a hurry too, and surely lacked time to abscond with cases of cash, or set out ten plastic bags of gasoline, before going off duty.

By 1:12 A.M. Monday, the vault fire alarm had summoned firemen, policemen, and Purolator employees to the scene. A few hours later, when it was determined that money was indeed missing, 1:12 A.M. marked the point before which the burglary occurred. Thus money had to have been taken between 9:34 Saturday night and 1:12 Monday morning.

Later on Monday morning, as soon as Purolator attempted to return to business and deliveries as usual, Hawthorne's bank received the padlocked containers, but some were empty. The question was, Whose money was stolen? Hawthorne racetrack money or First National Bank money? In other words, at what point did it cease being racetrack cash and become bank notes, charred or otherwise? Was Purolator acting as agent for the racetrack or the bank? Stratton thus needed to prove what he already knew — that the money (when found) had originally been Hawthorne racetrack money.

Therefore, the next step was to break down and study the racetrack's procedures for handling money. All racetrack employees put their own tiny mark on every bill they count. It can be a small *p* or a fancy hook, whatever. Every counter, though, knows his mark and can identify it, and even swear to it. According to the counters, they had put their marks on approximately $1.5 million and locked it in containers that only the bank could open. If Stratton could find any part of that money with those telltale etchings, they would tell their story. Not only that they came from the racetrack, but that they had originally been thrown in a vault *with* bank money. It would be difficult to claim that any Hawthorne-marked money, if and when found, was not from Purolator, since such money would be the only amount Hawthorne was missing. And some of Purolator's money was bank money — and bank money meant "enter the FBI."

If the burglars had headaches stealing the money, Stratton had his share acquiring the case. The state also has jurisdiction over bank robberies, and one of the assistant state's attorneys, Nick Ivarone, wanted the case for Illinois and his own career. According to Stratton, Ivarone "hated the FBI." But his sentiments were not shared by State's Attorney Bernard Carey, who once had been an FBI agent himself. Unfortunately he was out of town on Tuesday for the first joint meeting of state and federal attorneys in the assistant state's attorney's office. James Thompson, the U.S. attorney, was also absent, with the flu. Ivarone refused to share anything about the case with Stratton, and it was soon clear that nothing could be resolved without Carey or Thompson.

At last, on Thursday, October 24, Stratton was able to present his case for the FBI — and his carefully written complaint on Marrera, prepared but as yet unmentioned. (Approval by a U.S. attorney is needed before the FBI can make an arrest.) Those present in Thompson's office included Carey, Ed Nickels (heading the Chicago Police unit), the sheriff of Cook County, the chief of detectives, and the state's attorney's political adviser.

The logic of numbers — manpower, experience, and funds — in Stratton's opinion, further dictated the FBI's involvement. According to Deputy Chief Hanhardt, Stratton was right. In one month, for instance, the police in Chicago Area Two would have to deal with 300 robberies, ten of them bank jobs. They simply could not summon the concentrated manpower available to the FBI for a case the size of Purolator's. Even the state would have had difficulty marshaling the four special prosecutors and five FBI men assigned to the case. Another argument in favor of FBI jurisdiction was the subpoena costs of witnesses. The FBI at that time was able to spend $19 per day plus transportation for each witness, whereas the state paid witnesses nothing, and was sometimes forced to make a deal to save time and money. And finally, the FBI had a much higher rate of conviction for its cases.

The meeting was tense. U.S. Attorney Thompson sat silently with folded hands and listened to all concerned, with much of the aforesaid left unspoken. The state's attorneys cited all the information they already had from the IBI surveillance and ILIC investigation. As talk seemed to be going around in circles, Thompson suddenly said, "All right. I'll prosecute. O.K., Bernie?"

"Sure," said Carey. And it was settled.

At that point Stratton handed the complaint on Marrera to Thompson, who read it and said, "Fine. File it."

Then Carey instructed his people to give the FBI complete cooperation. However, it still took several days before the ILIC would admit that the "big score," the subject already of many hours of manpower and surveillance, *had already happened.* Once they decided this, they turned over several hundred pages of their reports on Gushi, Maniatis, the Marzanos, and the van. It was then that Stratton discovered that the FBI office in Florida had been notified some weeks earlier, thanks to Gushi's boast, that something big was supposed to happen and to watch for "these guys." They were still on the alert when Stratton sent word, repeating the ILIC's acknowledgment: "Hell — the big score already happened."

19

Bye-Bye Miami

Investigators checking on the Purolator theft said it had many elements that TV mystery viewers would find difficult to believe.

— October 24, 1974,
Chicago Sun-Times

Tony had a difficult time erasing the vision of Louie pulling out in a taxi with all that money on board. Charlie was already making plans as they returned to their rooms.

"Pete, you get ready to take off for home. We're leaving here."

They met five minutes later in the lobby. Charlie was paying their bill in cash, shaking his head that no, they didn't need a receipt for business purposes.

"Now we get a cab," he said, walking ahead of Pete and Tony.

Just then one pulled up. "We wanna go to Pompano," Charlie said, getting in the back. Pete got in the front out of habit, even though Louie was on his way to bank heaven in the islands.

"Flat rate, that far," the cabbie said before calling in the fare.

This particular driver must have just gotten up and still wanted to talk about the weather and Watergate. He wanted to let them know he still thought Nixon was the best president the country ever had. "Best living president," he amended. "He just got caught. Everybody does things. You only hear about the ones that get caught." Pete threw in a couple of yeahs at intervals to keep the man happy.

It was a bright Florida day — the kind that hurts your eyes. The sky was too blue and the light glinting off the cars in front was enough to burn off a hangover. They drove north weaving in and out of sight of the iridescent ocean beyond the high-rise hotels.

"Car twenty-one." Tony jumped as a sharp female voice intoned again, "Car twenty-one."

The cabbie reached for a button. "Whadya want?" Pete was sitting up straighter and Charlie leaned forward. The voice continued, "You're supposed to stop at the nearest phone booth and call in."

"Ah shit," the cabbie said. He continued driving. Pete's bald head had broken out in a glistening cap of sweat.

A few minutes later the voice came on again with the same message. As Pete turned an agonized face toward the back seat, the driver suddenly switched off the radio.

"Is that how you check in?" Tony asked, leaning forward. "Do they always do that? Say use a pay phone."

"No. This is something new. Fuck 'em."

They rode a while longer, but as they entered Fort Lauderdale about 11:30, Tony suggested they tell the driver to pull over. He didn't like that call.

"No," Charlie said and continued to stare out the window. Tony sat back. Charlie's noes didn't change. He wondered how such a hardhead, smart as he was, could ever work with the same bunch of guys more than once. Unless the regular crew liked not thinking. Maybe he didn't have a regular crew anymore since they didn't get in on this score.

In Pompano Tony pointed out a small shopping center just across from a Howard Johnson's. "Let's get out here. We can finish making plans." This time Charlie agreed and Pete shot out of the front seat.

"I'm getting the cabbie," Tony said, but Charlie elbowed him aside.

"You'd leave a mint and he'd remember us to his dying day."

"He'll remember a nickel trip even longer."

Charlie grunted, but his tip hit 15 percent on the nose.

With each of them hefting a suitcase, they ran across the highway to the Howard Johnson's coffee shop.

"I'll get change from the girl at the desk," Tony said as they entered the lobby.

"What girl?" Charlie asked. "I don't want no trouble."

"I just want change — quarters, dimes — Charlie, for the phone."

Tony headed straight for the brunette he had noticed when his eyes had first got accustomed to the change in light. She smiled wider as Tony told her he'd be back after a few calls. "You're the best thing I've seen in Florida so far," he said.

Tony called information at the Fort Lauderdale airport. Information regretted that there would be no flights to New York or Grand Cayman the rest of the afternoon. Then Tony called Miami's airport in Coral Gables. They had a 2:30 flight to New York's La Guardia with a connection to Chicago, and a 3:00 P.M. to Grand Cayman. Tony checked his watch. Noon. They'd be able to make it back easy — in a different cab. Then they could dump Pete and go find Louie. He wished they could put Pete on the boat he'd promised them — a slow one to China. No telling what Pete was going to do next.

He stopped at the counter to talk to the girl until he saw Charlie headed his way looking like a jealous husband.

"See ya when I get back," Tony said to the girl and followed Charlie back to their table.

"We're all booked out of Miami," he said.

"Miami," Pete exclaimed, his eyes bulging. "We just put Miami behind us."

Tony explained and ordered a club sandwich.

"We better get going," Pete said, giving his menu a push as he stood up.

"Soon as I have lunch," Tony said, pointing to Pete's seat. "I ain't had any food or sleep in three days."

Charlie settled back in the booth. He believed in eight hours a night beside his wife, and three meals a day. Pete produced a slip of paper from his wallet for Charlie to check for the tenth time — the Grand Cayman numbers — lawyer, hotel. If he heard anything he'd call — or wait to hear from Charlie.

Tony ordered pie.

"You gotta bar?" Pete asked the girl as the pie appeared.

"He don't want no bar," Charlie said. "Just the check. He don't want nothing more either," he said, pointing to Tony. Sure I do, Tony thought.

They found a cab outside the hotel.

"Can you turn your radio off?" Tony asked, leaning forward. "The goddamn static is ruining my hangover. It'll get you an extra five."

It took forty minutes to retrace their recent route back through Miami to the airport. Tony found an earlier flight for Pete and bustled him past two bars and onto the plane. Then he went back for Charlie and dragged him into an airport shop. "I only got what's on my back since Sunday night," Tony said, pulling at his shirt. "I feel like I'm still in the basement."

"Shut up," Charlie muttered, looking around fast.

"Everybody's got a basement."

"Not in Florida they don't."

The shop was small, flashy, and overstocked with plaid and flowered slacks. The clerk was wearing more cleavage than anything else. Tony bought two pairs of slacks he found hiding behind some flowers, some shirts, new shoes, and socks. Charlie bought two pairs of brown socks on sale.

"Why the new shoes?" Charlie asked.

"For them beaches," Tony said. "My feet need a change of scenery too."

Next they hit the drugstore, where Tony stopped in front of a display for hair dryers. "Hey — whadya think, Charlie? Maybe we get one of these we'll get to be as smart as Louie."

"Louie's smart enough for us," Charlie said, pointing Tony toward the girl at the cash register.

"Hey, haven't I seen you before," Tony asked, "at Howard Johnson's?" Tony could see her wanting it to be true.

"What you keep doing that for?" Charlie said, steering him toward the door. "They might remember seeing you if anyone starts putting out pictures for a pickup."

They arrived at their waiting area in plenty of time to notice that the average age of their traveling companions seemed to be about sixty-five.

"Think they're carrying cash?" Tony asked. "Can't squeeze much in a hearing aid or camera case."

"They're doing O.K.," Charlie said, but he looked them over just in case a Berwyn neighbor had turned up.

The plane ride renewed Tony's distrust of air travel. "Damned if I ever look at apple pie again," he groaned over his empty barf bag.

Tony accepted the stewardess's drink offer and felt the Scotch burn a neat hole through the apple pie and bacon lying in a tight lump below his ribs.

"Coke," Charlie said and glowered out the window.

"Costs the same whether you're sick or not," Tony said. "Which way you figure it's a bargain?"

Finally Charlie laughed.

They arrived in Georgetown, Grand Cayman, flying low over more water than Tony had ever seen in his life. He wondered how Louie had liked it in a little plane — if he had made it without a stopover in Majorca. They hustled past the other passengers in an unfair race to customs. After getting through that, they were off in a cab to the Holiday Inn. Tony noted in dismay the same retirement-age population — slow-moving old men and grouchy old ladies. Definitely no action here. And no shops. Only bank after bank after bank. And not much town either. Five minutes later, they were winding up the drive of the Holiday Inn about a mile out of town.

The driver pulled up to the lobby and handed Charlie a card. Charlie blankly looked at it and Tony took it and stuffed it in his pocket. He followed Charlie to the desk, where they checked in under their real names. If it ever went bad, they agreed, without needing to talk it out, there were advantages to looking like you had nothing to hide.

"We're meeting someone named Martin," Charlie said. "He here yet?"

"Martin," the clerk repeated, sending her brilliantly polished nails over the cards. "No Martin."

"How about Martine?" Charlie leaned over the counter. Same result.

"DeMartin," Charlie said, not a muscle moving in his face.

The girl gave him a funny look, her nails drumming on

the counter. "A friend, huh?" Again her nails rifled the cards. "Next?"

"Hell, let's get some sleep," Tony said. "It's a small island. We'll find him."

Tony didn't add what they knew — it wasn't finding Louie that mattered. It was finding the money.

20

Tax Havens: History Repeats Itself

"If the money all burned up, who'd ever think any of it was taken? It would have been the perfect crime," said former Cook County Sheriff Joseph I. Woods, now senior vice president, Midwest Group, of Purolator.

— October 27, 1974,
Chicago Tribune

On October 15, 1974, nine days before the Purolator robbery and thirteen days before Marzano and company landed on Grand Cayman, *Forbes* magazine had printed an article on tax havens titled "No Hiding Place Down There?" It mentioned exotic places like Liechtenstein and Hong Kong and balmy places like the Bahamas where frightened American money could go to hide. There, it could be washed clean of any taint and nestle snugly under the cover of an anonymous numbered account or bland corporate name — where it would multiply in peace.

The previous year, on February 3, 1973, *Business Week* had run a piece called "How to Set Up a Foreign Tax

Haven." It was directed toward the average grandfather who wished to leave a good supply of cash as unostentatiously as possible to his descendants. (About the time these articles appeared, Congress was supposedly getting ready to lower a boom on tax havens — a boom that is, however, still suspended.)

Charlie Marzano, a man looking forward to a large cash flow in the fall of 1974, probably never read these articles, but he was able to get in touch with someone who — most likely — had. Charlie was afraid of the negative effect that damp and mildew have on large amounts of paper buried under cellars. Then, there were such things as nosy neighbors. And, of course, inflation. So he set up a meeting with Louis DiFonzo, who knew all about the problems of sensitive money.

In that meeting DiFonzo touched on some of the options available to a man with Charlie's problems. There is such a thing as a "living accumulation trust," which pays no income taxes on interest and, with high interest, multiplies like a Keogh account gone crazy. The person who establishes the trust should, of course, notify the Internal Revenue Service of its existence so that his beneficiaries can pay the taxes due when they collect their inheritance. The laws, however, are constantly changing — and if not the laws, the IRS's interpretation of them.

For this reason, lawyers or financial advisers frequently aim for the lowest level of visibility and the highest level of complexity in the money's disposition, to discourage investigation.

The government still has its troubles. As recently as April 1979, the House Ways and Means Committee held two days of hearings on the growing number of Americans who use offshore tax havens. One of the members, Congressman Jake Pickle (a Texas Democrat), summarized the proceedings by saying "We don't know who's doing what to whom in which direction." Some part of the billions of dollars involved never in fact leaves the United States. There has been a great growth in U.S. bank branches in the Cayman Islands, and testimony before the committee showed that many of the branches were only shells, with accounts and management still maintained in the head office of the American bank. It was noted that the Cayman Islands had only one or two banks and insignificant offshore business in 1964. By December 1977, however, with a population of 14,000, the islands had 237 banks, 8158 registered companies, and more Telex machines per capita than any other place in the world.

M. Carr Ferguson, an assistant attorney general in the Justice Department, was quoted as saying that it was getting to be more and more difficult to draw the line between the aggressive taxpayer and the fraud. This is so because, in U.S. law, there is a difference between tax evasion and tax avoidance. The former is secret, sticky — and illegal. The latter is not exactly encouraged but is sometimes condoned. An American business, for example, might be able to operate more competitively if it set up a subsidiary in a nation with low taxes. Eventually, though, the U.S. government will benefit from the financial health of the parent corporation.

According to Marshall Langer, author of *How To Use Foreign Tax Havens,* there is always a day of reckoning for those individuals or firms who employ tax havens. "They offer deferral rather than complete freedom from taxes," he says.

But Americans are used to living on a deferral system — our long-unbalanced national budget being the most visible example. People seem to be confident that if their grandchildren receive a tax bill with their inheritance, they, too, will find some way to defer payments. As tax lawyers point out, taxes deferred mean an interest-free loan from the government. Those secluded dollars and their interest can be reinvested over the years to yield gains that would outweigh the disadvantage of any future tax.

Louie, however, touched only lightly on the complexities. His main message was to outline the ideal tax haven:

First, safety. That means a politically and economically stable country. There are some countries that will give a written guarantee against future taxes on your deposits, if you ask for it. (If you guess wrong, that guarantee could end up as valuable as a Batista government bond.)

Second, secrecy. Some countries in the Caribbean, such as the Bahamas, the Cayman Islands, and the Netherlands Antilles, are called loophole countries. Their bank secrecy laws make them even closer-mouthed than the silent Swiss. A Grand Cayman banking or government official is subject to a fine and a sentence if he says much more than hello and goodbye.

Third, convenience. Hong Kong is colorful, but the Cayman Islands are about 500 miles due south of Miami.

Fourth, inaccessibility. As a federal investigator once put it, "Our subpoena has a twelve-mile offshore limit." And, when the IRS does practice its own idea of hot pursuit, it may end up in confusion. One of its biggest investigations of tax havens was aimed at the Castle Bank in Grand Cayman. IRS agents broke into the hotel room of a bank official and borrowed his briefcase long enough to photograph its contents. But the case has dragged on — with the IRS now maintaining that it didn't really need the briefcase for its proof — and, according to recent articles, no charge of illegality against the heavy depositors in the bank has yet been proved.

So Charlie, with the guidance of Louis DiFonzo, was about to undertake a financial maneuver familiar to a good many actors, doctors, businessmen, and gamblers in the United States. DiFonzo was not aware how Charlie meant to get rich suddenly. His only concern was to make the money clean and to find it a discreet home where it could thrive and beget offspring.

The Cayman Islands — Grand Cayman, Little Cayman, and Cayman Brac — lie approximately 180 miles northwest of Jamaica. They were sighted by Columbus in May 1503 and recorded in his ship's log. He did not go ashore, but he did name the islands Las Tortugas. The islands, once a dependency of Jamaica, are now a British dependency.

The early foreign inhabitants were mixed groups of shipwrecked sailors, marooned mariners, and pirates. No serious settlement took place till the early eighteenth century, and no rapid advances were made until 1940, when modern transportation brought the Cayman Islands into frequent contact with the outside world.

Grand Cayman is the land of sunshine, priceless black coral, and pirates' hoards — past and present. One of the famous landmarks is Pedro Castle, sitting on the end of Great Pedro Point, built by slaves in 1631. The famous buccaneer Henry Morgan used Pedro Castle as his headquarters and resting place while he planned raids on Cuba, Puerto Bello, Cartagena, and Panama. The North Sound, on the other side of the long, narrow island, was the gathering area for his fleet. His total plunder from these raids has been estimated at more than $3.5 million. More than 400 wrecks have been established as lost in these waters — 325 in known locations. The "wreck of the Ten Sails," one of the island's greatest disasters, took place in 1798 at Gun Bay. All ten ships of a fleet were lost. A more recent wreck, in the 1940s, carried a most unusual "treasure": the ship was filled with rice. The rice began to swell and drifted away — leaving in its wake the slowly expanding hull, which had opened like a split fish. Travel brochures are anxious to assure their potential customers that some of the old treasures may still be hidden on these islands. And each year several elaborate efforts are made to resurrect a pirate's treasure. The difference between then and now is that Morgan's treasure, wherever it might be deposited, isn't drawing 12 percent interest.

Today's pirates have raised the craft of depositing money on Grand Cayman to a more respectable level. The eye patches and swords have been replaced by expensive three-piece suits and credit cards. The decendants of the old wooden ships that brought home the plunder are winged jets that follow the airways from Miami. The elaborate trenches, tunnels, and underwater caves for making the treasure secure, which required days of backbreaking labor, have been replaced by one small sheet of paper — the deposit slip — and the amount of energy required to flourish a ball-point pen.

21

Safekeeping

It is believed that the $1.5 million is still somewhere on the island, either in one of Grand Cayman's 178 banks or buried somewhere under its beaches.

— October 31, 1974,
Chicago Tribune

The Grand Cayman Holiday Inn lies on the eastern coast, across the island from North Sound. It is a sprawling labyrinth of tennis courts, stucco buildings, and shrubbery that its cousin in Peoria would never recognize. During Tony's stay the bars were the central meeting place on the island — the "in" place, and the bar by the pool had the distinction of being literally poolside, requiring the customers merely to slip onto underwater stools to order a slushy tropical cocktail. Tony could see the aqua circle from his terrace and that was where he wanted to be. But business first.

After a full, if not worry-free, night's sleep, Tony felt better — ready for his new clothes. Charlie pulled a second pair of his too-short slacks out of his bag and they dressed. They didn't mention Louie. Yet.

At the registration desk they went through all the names

again for a different blonde clerk. "Your — ah, friend's expected? Huh?" No messages, no Martin. Charlie was staring at the girl.

"Come on." Tony gave him a push, though he, too, felt paralyzed with dread.

"I'm through fucking around," Charlie said, pulling a slip of paper out of his wallet. "I'm calling that lawyer right now."

Just as Charlie dialed the number Tony poked him in the arm. "Hang up. There he is."

Charlie slammed the receiver in place as Louie noticed Tony and changed direction. There was a satisfied smile below his neat mustache. Tony wanted to hit him.

"Where the hell you staying?" Charlie growled.

"Here." Louie's gesture took in the lobby and the bored desk clerk watching from across the room.

"There ain't no Martin here."

"I know. I used my own name. Seemed like a good idea — especially when I catch you all up on everything that's happened so far." (Louie's decision to use his own name was to prove crucial when he later had some explaining to do. "Why wouldn't I use my own name?" he would say. "I was just setting up a business transaction — that wasn't dishonest.")

Charlie let it drop and they followed Louie to the inevitable coffee shop — this one overlooking the beach and the fake-blue water.

Tony felt a sort of grudging respect for Louie now that they had located him. He could have run off with the million — knowing they probably wouldn't have reported it to the police. (Three years later someone made the comment that Louie was dumb not to have taken the money and run. Tony disagreed. "There has to be some honor somewhere. Thieves can't steal from their partners. Then we'd have complete chaos. There has to be some organization.")

"What happened going through customs?" Charlie asked when orders had been taken.

Louie shrugged. "I got someone to help me heave the cases up on the table. It looks like I'm bringing enough stuff to live here for a year. The customs guy is bored and looking past me like he's watching TV over my shoulder. 'Any alcohol or contraband?' he asks, finally looking at the cases.

"I say, 'No.'

" 'Mind if I look?' he says, already opening the first case. The money's just sitting there, no clothes, no shoes, toothbrush, just your everyday United States negotiable cash. The guy never blinks. Just like I predicted, he feels around, along the sides, underneath. He closes it up and pulls the second case over. 'Any alcohol or contraband in this one?' he asks, not waiting for an answer. Then he pokes around in all that money as if he were looking for something really valuable, like a pint of Scotch. I'm wondering what would make him react. He closes up the second bag, fitting the lid tight. Then he pulls the big fold-over bag in front of us. It's tied up tight in the middle — the money's bunched at both ends like a fat woman in a belt. 'What's in there?' he asks, forgetting his alcohol and contraband line. 'More of the same,' I tell him. He doesn't say anything, just looks at me.

" 'You know,' I say, 'the same as in the other bag. Money.'

"He gives the bag a poke or two and waves it through. Didn't even look in the last bag. That's probably all he ever sees every day. Money." Louie shrugged as if that was all he ever saw too.

Tony could feel his back relax at the end of Louie's story. "That was it?" he said. "We could've done that." But it was probably a good idea that Louie had.

"So that was it, as far as customs is concerned," Louie said, smoothing the tablecloth.

"But you're still in the airport — then what?" Charlie leaned forward.

"So I phoned my lawyer, told him to make sure the bank stayed open. The cabbie wanted to take me to a hotel first.

" 'Just drive,' I said. I gave him the name of the bank and said, 'I have to make closing time.'

" 'You missed it already,' he said.

" 'I don't like crowds,' I told him, and he finally shut up.

"The bank looked about the size of a first-class Chicago hot-dog stand — with a little more paint and polish. The president himself unlocked the door and helped me lug the bags into his office. Nice place — wooden desk, pictures of his wife and kids, coupla plants, and a goddamn six-foot safe. I waited to be taken to the vault but the banker handed me a deposit slip, then started fiddling with the T-handle on the safe. You know, the old-fashioned kind."

"Christ," Tony said, seeing it.

Charlie covered his eyes.

"Anyway, he got it open and started stuffing the cases inside. The bank doesn't even have a burglar alarm. Nothing."

"They don't work too well anyway," Tony said.

Louie didn't smile. "So I left the money and went to see Eric Cranston." Louie's shoulder pads rose and fell as he shrugged elaborately.

"So now what happens?" Charlie asked. Tony could tell that Charlie didn't like asking Louie for instructions. And he didn't like hearing Louie's stories about moving the money around. Charlie probably wished he was sitting on it — the burglar himself makes the best alarm.

"Nothing right now," Louie said. "Tonight we go to the bank. The guy is nervous with all that cash not counted and he wants it out of there. Then there's a million papers to fill out. You guys do some relaxing — swim, lay on the beach."

"Relax!" Tony's coffee cup banged down as his irritation with Louie returned.

"Easy," Charlie said. "Louie, you go do your thing. We'll meet here for dinner. No telephone calls." Louie looked startled but nodded. He'd heard it before. They watched him leave.

"He's just a cog," Charlie said. "Like an accountant. An adding machine. No more."

Tony propelled Charlie toward the cabstand saying it had to be livelier in town than at the old folks' home. He knew Charlie would go along just to see he didn't grab a phone line or a bust line. He couldn't figure what Charlie was worried about. Did he think Tony would pull out if he saw his name in print? Maybe call the IBI to see how their investigation was going?

A mile and a half down the road they came to a town — a series of banks with a few small shops tucked in beside them.

"Stop here," Tony called to the cabbie. "I think I see a store."

"Yes, sir," the driver said, pocketing Tony's $5 tip. "Should I come back for you, sir?"

"No," Charlie said, slamming the door.

Tony's shopping spree went sour with Charlie along. In Chicago, he'd have had a friend, maybe a couple of girls, to sit around and tell him how he looked. Talk about the fit, the color. Then they'd stop for a drink between stores. He'd buy two of something if he liked it enough. Give the tailor a big tip. Shopping with Charlie in Grand Cayman was like poking vegetables in the old country. "They probably mark everything up five times here," Charlie said, pushing his way through a rack of mod suits while Tony tried one on.

"They gotta make money too," Tony said over his shoulder at the mirror.

"You got any other places around here?" Charlie asked the man kneeling at Tony's feet. The fitted jackets and shirts weren't made for Charlie's bulky build.

The man pointed them to a store down the block where Charlie held up a couple of pairs of trousers. "Nice, huh?"

But for Tony the shopping was over.

"Relax," Charlie said as they walked around the downtown area — actually only one street of small wooden establishments. "This is the islands." He slowed his pace to window-shop at a bank."

"There's nothing to do."

"That's relaxing," Charlie said.

"That's boring," Tony snorted. "And I get to worrying about my car being left behind with them guns in it."

"It's in a private airport. Nobody knows it's there."

"Gushi knows."

"He's the only one. So nobody knows it's there, like I said. Right now I just want to see the money. We shoulda checked the papers this morning for any burglaries here during the night. What bank was Louie doing business at?"

"First National something."

"That's not funny."

"Louie knows. He'll want to take us anyway — he likes being in charge."

When they returned to the Holiday Inn Tony tried to stop at the bar but Charlie vetoed it. Once in their rooms Tony exploded.

"I hate this place. No women; I don't want no Jamaicans or hookers. I can't drink. I think I'll leave."

"Look, we don't want anyone remembering us. We only got a few days to go."

So Tony went for a fast swim and then sat poolside at the bar. Charlie hadn't thought about that.

A little later Louie phoned to say that the banker was getting nervous. He wanted them all down at the bank. "The

Cayman National," he repeated. "The banker says there is more in those suitcases then he has in the whole bank and he wants it out of there."

"Maybe he thought we looked like hoods," Tony said. The whole thing was beginning to seem unreal. Buying things with hundred-dollar bills a thousand miles from Chicago. He'd have had more fun staying in town.

The Cayman National, as did most of the Grand Cayman banks, acted as a temporary repository for money. Every day funds were transferred to the home country of each foreign branch bank, while the Grand Cayman banks invested their funds out of the country too. Withdrawals were usually paper transfers or transactions, so it wasn't necessary to keep large amounts of cash on hand. Although not one of the large banks, the Cayman National was later to have one of the corporate accounts that Louie was creating. In the meantime, the bank had promised to hold the money just till morning because it did not have adequate storage or counting facilities.

When Tony and Charlie arrived, the banker took them and Louie in to view the safe and its contents. Tony and Charlie identified the suitcases. No one sat down.

"How much is in there?" the banker asked, pointing to the bags, then wringing his hands.

"A million or so," Tony replied with a shrug. "How should we know?"

"Is it not counted?" The banker looked appalled and moved around behind his desk.

"That's what you banks are for," Tony said. "We tried to give you the hundreds, to make it easier and lighter. We just sort of multiplied the packages by the bills we figured in each block."

The banker's eyelids fluttered and he looked ill. "All my employees have gone home. Security . . ."

"Don't worry — we'll have it out of here tomorrow,"

Louie interjected. "The Swiss National can take it then."

"As soon as possible," the banker said. He moved to close the safe door and stood with his back against it.

"Sure took a genius to pick this bank," Tony muttered to Charlie. "They don't like money."

Eventually it was agreed that the banker would hold the money one more night, but he insisted they return for it by 4:00 P.M. the next day.

"We'll be here," Charlie said. He gestured Louie aside to question him about the corporate accounts.

Tony, alone with the banker, said, "Who knows? We may need a loan. I got my eye on a restaurant in Chicago. A nightclub. Maybe need three, four hundred thousand."

The banker nodded. Now they were talking his language — loans. They started walking to the door together.

"So how would it work?" Tony asked.

The banker looked judicious. They paid 12 percent on a corporate account, so one method required them to hold back 1 percent and pass on 11 percent, "depending on the size of the loan — "

"What loan?" Charlie demanded, joining them.

"Nothing." Tony waved the banker off. "We're just talking about how you borrow money. Say twelve percent of a million is a hundred twenty grand a year. So we pay ten thousand back if we borrow — "

"We ain't borrowing," Charlie said. "We're investing. You start borrowing and pretty soon it's all gone. Sixty thousand a year is plenty to spend without no borrowing, and then the million is always there for a rainy day."

"You wouldn't call it a rainy day if you was drowning," Tony complained.

But the visit to his money had put Charlie in a better humor. "I just know when you got a million bucks, there ain't no such thing as a rainy day."

"There's still a lot of work — " Louie began.

"What'd you expect for fifty grand?" Tony said, anger boiling in him.

Louie ignored him. "Let's get back to the hotel. How do you feel about duck in orange sauce? Gotta order it ahead."

Charlie wouldn't meet Tony's eye. Duck!

"They have some good wines," Louie said, already hailing a cab. "I'm going to drop by the lawyer's office first. I'll call the maître d' from there."

Tony looked out the window at the pastel island buildings. A back tooth was beginning to ache, and if he didn't get a drink soon, or get rid of Louie, the top of his head would come off.

They dropped Louie first, and then, this time, Charlie gave in on the bar.

22

One Deposit, Two Deposits, Three Deposits, Four

DID TV SHOW LEAD GANG TO CAYMANS?

Federal investigators believe the Purolator gang got the idea of stashing cash in secret bank accounts from a TV show. The NBC program "First Tuesday" told in detail how Grand Cayman Island banks welcome both clean and tainted cash. One banker, interviewed about the illegitimate money being deposited, replied, "We're bankers, not policemen." But some policemen, notably FBI men, are working to break the coded-account secrecy in the Purolator case.

— November 3, 1974,
Chicago Sun-Times

Louie and Charlie played the wine game at dinner to Tony's disgust. Charlie had insisted they all eat together, although Tony had wanted to just sit in the bar until he couldn't feel anything, not even his tooth.

Their food arrived with the first bottle, which Louie pronounced acceptable after sipping it slowly, his eyes on the ceiling. The second-course wine could not be poured until

Louie returned from the men's room. Tony finally turned to the hovering waiter. "Just put the bottle down and get out of here."

The wine tasted the same as any he'd ever had. Louie and Charlie probably didn't know the difference either. As an outlet for his annoyance, Tony kept ordering the $100 bottles of wine and drinking them almost by himself. Louie and Charlie nodded sagely at each new bottle. Someone steered Tony to bed.

Thursday morning, Louie was already at the lawyer's office by the time Charlie and Tony appeared to blink painfully at breakfast.

"What the hell's he doing?" Tony asked.

"There's a lot of paperwork," Charlie said. "It's got to be done right."

They lounged through the remainder of the morning and early afternoon. Tony drank in the swimming-pool bar without much effect. When Louie finally motioned to him from the patio around 2:30, Tony felt as if his nerves were standing outside his skin. Charlie had tensed, too, his bull neck reddening from more than the tropical sun. Louie was oblivious as he hustled them to a table in a corner of the patio, spreading papers over the Formica. Tony pulled up a chair, tiny drops of water falling from his shoulders onto the table. Louie brushed them away with a towel Charlie had thrown over a chair.

"Just sign wherever there's an X — don't skip any," Louie instructed them. Tony signed one and it disappeared into Louie's pile.

"Just one fuckin' minute," Tony said. "What're we signing?"

Louie flushed and straightened up. "I know my business."

"I ain't signing no more till I know what it says." Tony threw the pen down and stood up. Charlie shrugged.

"There's no way you'd understand any of this," Louie said with contempt. "And there ain't no time — "

"Then get your friggin' lawyer friend to explain it, if you can't. What's the big deal with all us getting together?"

"The less you're seen the better," Louie said.

Tony moved around the table fast, but before he could throw a punch Charlie had leaned over and grabbed his arm.

"Siddown," he said, pulling Tony back to his chair.

"This wiseass ain't gettin' my name on a piece of toilet paper. I'm getting out of here right now — just give me my share and I'm leaving. I don't need his shit. And before I go I'm gonna take him apart."

"Take it easy," Charlie began, but Louie interrupted.

"Just a minute," he said softly, leaning forward, putting the cap on the pen. "I'm sorry. I mean it." His gaze on Tony was steady.

Tony looked at him suspiciously.

"No, I mean it." Louie's eyes were red-rimmed. "We're all a little edgy. I've just been reading stuff so much — going over all the possibilities." He looked at Charlie for corroboration.

"He's been working too hard," Charlie said. "But he'll tell us what's going on."

Tony settled back into his chair, but waited to see if Louie was just pulling a different kind of stall. A good con should be able to fake a shift in emotions, playing a mark like a fish. He was sure Louie had the skill — he just didn't want to be Louie's mark.

But Louie was apparently sincere. He went over each batch of papers, indicating the creation of five separate corporate accounts, with five separate names. Charlie's signature was required on all five in order to withdraw funds or receive interest. Tony and Louie shared ownership with

Charlie — that is, Charlie alone could release funds, or Tony and Louie together could withdraw the contents should Charlie be unavailable. They would all share in all the interest. But the deal had definitely changed. Louie had exchanged his 10 percent laundry fee for an annuity. Tony looked over at Charlie as Louie paused in his monologue.

"That's a lot of paperwork," Tony said.

Charlie nodded, hearing the question in Tony's voice.

That was enough for Tony. He and Charlie trusted each other and if Charlie said Louie is in, he's in.

As Louie continued to leaf through the papers, Tony quickly calculated that he and Louie would each be getting about $40,000 a year. He had to admit that Louie had come through in hauling the money down, being where he said he'd be, doing what he was supposed to do. He felt his respect for Louie grow. Maybe Gushi had done Charlie a favor bringing Louie in. Maybe there were future possibilities with a man like that — his kind of financial know-how. Like having a lawyer in the family.

Just after four o'clock they all returned to the Cayman National to oversee the transfer to the Swiss National. The suitcases, as bulging and mismatched as immigrant luggage, were walked across the street to where six tellers waited in their cages to check Charlie and Tony's hurried computations.

Louie ushered Tony and Charlie upstairs to an office adjoining the one in which he continued to work separately with Eric Cranston. Tony was no longer interested in the legal language and merely glanced at the papers Louie brought out for signatures.

When Charlie, too, disappeared for a few minutes, Tony decided to phone a close friend in Chicago.

"Anything going on?" Tony asked.

J.D. had not known any details of Tony's doings the past

few months, but newspaper headlines and Tony's absence provided clues to Tony's concern. J.D. narrated a few anecdotes about a newly cemented garage or warehouse on the South Side being dug up. "Then after the police did all the work, they discovered the cementing had been done the day before the big Purolator robbery — which is the biggest thing in town." They got a good laugh out of that. Then J.D. said Maniatis had been picked up about something. And Charlie was still wanted on a fake-driver's-license charge, and what the hell was all that about? He didn't expect an answer, or further information.

"Hey, thanks." Tony was signing off. "Will you call my sister and tell her I'm all right and I'll be home soon?" He was following the unwritten code: do not involve your friends unnecessarily, for their own protection. J.D. was entitled to guess his head off, but hunches were not allowed as evidence in court.

When Charlie joined him, Tony said he'd called home.

"I told you . . . shit, what'd they say?"

Tony began relating the story about the warehouse on the South Side. Then he mentioned the license warrant story, but Charlie shrugged it off. Even if Gushi was picked up, he didn't know any details about the burglary. He had $400,000 keeping his mouth under control. And even though Marrera would be questioned hard, they felt his alibi would hold up. Hell, he'd say he didn't have any vault combination. If someone set a fire inside it, they must have left behind a delayed fuse set before he came on duty, because the vault was locked when he arrived — his coworkers could testify to that. He knew what to say. And being questioned was no big deal for Marrera — he'd been through that before. Or being fired. He could even act angry. After all — he didn't leave his post. The others did.

Finally Charlie and Tony grew tired of watching Louie

and Cranston through the crack of the door to the conference room. The next time Louie appeared with some papers
they said they'd see him back at the hotel.

About eight, a tired Louie arrived with a receipt for
$1,165,000. It was about $100,000 more than they had expected. They decided to have a signing party, a special dinner. "Make it money under glass," Tony said, and Louie
punched him in the arm. When somebody makes you rich,
his imperfections tend to fade. They had a lot in common
now: One-third of the 12 percent interest on $1,165,000.
That was enough to stir up anybody's appetite.

It was at this point that scenes were beginning to repeat
themselves and the days were like reruns of last year's show.
Charlie shopping — this time for pajamas. Tony and Charlie, dressed up, sitting on the bed in Louie's room and waiting while Louie maneuvered his hair dryer. Louie blowing
the important hairs into just the right fluffiness to hide his
bald spot. Louie putting on cologne, a freshly laundered
shirt, gold cuff links, and finally, a navy blue blazer with
silver buttons.

Going outside the hotel to get a taxi to *the* restaurant, the
only one that was supposed to be any good. Getting ushered
to a table, pretending to study the wine list and not knowing
one kind from another except by the prices. Ordering the
$100 one. After dinner, listening to a singer billed as "the
barefoot man," and, sure enough, he did have a pair of big
bare feet, propped on the rungs of the high stool he sat on.

At night Tony dreamed about somebody with a flashlight
in a parking lot back in Ohio coming to open the trunk of
his car.

The next day he told Charlie he was about ready to get on
a plane and fly home. But Charlie said there were just a few
more papers to sign.

That afternoon they signed a new batch of papers. That

night they went to *the* restaurant and drank $300 worth of wine with their steak. Charlie went to bed and Tony and Louie looked around for something to do. The best they could find was a walk on the beach and, at last, they sat down and listened to the soft noise of the surf. And Louie began to talk. It was the first time Tony had ever had any personal talk with Louie and, to his surprise, he found that they had a lot in common. Louie had some pretty good stories.

Some of them were about the time he dealt in silver futures. He told Tony about the commodities market, explained selling short. Tony laughed with surprise as Louie explained how he'd smooth-talked bankers into parting with their own money.

"I didn't make no half million," Tony said. "But I get by." He wanted to impress Louie, let him know he was just as smart. "I made a few scores you could put in a book. One I can remember goes back a long ways when I was teamed up with Frankie.

"This Frankie, he was a big guy, scars over the eye where he's been hit, broken knuckles where he did the hitting. We're out drivin' in this sort of Greek neighborhood where he's pulled a few stickups — grocery stores, gas stations. He acts like it's his turf, he has to check it out now and then, you know what I mean?"

Louie said, "Uh-huh."

"Well, we're gettin' near a friend's gas station. His name's Nick and it was an Enco he just bought. It'd been having a real string of bad luck the past year. Five stickups in eight months. A friend and I pulled the last one, figuring to run the owner out of business so Nick could buy it cheap. Just like he thought, the guy gets disgusted, can't get no more insurance, so he sells and Nick buys him out. I help him negotiate. We got a good price, too. We all work it for him occasionally. He only got stuck up once since. I was in the back that time, sleeping. It's real late and this black dude comes in, takes the pistol off Nick, *and* all the cash. But Nick don't finger him in the line-up the next week. He won't do that to a guy in the same line of work, he says.

"So anyway, this other night with Frankie, he's talking about needing some cash and me going along with him. 'Just hold the pistol and sit in the car,' he says. It's one-thirty in the morning and we been drinkin' and the last thing I want to do is stick up some all-night grocery for a fuckin' eighty-three dollars, which is what he says he came off with last time.

"Besides, I'm still hungry and when we get to Nick's station we see this little hot-dog stand across the street is still open, just Lou, the owner, is in there cleaning up, getting ready to close. It was the kinda place you stand at the counter outside. So we get a coupla dogs, and I know I don't want to stick up no place with Frankie and his pistol. I like to use brains, not muscle. Besides, you can get hurt with a pistol.

"Anyway, I'm standing there, eating my hot dog, and looking across the street at Nick's gas station, and he's not there, got someone new. And then I remember he told me he just hired the guy by phone today. Never saw him. A guy named Fred, supposed to be honest as a fuckin' fool, just laid off the mill a few months back. Of course, Nick can't have no crook working nights for him all alone.

"That's when I got the idea. 'Hey,' I say to Frankie. 'You ever do a robbery by telephone?' He looks at me like I'm missing marbles. I get some change, pull out my address book, look up the number. 'Come on,' I tell him. 'We're gonna rob a place by telephone.'

"There's a phone booth on the corner, next to the stand, so I walk over, Frankie following, dripping mustard. I leave the door open so he can hear. 'Just watch Nick's place across the street,' I tell him. 'Keep an eye on the guy in there.'

"I dial the number and after a few rings we can see this guy, Fred, going to the phone and answering.

" 'Fred,' I say. 'This is Nick. How's it goin'?' Fred says, 'O.K., not too busy.' I say, 'Listen. I know we haven't had a chance to meet yet, but I need you to do me a favor. I've been gambling. I owe some people who're connected. And they want their money now, see?'

" 'Yeah.' He sees. We can see him nodding his head.

" 'Here's what I want you to do,' I say. 'You know that alley out back? I want you to get all the tires together, batteries, tools, and put them out back. In the alley. Put the tires in fives so this guy can carry them easy. Then I want you to put whatever money there is out back, too. Put it in between the first stack of tires nearest the garage. Hold ten dollars out for making change tomorrow morning.' We can see this customer pulling into the station. It's a Lincoln pulls up to the pumps and starts peering in at Fred, who's talking on the phone. The guy starts honking his horn.

" 'There's a customer out there,' Fred says.

" 'Fuck'im,' I say. 'This guy I owe is comin' there in under an hour and that stuff better be ready. You don't mess around with this guy. So don't wait on any more customers tonight no matter what. You do what I say, then go back in the station and lock the door. Don't look out, but lock yourself in. You don't want to see anything. Know what I mean? Just do what I say. Got it?'

"He nods, looking around the station, figuring how much work he's got to do in one hour. 'Yeah,' he says. 'I got it. Jesus.'

"So we hang up and die laughing. We can't believe it. He gets to work hauling the stuff out the door to the back alley.

Cars come in and honk, see the lights, but he just keeps on emptying the place. Frankie and I go back to the stand, tell Lou we need another hot dog to get us through the night. He grumbles but turns the grill on again. Meantime we can see the guy sweatin' away across the street. Lou don't get what's so funny. We're laughin' fit to die. Sure enough, when he gets the last tire and tool out back, he locks himself in. Then he stands inside there looking out the window. And guys are honking — they see him in there and don't know why he don't come out and fill 'em up. That's really the best part. We just double over.

"Anyway, we leave Lou's and drive around the block to the back of the station and load up the trunk. Have to make two trips, and stuff things in the back seat, too. Have to get Frankie's car to haul away the second load, and stash it in his garage till we can move it a couple days later. Made five, six hundred on it. 'Christ,' Frankie keeps sayin'. 'It's the easiest fuckin' money I ever made.' I want to tell him, see? You don't need no gun. But I don't say it. Maybe he does."

Louie whistled in appreciation. "That ought to be on TV," he said.

"Yeah," Tony said. "There's more. The next morning Frankie and I just happen to drop by the station to be there when Nick gets in. We see he's screaming at Fred to unlock the fuckin' door. Then he's looking through the glass, and shoves the door open so hard Fred falls back on the desk. We're right behind him by now.

" 'Where the hell's everything?' he screams. 'Where's my inventory?' He waves his arms wild at the empty shelves and tire racks.

" 'Whadya mean?' Fred says. 'I put it all out back like you said.'

" 'Out back? Like I said?' Nick is pounding his fist into the palm of his hand like he's wishing it was Fred's face. He goes out back and Fred and Frankie and I follow him. Nothin' there except a bunch of garbage cans. A little light starts to dawn in Fred's eyes and he starts to shake a little. Nick hauls him back in the garage and sits him down like they're back in the police station. Frankie and I stay back a few feet while Fred stutters out his story, and shows Nick the ten dollars in receipts from the night. We can hardly keep a straight face. Frankie's rubbing his mouth like his teeth are itching. Nick screams some more and then he calms down. The light seems to be dawning in his head, too, but he just glances at us; he don't say anything. We don't catch his eye either.

"You know," Tony told Louie, "Nick never fired the guy. I knew he wouldn't. He figured Fred was not only honest, but now too fuckin' scared to lift a quart of oil off him. Coupla months later, I was sayin' I could use some money, and Nick said, 'Why don't you just phone and have it delivered.' But he wasn't mad. Got some back with insurance. He knew we couldn'tve planned it. Just a crazy thing to try."

Louie loved it. "You know," he said, "we think a lot alike. "We'd make a good team."

Tony nodded as they turned to walk back the way they'd come. "Yeah. I think so, too. And now, if everything goes well, we got the leverage. Money gives you time to think. No rush. Time to plan schemes — not robberies."

"Like they say," Louie said, "it takes money to make money."

"Yeah, I been thinking of a traveler's check thing. Maybe get them under new I.D.s Get maybe ten thousand worth. Then give 'em to someone else, with the I.D.s, and report them stolen. Or run ads for phony stocks. Or throw our own money in a phony corporation. Build it up. Stock goes up. You dump it — end up with twenty million. You'd know how," he said to Louie.

Louie nodded. "You got people you can turn to, right? Wire money to?"

Tony agreed. He knew what guys were looking to turn that kind of buck. One advantage he had over Louie's nice middle-class background. He, Tony, had grown up with the future cons. He had a network of old boys just like the corporate crowd.

23

Home Sweet ——— Oops

Jesse James had it good.

— J.D.

On Saturday, October 26, 1974, Tony packed one of the now empty suitcases and said goodbye to Grand Cayman, its banks and beaches. His tooth was twanging and he couldn't find any TV or drinking buddies to distract him. Thoughts of the guns in his car in Ohio competed with fears of Pete's ability to stand up under questioning. Charlie told him to keep his eyes peeled when he got home. Tony booked himself on the first flight to Miami and took a cab to the airport, where he went directly to the men's room. He ripped up his remaining Grand Cayman "expense" money, which he had just realized he still had on him, and flushed it down the toilet — about $500 or $600. He'd take a vacation later when the heat was off.

Then he settled himself in the bar to drink until he was numb to the pain in his tooth, and the pain in his gut that preceded any flight. Once he got on the plane, the short hop to Miami passed in a haze of stewardesses, clouds, and little bottles that regularly renewed themselves.

It was raining in Miami. He made a few calls home to ask if his name was being brought up anywhere. It was not. He decided he wasn't up to dragging out his transportation home on a bus or train and phoned his sister that he'd be getting in that night. At O'Hare he took a cab to within a few blocks of Marty's house. Marty was a "legitimate person" — no illegal activities — and therefore the police weren't likely to be watching him. And Tony took a chance on Marty being home and surprising him — hoping to tell by his reaction if anything was up.

Marty answered the door and his guarded reaction confirmed Tony's suspicion that his part in the robbery was strongly suspected. As Marty referred to the *Tribune* articles on the big score in town his voice held a note of compliment as if to say "I know you had something important to do with it." It didn't take much putting together: Tony and Charlie had been hanging out together for weeks. Suddenly they're both gone on vacation. There's a big heist and Charlie's driver's license is a big deal.

So Marty knew.

Tony checked with his sister and then had Marty drop him off a few blocks from her house so he could look around again. Everything seemed strange, somehow changed, as if he'd been away years instead of just a few days. Finally, when he thought it safe, he took his suitcase inside. Therese was knee-deep in messages. Everybody was calling: Gino Martelli was calling almost every day. Hadn't seen him since last Sunday's spaghetti dinner.

Tony phoned Gino and made plans to meet him for a sandwich later. He thought he heard the old question in his friend's voice: Is this someone it might be really good to know — or does he spell danger?

When Tony arrived at Gino's the *Tribune* was lying casually on the couch.

"Hey, look at this," Gino said, bringing him a vodka and tonic. "Whad'ya think of this here score?"

Tony peered at the headline about the warrant for Marrera's arrest. "That's something, all right," Tony agreed. The look on Gino's face would be repeated many times in the next few days as old friends and old not-so-friends tried to read in Tony's face the answers they suspected they knew to their unasked questions. Was this guy in on the heist? Does he have his hands on any of the millions? Tony was friendly but noncommittal.

But he couldn't relax — he couldn't get rid of the image of his car nestling right next to Louie's Lincoln somewhere in Ohio. And his mind burrowed right inside the trunk to where the guns and walkie-talkies were piled. He had to do something about his car. But Gino was almost straight, had gotten himself a college education, courtesy of the penal system. This was no time to involve him in anything.

First thing next morning he called J.D. "We got to drive to Ohio to get my car," he told J.D.

"Whadya mean Ohio?" J.D. asked.

An hour later J.D. was at the curb honking his horn for Tony. "How we supposed to find a car when you don't even know which airport in which city. I shoulda brought a suitcase."

"I know it wasn't Cleveland," Tony said, slamming the door.

"Great." J.D. stared at him in disbelief.

"Let's get started. I know we went to Indianapolis, but then I was so whacked out we just followed the car in front. I'll recognize something. I know we turned left at Indianapolis."

"You know how many lefts —?" J.D. complained.

"Just drive."

As they drove south on the expressway toward the mills

of Gary and the gray skyline, Tony explained his problem. They might be open to a charge of crossing state lines with weapons. In Ohio, a tough state, that conviction alone could mean twenty-five years. He didn't mention that that would be a big lever for the IBI to use to get info on Purolator. Tony didn't mention Purolator by name. But J.D. said he heard that Marrera had been picked up at his in-laws'. J.D.'s own family was waiting at home for him for his birthday party. They would celebrate without him; he shrugged.

Or, if anybody asked, *with* him.

"Marrera's in the Rockford Jail," J.D. said. "Figures now that he's a suspect." Tony agreed with him.

"Those lie tests don't matter a fuckin' bit," J.D. added. "Can't use them in court."

Tony was looking hard out the window. "It's coming up," he said. "There. See that sign for the turnoff to Indianapolis. Take that."

"That's Sixty-five. It don't take you to Ohio," J.D. said, slowing down.

"It will," Tony said. "Quit the fuckin' worrying. I can get us there all right, I just don't know where we're going."

"Christ! Did you hear what you said?" J.D. shook his head.

"Drive." Tony lapsed into silence, and finally sleep. Until J.D.'s voice broke through.

"Hey, wake up. There's your first landmark," J.D. said. "Indianapolis. We go to California or New York?"

"Take that there by-pass. East," Tony said, pointing to a green highway sign. "It's a while yet. Then we gotta look for tall buildings near the highway."

"You gotta be kiddin'. Ya thinking of a lady holding a torch, maybe?"

"It's this way. Maybe Cincinnati. Dayton. Just lemme look."

They drove on. "It's gonna be dark soon. Will you know it in the dark?"

"Yeah, I'll know it." Tony continued to peer out the window. The flat countryside disappeared into the evening dusk.

A little after 6:00 P.M. Tony shouted, "Turn here. Where it says COLUMBUS."

"Christ," J.D. said, but there was relief in his voice.

"Yeah, yeah," Tony said. "I remember these streets. Just keep going for a while. See those buildings? This is it."

When they passed the liquor store Pete had dashed into, Tony cheered. "Follow the AIRPORT signs," Tony said. They both noticed a blonde girl hitchhiking. "Next time," Tony said as they passed her by. But not bad, they agreed. Tony lit a cigarette, his fifth in the past hour. He could feel his chest tighten as they drew nearer and nearer to the airport, pulled as if by some invisible lasso. It was just possible that the cars would be staked out and the FBI would be waiting for them.

"We can't just drive up to the fuckin' car," Tony said, hunching forward. "When we get there, just keep drivin' around the lot till I tell you it's O.K. Don't stop."

J.D. grunted. Tony could tell it was getting to him too.

By the time they reached the airport lot it was pitch black. They drove in the gate past the office to make a sweep of the lot. As they drove slowly around, Tony counted just three cars parked there. His and Louie's were next to each other; the third some way off. Empty. There was nothing else in sight. They passed the office a second time. Tony could see only one man at a desk, reading.

"O.K., now pull up to my car and stop right behind it. Keep the motor going. I'll jump out, open the trunk, and throw the stuff in your back window. You just take off. Don't stop anywhere. We'll meet on that main strip we was just on. Where that girl was walking."

"Gotcha," J.D. said, running his hand over his thick black hair. He pulled up behind Tony's Ford as directed. Tony got out and put the key in the trunk as J.D. let the car edge forward, bringing the back window even with Tony's trunk. Tony grabbed blindly, felt for the leather case holding the pistols, and threw them in the back of J.D.'s car. Then he felt around for the walkie-talkies and threw those in too. "O.K. Move out," Tony whispered, and J.D.'s car picked up speed and cleared the gates in seconds. Tony waited.

No one followed him.

No lights flashed.

Tony closed his trunk with a soft thud. He lit a cigarette and stood there in the dim light. Then he walked over to the Executive Jet office and checked through the window. Only one man behind the counter. Tony identified himself and pointed to the key hanging on the grimy board. The guy pulled it off the hook and handed it over. "Gotta slow night here," Tony said.

"They're all slow," the man replied, peering out the window toward Tony's car. Tony hoped he wasn't seeing anything unusual.

"See ya," he called. He made himself walk to the car without looking around. He slid under the wheel and put the key in the ignition. Nothing in his rearview mirror. Then his foot hit something under the seat. Shit. One of the walkie-talkies.

He headed for the main street that reminded him of Chicago's State Street. That was one of the things he'd remembered — and how it'd snaked right off the highway. Now all he had to do was find J.D.

He drove to the main part of town, up and down the street, as slowly as he dared. Then he turned and took it again. His hands grew slippery and he tightened them on the wheel. He didn't want J.D. caught with the heat. It meant

big trouble to be jackpotted in an Ohio town. Especially
when you're from Chicago. He hoped J.D. stopped somewhere and dumped them. Tony would have done that. He
remembered the walkie-talkie. He spotted a Holiday Inn
and drove around the back. He parked and wiped off the
walkie-talkie with his sleeve. No one around. He pulled out
his overflowing ashtray and dumped the butts along with
the talkie in a large garbage container and threw some stray
boxes on top.

Then he returned to the street. After the third time, he
pulled in to McDonald's for coffee; maybe he could figure
which way J.D. might have gone. The blonde hitchhiker was
eating at a small table. Tony sat down at the table next to
her and sipped at his coffee.

"You was hitching a while ago, weren't you?" he said to
her.

"Yeah," she said to him — liking what she saw. Tony
was used to that. "You saw me?"

"Let's get a couple more coffees to go; maybe you can tell
me how to get back to Chicago."

The girl flipped her hair away from her face. "Sure," she
said. No make-up, but pretty.

As they walked to his car, Tony explained he wanted to
just drive up the main street once more. "Looking for a
friend," he said. Her name was Gilly. She had long red
fingernails and two books in her purse, which flopped open
on the floor of the car. She started talking about some boots
she wanted to buy. Real leather and cost $40 or $50. Tony
nodded, checking out the cars on the street, squinting into
the oncoming lights.

"What do you do?" he asked, his eyes still on the street.
But all she could talk about was the boots. Real leather.
Christ, what a time to get hit by a broad — a pair of fucking
boots. Finally he told her he was sorry but he really had to
leave for Chicago.

"Oh, hell," she said. "Just take me home. You can get on the highway from there. What's your hurry?" she asked, leaning around to smile into his face. Her long hair was swinging against the dash.

"I gotta see someone," he said.

Once on the highway, pointed again at Indianapolis, Tony felt the same weariness from yesterday's flight overtake him. He pulled into the second truck stop, automatically glanced around for J.D., then fell asleep. He woke after midnight, and drove straight through until he reached J.D.'s house at four in the morning. J.D. had just gotten home a half hour earlier — couldn't figure how they'd missed each other. But Tony had guessed right about one thing. J.D. had dumped the guns. At another Holiday Inn. Let the Columbus police or garbage departments figure that one out.

"And I found the blonde. She only wanted boots." Tony grimaced.

"That's what they all say." J.D. lowered his voice. "Hey, the papers are putting out that the Purolator loot might be on the way to Florida in a blue Chevy bakery truck."

"Need new glasses," Tony said.

"They're also making a fuss over Gushi's discount operations. Funny time to hit those."

Tony shook his head. Gushi might have a reputation as a standup guy, but there was a hell of a lot they could hold over him. The memory of dragging the duffel bags down the basement steps suddenly overcame him. Shit. All those stacks and stacks of nothing more than numbers on a piece of paper — even though it was a deposit slip.

"I gotta get some sleep," he said. "I'm starting to dream standing up."

24

Cat and Mouse

The drama is over, and the original performance was a smashing success. Now the cast of characters must come forward to make their reluctant curtain call.

— October 30, 1974,
Chicago Tribune

Monday noon, October 28, 1974. Tony was out cruising the streets. See and be seen so the phone would start ringing again with "Where you been? Whadya doin'?" He was also trying to put Sunday's newspaper headlines out of his mind: 4.3 MILLION THEFT PLOT WILDER THAN TV. But the one that bothered him most was NAB $4 MILLION SUSPECT IN OAK PARK. Marrera had been picked up at his in-laws' house. And one of the articles had said the ILIC had known something was going down for a long time. Charlie was on their list. Gushi had been questioned already. And the reward was an all-time high of $175,000. At least Tony had his car, minus the guns, back in town.

It occurred to him that before there was an indictment, any mention of his name, he could leave town. Run away. But where would he go? You need friends, money, a plan. A place to stay. Someone to hide you. To buy food. Get the papers. If it had been a small score, maybe, just maybe, he could have parked himself in another state. There might be one warrant out, but no one is really looking hard for you. But in a $4 million theft, it's not so easy. There are bulletins all over. You're looking over your shoulder all the time. And Tony knew he wasn't the type to blend into a small town — his face on posters, TV. This time the FBI wasn't going to give up. They wouldn't mind spending millions to avoid admitting to the public that a guy can steal millions and disappear. And besides, running is just another jail. But still, it was tempting to take off and leave Chicago in the dust.

Suddenly a man darted into the middle of the street and flagged him down. A guy he knew named Joe. "Bailey's been trying to find you. He called me, and I been calling all over. Finally left word with your sister." Joe leaned an arm on Tony's door and hunched over it, peering into the back seat.

"Bailey?" Tony didn't like Joe looking around. The Purolator reward came to mind.

"Yeah, Bailey. You get in touch with him. He wants to see you in his office," Joe said, hitting the side of the car before he backed off.

Tony nodded and pulled away, but he didn't call Bailey. He hadn't seen Bailey — his lawyer from years ago — for ages. Hadn't needed to. So why did Bailey want to see him — and how did Joe — ? Then he remembered that Bailey was Joe's attorney too.

His sister confirmed Joe's message. She sounded worried. But Tony didn't call Bailey right away — he didn't want to sound as if he were in trouble. He waited until later that evening and then phoned Bailey at home.

"I'd like you to come down to my office tomorrow,"

Bailey said. "And listen. Don't say anything to Joe. You can't trust him."

"I know," Tony said. "I'll be there."

Tony had been Robert Bailey's second client more than ten years ago. Another friend of Tony's had been his first. Tony knew he was the kind of lawyer who, when he says he has to see you, he has to see you. They liked each other, had gone out drinking a few times. Bailey had come to Chicago from Washington to head a federal strike force to clean up narcotics and then had become an assistant U.S. attorney. He did his Chicago job well, but then, Tony understood, didn't get the position he had been promised and therefore went into private practice.

Tuesday morning Tony walked into Bailey's office. He still looked the same, his hair cropped short, all business. His style of questioning hadn't changed much either.

"First thing," Bailey said, pointing him to a chair. "Are you related to Charlie, the one they're looking for on the driver's license charge?"

"Yeah. He's my cousin."

Bailey nodded. "Now, before I ask you anything else: now that Joe delivered my message, don't talk to him anymore."

"O.K. I won't."

"And I'm going to come right out with it. And you tell me the truth. Did you have anything to do with Purolator?"

"Of course not," Tony said, stretching out his legs. "Why you asking me?" Even though he trusted Bailey, Tony's reply was automatic. He had never been involved in anything this big before. Nor had Bailey.

"The FBI's been calling me. They want to talk to you. Did you know Pete Gushi?" Bailey leaned back in his chair.

"Yeah, what about it?"

Bailey shrugged. "Why would they be calling for you if he wasn't saying something?"

Tony was silent, then said, "You're probably right. So if

something goes wrong, you'll handle my case, O.K.? Only no more questions right now."

"Fine." Bailey sat up to his desk and pulled a pad of paper with some phone numbers closer to hand. "I told them you won't come into the office without me. And I said I'd call them back at one o'clock. You call me then."

Tony nodded. Something going wrong was beginning to sound likely.

Tony went across the street for a sandwich and a few drinks to pass the time.

He still couldn't figure Pete for talking — hoped to hell he wasn't. Lots of guys held off talking for a long time, months even, to give their friends time to work things out one way or another. Surely Pete could do that. Give them a few months. But already Tony felt unguarded. A little after one he phoned Bailey.

"I told them I'd come across the street with you. That I represent you," Bailey said. "Then they said they changed their minds — forget about it. They don't want to talk to you. But I think you better check in with me every morning and afternoon from now on. I want to know where you're at — in the streets, wherever. This isn't normal."

They didn't need to tell each other that something was wrong.

Tony called Bailey back again at four that day. "They want to talk to you now, so you better get down here."

When Tony arrived at Bailey's office, two secretaries met him and rushed him off to another floor into a different office. "Coffee, Mr. Marzano? Mr. Bailey will be here soon."

When Bailey came up he said, "You want to go over?"

"If you go with me," Tony said, trying to be nonchalant, but the coffee was turning to lye in his stomach.

Bailey phoned the FBI from that office. "My man's here now," he said. "I can bring him over."

Tony watched his face as he listened, hung up.

"Changed their minds again," Bailey said, his voice exasperated. "So you keep in touch like before."

They both knew that Bailey was trying to keep Tony from getting grabbed on the streets. He stood a good chance of eventually making bond if Bailey could show he kept coming in, wasn't trying to run. But there was no point in going in ahead of time.

Early Wednesday morning Tony called again. Nothing yet. Except that he knew Bailey's number by heart.

At three in the afternoon he was in an Elmwood Park restaurant, drinking with Marty and two girls. They were talking about flying to Vegas for the weekend, on Tony, who still had some non–Grand Cayman money left. He was about to send Lori, Marty's girl friend, to an agent for tickets, when he decided to call Bailey again.

As Tony left the table he could hear Marty telling the girls what a great guy Tony was, how you could depend on him to share whatever he had with his friends. Girl friends too, he said, patting Sara's arm.

Tony called his sister first. She was frantic. Bailey had called and said it was very important that Tony call him immediately. She repeated *very important*. Tony regretted the worry in her voice and told her, "Hey, not to worry, let him do it."

Bailey said, "I got something to tell you."

"What?"

"They got a warrant out for your arrest. So get in here as soon as possible. I'll turn you in."

"No way." Tony thought of his plans. If he couldn't have the weekend, at least he wanted this one night. "No," he repeated. "I ain't going in today."

"If you're not coming in," Bailey said, unperturbed, "then I don't want you out on the street. Anywhere you can get picked up. You stay somewhere till I get you in my hands to bring you in."

"I'll be in your office ten tomorrow."

"O.K. I'll call them now and say I'll have my man here at ten, so they know." He hesitated. "But that don't mean they won't be looking for you."

"Thanks, I know," Tony said, swinging around to look at his party. "See you tomorrow."

He rejoined Marty and the girls and broke part of the news. "We'll have dinner and go back to Marty's." He and Marty went way back, so he could hole up there till morning. Things could be worse. He told Sara they'd make Vegas some other time.

On the way to Marty's house, Marty insisted that Tony slouch down in the back seat of the car "just in case." So Marty was getting scared even though no one was out looking for Tony — yet.

They got to Marty's house in time for the evening news. The first thing flashed before them was Tony's face and a hard voice saying "This man is a fugitive. He is being sought in connection with the Purolator robbery. Two of his companions are being held in custody, and two others have been apprehended on the island of Grand Cayman, just as they were leaving for Costa Rica. If you have infor.nation — " Tony snapped it off. So Louie and Charlie had been picked up.

"They're looking for you," Marty said. He was sweating and wiping his neck.

"Well, they won't look here."

"They probably have a list of your friends." His voice had become a whine. The girls were silent.

Tony stopped his pacing in front of Marty. "I'd leave, but I can't run around this neighborhood and I left my car at my sister's." Marty lived only a block from Tony's mother. "Let's all have a drink."

"Good idea," Lori said. She brought back two bottles from the kitchen. Sara carried glasses and a tray of ice.

Tony felt trapped. Then he remembered a place J.D. might be. "Listen," he said. "Nobody knows Lori. She can go looking for J.D. and bring him back here. Then we can figure out where to go next." Tony couldn't call, in case J.D.'s phone was tapped.

Marty practically shoved Lori out of the house, grabbing the drink out of her hand. They watched the car pull away.

Tony felt himself using up all the good effects of the alcohol in the effort to remain calm. They all had another drink. An hour had passed when the telephone's ring shot the three of them out of their seats.

"I better get it," Marty said, drying his hands on the side of his pants.

"Being's it's your house," Tony said.

Sara gave a small titter but it died quickly. Tony could see the sweat stains growing under Marty's arm; his forehead glistened.

"It's Lori," Marty said, staring wildly at Tony. "The police pulled her over near here, shoved a light in her face. She's hysterical."

"Goddammit," Tony said, and he pulled the receiver away from Marty. "Now calm down, Lori. Just tell me what happened."

Apparently, everyone in the neighborhood was being pulled over, they finally told Lori when they let her go. Besides, she was double-parked. Nothing personal. She found J.D. But he didn't trust her. In her condition, who would? J.D. said he didn't want to get in no car with her and be dropped off any place by her. She was probably followed, he told her. Her voice broke. Now what?

"Never mind," Tony said, feeling sorry for her in spite of his own fear. "You did O.K. Come on back here. If you get stopped again just remember you don't know nothing."

He hung up. He tried to ignore Marty as he made another

drink for Sara and himself. But Marty couldn't stay still. And he kept talking about being clean, and not needing any trouble. He never said he didn't need a trip to Vegas, Tony thought, but why say it aloud? You never knew about someone until the crunch came — and who went around looking for crunches just to identify some friends? He and Sara sat on the couch. She had stopped smiling, although she was still trying to please him with distracting comments. He squeezed her hand and turned all her rings around. She giggled. Marty was still pacing up and down and finally turned on the TV again. They must have watched some programs for a while, but Tony couldn't account for the passing of time. At 9:30 he decided he couldn't stand Marty's pacing anymore. He had to get out of this cage.

"I'll call you sometime," he said to Sara. "It woulda been nice." She looked disappointed and her chin trembled. To Marty he said, "I'm getting out of here so you can stop that crying." Before Marty could protest, Tony had walked out of the house, down the stairs, jumped over a side fence into an alley, and walked eight blocks, heading toward Cicero Avenue looking for a cab.

A police car came slowly along the street but didn't stop. Tony kept walking. At Sixteenth and Cicero he stopped in at a small restaurant and motel. He'd call a cab from there — at least he'd be off the street.

Two phones stood on an open counter in the dark lobby, next to a short hall that led to a restaurant. A TV droned from the top of the bar. Another man was talking on the phone, looking at the TV. Tony asked for change and began dialing. They both stood watching the television — the line was ringing. Tony was suddenly looking at his own face and realized it was the ten o'clock news. He turned to the man, who had also turned to look at him. Tony shrugged, hung up the phone, and walked slowly out the door. Then he ran

down one street, and careened down a side street, off Cicero. Just as he turned the corner he saw a cab dropping off
two women. He whistled it to wait.

The cabbie pushed up his meter bar as Tony gave the
name of his cousin's bar. He lived downstairs from Tony's
mother, but he kept another apartment no one knew
about — except Tony.

The cousin took him into the kitchen and gave him a key.
No questions asked. Just a slap on the back and "good
luck."

Tony took his first easy breath in hours behind the closed
door. Then he phoned J.D.'s house and found him in. "Can
you come over?" he asked. He needed to talk to someone. It
was important that someone knew where you were, and
what was happening. J.D. and Gino would be his line to the
outside, once Tony was inside. He had to fill J.D. in on all
the details — like where he could lay his hands on some
money. It costs to go to jail, and Tony needed to cover his
expenses.

It was 3 A.M. as Tony pulled the curtains and they sat
there drinking and smoking. He told J.D. about Marty. "I
told him I just needed to stay there the night so I could
make bond the next morning. Lori had this cute friend
there. I said I wasn't running out on a warrant. I've spent
thousands on that guy. He sees one fucking picture on TV
and goes to pieces."

"Piece of shit," J.D. said calmly. "Forget him. Let's make
plans."

At eight o'clock Thursday morning, after trying to sleep and
dozing maybe a couple of hours after J.D. left, Tony got up
and had coffee with his cousin. There was still time to run
away, and Tony had again thought about it. But now there
was an indictment, so common sense said stay put, walk in
before they get you.

"I'm going to call a cab and turn myself in," he told his cousin. "Don't know if I'll ever be in the streets again. I could get a hundred years." He didn't know what he was saying. But he knew he could no longer stand the constant hopes and fears of the past few days — the expectation of being caught and at the same time trying to figure how to minimize the impact. Besides, if he walked in he had a better chance of pulling a decent bond.

He thanked his cousin and took a cab to the back of Bailey's building. Bailey had told the U.S. attorney that he'd be coming in with Tony that morning, but neither of them trusted the feds not to try to bring him in anyway. When Tony reached Bailey's office he was whisked upstairs.

Bailey showed up fifteen minutes later and motioned with his head. They left the building and walked across the street. Once they were in the anteroom outside Stratton's office, an agent said to wait a few minutes. "It'll be routine," Bailey told Tony. "I'll see you later." They both knew Tony would say nothing.

When Ramon Stratton came out for him, he also knew Tony wouldn't say anything. But Stratton had to try. He took Tony back to the interrogation room for the routine request for answers to a not-so-routine burglary.

"Well, Bill. You really got your tit in the wringer this time," Stratton said, sitting on the edge of the desk. Stratton must have heard Bailey call him Bill — he was the only one to do so, Tony thought.

He remained silent. This was the easy part.

"Got anything you'd like to tell us?" Stratton asked, but in a perfunctory tone.

Tony shook his head.

Before they locked him up, Tony was taken before Federal Magistrate James T. Balog for bond to be set. Tony was astounded to see the room crammed with people: TV reporters, newspaper people, everybody wanting a look at the last member of the Purolator team to be picked up. He knew he was going to get the book thrown at him — no way was he going to get reasonable bond with the world watching. You may be innocent till proven guilty, but he knew you still could be locked up till proven guilty. Bailey was summoned and a minidebate was conducted before the packed house. Assistant U.S. Attorney James Breen pointed out that this was the biggest robbery ever in the United States. Millions were still missing. This man, William Anthony Marzano, and his confederates tried to blow up Purolator. He is not a stable person; he is unemployed and divorced. He would run, given the chance, if his bond was set low.

Bailey rebutted. William Anthony Marzano had been on trial before in U.S. District Court. Many times, in fact, and he never had missed a court appearance. Then, when notified that the FBI wanted to talk to him, he came to Bailey's office several times in one week, only to find that the FBI had changed its mind. When the warrant for his arrest came through, Bailey had called Tony's sister, with whom Tony lives, and he said he'd turn himself in the very next morning. And he did.

Tony hardly listened. He believed that the federal magistrate was a puppet who would go along with the FBI and the U.S. attorneys no matter what.

The judge asked Tony, "Do you work?"

Tony explained that he had worked in the cartage business, but his truck was stolen a few months ago.

"Where's your wife?" the judge asked.

"In Florida," Tony said. "Clearwater, I think. We're separated."

"You are not a stable man," the judge announced. "I'm setting your bond at four hundred thousand dollars cash."

"We'll get another hearing," Bailey told Tony.

They went back to the FBI offices for the usual booking procedure — not too different from the one almost ten years ago when the FBI had charged Tony with interstate cartage theft. In fact, they had charged him two separate times, two years in a row. The first time, the case had been dismissed quickly by the judge. Bailey had handled the second one just right. And although arrested many times afterward by local and state representatives, Tony had had no further dealings with the FBI — until today. The procedure hadn't changed: the emptying of pockets, the fingerprinting, the walks down the halls into large rooms or small offices. As he was being brought back to Stratton's desk, Tony remembered the saying "You don't beat the FBI." Well, he'd done it twice. He knew there would not be the charm of a third time.

"Anything to say?" Stratton asked again, checking through the booking papers.

Tony shook his head. "Not without my lawyer."

"Your car is parked a couple of blocks from your sister's house," Stratton said, and Tony nodded. He had figured they would have staked out that area.

"We can tow it in. Or, you can give me the keys, and sign papers to release the car to us."

"I'll sign the papers, if you promise not to impound it, and if you give it back to my sister."

"Anything you want," Stratton said. "Soon as we finish with it, it goes right back to Therese."

Stratton let him use the phone to call Therese and tell her to give the keys to Stratton's men. Then they took him to another office where a couple of FBI and IBI agents were waiting. They were writing down the serial numbers of the two fifties and smaller bills that Tony had had with him and turned over earlier. He signed the FBI release while the agent said, "You got problems, Bill. You sure you haven't got anything to say?"

The IBI agents said nothing. Tony followed suit.

"Well," one of the agents said, throwing down a pen, "he's printed, booked. Lock him up."

They took him to the federal lockup for a couple of hours.

"We're waiting to hear where you're going to," a marshal told him, leaning against the bars. By four o'clock the same marshal was tired of waiting and impatiently called down for instructions. He took Tony out to the phone with him so he could call his sister as soon as his destination was known. The marshal was talking to a loud mouthed guy who finally said, "Take him to county jail."

"Know where you're going?" the marshal laughed, holding the phone away from his ear.

"Yeah," Tony said and called his sister.

He was put back in the lockup for a short while until a different marshal came to take him away. It seemed strange to be watched so closely, Tony thought. He had tried to come in two or three times that week, and had walked right in today — yet they still acted as if he were about to take off. Nice guys — the fuckin' FBI.

25

One Pickup After Another

The story of Marzano's last days in the sun of Grand Cayman Island — from paying even the slightest expense with a $100 bill to suspecting that laundry workers had made off with his pajamas — was told to the *Tribune* by George Salati, Holiday Inn manager.

Marzano eventually got his pajamas back from the laundry, but not before the wait almost tripped him up with the local authorities and prowling FBI agents who were seeking him.

"He raised an awful fuss about the pajamas and demanded that I personally look for them," said Salati.

The pajamas were returned to Marzano only hours before authorities closed in on his hotel hideout and found both him and DiFonzo missing.

"He [Marzano] liked to sun-bathe and take a dip in our pool," said Salati. "Outside of that and ordering meals of steak with wine, I can't recall anything else except his curiosity about pirates. You know, Blackbeard himself used to come here."

— November 1, 1974,
Chicago Tribune

The "Super-Heist," as one *Chicago Sun-Times* headline termed it, starting October 22, 1974, took over the front pages of all local newspapers. It was the biggest case Chicago journalism had seen in years and produced exhaustive news coverage and wild speculation as each day editors called for new and dramatic copy. John O'Brien, a *Tribune* reporter and a friend of Ramon Stratton's, followed the case from start to finish, and his thorough, fast-breaking stories appeared day after day. Pushed to page two were the Nixon-tapes disclosures, the search for Patty Hearst, and jury selection for the trial of the Ohio National Guardsmen in the shooting of Kent State students. The sympathy the Chicago man in the street later expressed for the burglars, according to televised interviews, may have resulted from the above juxtaposition of events.

At any rate, Ramon Stratton did not share the public's enthusiasm for the grand theft. Now that the FBI had been granted jurisdiction, he was busy coordinating detective assignments and the information-gathering machinery that would provide the underpinnings of the government's case. He sifted all reports, plus those passed along by the other state agencies, noting relevant pieces of information that would result in a clear design of proof. Marrera and Marzano were like two ends of a magnet attracting and holding particles named Gushi, Maniatis, DiFonzo, and still another Marzano. Linked originally by the Evanston gold theft, the first two drew in the other names as a result of the ILIC surveillance on Gushi and friends.

On Wednesday, October 23, Peter Gushi and James Maniatis were picked up for questioning. The latter was taken before the grand jury in connection with the impounded Ford Econoline van found outside his home. This van was assumed to be the same one that IBI Superintendent Wayne Kerstetter had ordered followed until the surveillance was called off. Now it was being sifted by the police crime laboratory for scrapings that might provide a clue. Traces of red paint had already been found in the van, and some money containers in the Purolator vault were painted red. Gushi did not appear before the grand jury at this time, but was released after inconclusive questioning. Just enough to give him more nightmares.

Meanwhile, the newspapers reported varying amounts stolen and left behind in the vault. On Wednesday they announced that only $16,000 remained in the vault after $3.8 million was taken. On Thursday, October 24, newspapers revised the figure left behind up to $21 million. Police Captain Victor Vrdolyak, commissioner of the General Assignment Division, said he was told that about $25 million in four-by-four-by-two containers, or tankers, was in the vault when the burglars struck. (Purolator requested that the public not be told the exact amount in the vault at any one time.)

Stratton, meanwhile, was increasingly irritated by leaks he suspected were coming from an assistant state's attorney's office. The FBI had promised to keep the state informed daily, and U.S. Attorney James Thompson, who now issued his own statements, was accusing Stratton of further leaks. To delay the passage of information, Stratton began sending reports to the Chicago Police. It then took at least a day or two, in the normal course of communication, before they in turn informed the state's people. Eventually Chicago Police created a so-called news blackout about the crime by referring all reporter's questions to Ralph Berkowitz, first assistant state's attorney. Soon after, federal forces also clamped a news lid on their information.

On Friday, October 25, five days after the discovery of the burglary, Stratton obtained a warrant for Marrera's arrest. Charges against Marrera were "participating in a bank burglary, bank larceny, and use of explosive devices." Because the FBI in Washington is kept informed with daily reports and summaries, the charges were announced simultaneously by Clarence M. Kelley in Washington, D.C., and U.S. Attorney Thompson and State's Attorney Carey in Chicago. Richard Held, special agent in charge of the Chicago FBI office, leaving no publicity stone unturned, revised the amount stolen from $3.9 million to more than $4 million. The FBI further stated that the suspect was likely to be armed and extremely dangerous. A nationwide pickup order was issued and a manhunt ensued, employing 300 men pulled off other duties to concentrate on the search for Marrera. He probably heard the news report of this, and thus he wasn't at home when the police came to arrest him. Meanwhile, the police were still questioning Gushi, whose store was described in newspaper reports as the headquarters for a major fencing operation.

Stratton wasn't particularly worried about proving his case. He believed that Marrera eventually would talk as the evidence piled up. "The evidence comes down to the fact that the money went in — and out — while Marrera was watching over it," Stratton said. Given the bulk of the money it was hard to imagine someone sneaking it out in a lunch box. It was equally hard to imagine bags of gasoline appearing overnight in locked vaults that showed no sign of forced entry. In addition, there was the fact that Marrera had sent the woman alarm-board watcher home four hours early, and suggested the runner catch a movie.

A little after midnight Saturday, the Chicago Police located Marrera in the home of his in-laws. Police were told that Marrera was asleep, but that since the matter seemed urgent they would wake him. As the police gathered outside in the chill night, their car lights flashing, Marrera finally appeared at a second-story window.

"You got a warrant with you?" he called down to Area Six General Assignment Sergeant Kelley.

"Get the FBI over here with a warrant," Kelley called to another detective, who radioed the request to Stratton's office.

When the FBI agents arrived, Kelley took them into the small yard and yelled, "They're here. You coming out now?"

"I want to check the I.D.s," Marrera's wife called back. Under Marrera's direction she phoned Stratton for the names of the agents he'd sent over and a description of each. Then she reappeared at the window and shouted down that she wanted to see identification. Covered by the Chicago Police, in case Marrera should try anything, the agents went to the door and flashed their I.D. cards for Mrs. Marrera's approval. Only when satisfied that they were truly FBI did Marrera come downstairs, out the door, and surrender.

Marrera later told Stratton that he'd planned to surrender Tuesday (federal offices would be closed Monday for Veterans Day). He said he was going to turn himself in, post bond, and then go back into hiding — for his *own* protection, he intimated. Stratton immediately arranged for federal marshals to escort Marrera to Rockford Jail in Winnebago County, about twenty miles northwest of Chicago. He didn't want anyone — underworld enemies or erstwhile friends — to know where Marrera was. Just in case. "When somebody is accused of stealing four million dollars," Stratton said emphatically, "he's sure game for anyone who wants to take it away from him." For the moment, Stratton had no more questioning sessions planned with Marrera, who was "stonewalling it" and not worth Stratton's time. Unfortunately, every night as a matter of course, all jails put on the state teletype network the names of new prisoners. Stratton, still at his desk, read, "Ralph Marrera, Winnebago County Jail, Rockford, IL."

"Oh my God," he remembers commenting to the empty

room before he called U.S. Marshal John Tower at 2:00 A.M. "The cat is out of the bag — they put it on the state tele- type." (Stratton often called the marshal's home at 2:00 A.M., because when he was at his desk working he felt no pang at awakening a fellow federal employee.)

On Monday, October 28, Marrera was driven back to Chicago and arraigned before U.S. Magistrate Carl Sussman on theft charges for the purpose of setting bond. Under questioning by the judge, Marrera admitted meeting Charlie Marzano for breakfast every other day at Connie's Restau- rant at Thirty-fourth and Harlem in Berwyn (and what was wrong with friends having breakfast together?). Assistant U.S. Attorneys Michael King and James Breen asked for a high cash bond to keep Marrera in jail for safekeeping. U.S. Attorney Thompson said Marrera "obviously knows so much there's a real concern that either his confederates may want to bump him off, or some other hoods trying to learn where the loot is may find him and 'squeeze' him too hard." Over the objections of Marrera's lawyer, bond was set at $400,000 cash or corporate securities. Marrera was then transported back to Rockford — though this time it wasn't a secret.

Meanwhile, Stratton got another break. He'd gone back to his desk to continue sifting through stacks of material regularly passed along by all law-enforcement agencies "just in case something might have to do with Purolator." This time it was the Columbus, Ohio, police just doing their job. An employee of an airplane charter company, Executive Jet Service in Columbus, had noticed a Lincoln Continental parked in an odd place in its airport lot. The car had Illinois license plates and was perhaps abandoned; he had called the police. They investigated and sent an inquiry along to the Il- linois State Police, who passed the inquiry along to the Chi- cago Police. The Chicago Police duly passed the information along to the FBI. There the license plate number crossed Stratton's desk. Stratton, who recites U.S. titles and code numbers with less hesitation than the rest of the world recalls its own phone numbers, recognized it as belonging to the last strange car seen at Gushi's place the Saturday before the burglary. A quick flip through the recent IBI and ILIC reports confirmed his memory. The car had been rented by Louis DiFonzo and was seen parked outside Pete Gushi's home.

Stratton phoned the senior resident agent at Columbus, Bud (Wilfred) Goodwin, and gave him the necessary information for a probable-cause search warrant for the car. "Check the airport," he said. "They must have flown from there." Stratton's Chicago agents traced the license plates to the leasing company, which had indeed leased it to DiFonzo. Stratton then tensely waited for the Columbus report.

In a few hours Goodwin gave Stratton the details: an Executive Jet Service employee remembered chartering a Lear jet to four men with heavy luggage and growths of beard. They had originally planned to fly to Grand Cayman Island but had switched their plans and landed in Miami. They left the Miami airport in a cab. One cab.

Stratton immediately notified the Miami office and their agents took over. They traced the foursome to the Colonnade, but nobody remembered any of them registering there. Finally they found the cab driver who had picked up four men from the Colonnade and taken them to the Airport Tower Hotel. The desk clerk recognized pictures of the Marzanos, DiFonzo, and Gushi. After checking his records, he said, "That was the Keith Anderson group."

Further checking located the Robert Grass Jet Service with its charter-flight record of Louie and his eighty-minute private plane trip out of Fort Lauderdale at the cost of $1233. The Marzanos were found on the commercial air-

line's manifest listing travelers to Grand Cayman. When
Stratton had this information, he requested the Miami FBI
office to send two agents to Grand Cayman.

Less than twenty-four hours after Stratton's first call, the
Miami agents phoned the superintendent of police on Grand
Cayman, Derrick Tricker, to inform him that wanted criminals were in his haven. Tricker said they could come over,
without firearms. The agents flew down to Grand Cayman
Wednesday morning, October 30, to confer with Tricker in
person. When they arrived, Tricker told them they were
guests of his country — they could accompany him, but they
were to remember that they had no jurisdiction. They were
to say nothing, do nothing. He would handle the entire investigation.

The agents reported back that Derrick Tricker is "Mr.
Law" on Grand Cayman and rules with the knowledge of
exactly what comes in and goes out. Shortly after DiFonzo's
arrival Superintendent Tricker was well aware that his customs had cleared a large sum of American dollars. Aware
but not impressed. The week before that, $8 million had
lumbered through customs in one shepherded flock. By the
time the FBI agents arrived, Tricker had already notified airport authorities to report any suspicious departures, specifically those of Mr. Marzano and Mr. DiFonzo.

In the meantime, Monday afternoon, back at Chicago's
Civic Center, State's Attorney Bernard Carey and Charles
Siragusa, head of the ILIC, had announced new indictments
by the grant jury. They charged Peter Gushi and James
Maniatis, along with three other men, with allegedly operat-
ing a stolen goods ring doing a business of $5 million a year.
Gushi's indictments focused specifically on the theft of
$12,000 cash and some traveler's checks from a Sterling
Heights, Michigan, bank on July 27, and the theft of an es-
timated $1 million in jewels and merchandise from the Dun-

hill Company in Oak Forest on July 24. Gushi and Maniatis were also indicted for selling 1500 wrist watches from Dunhill's valued at $37,000.

Members of the Chicago Police and several IBI agents led by Wayne Kerstetter arrested Gushi and Maniatis in the Family Discount Store on 111th Street in Worth, Illinois. Two hours later, as Gushi and Maniatis left after making bond by posting $10,000 each, Gushi was picked up outside police headquarters. This time he was held without bond, pending the filing of charges relating to the Purolator theft before a U.S. magistrate. The heat was finally on.

Stratton went into the interrogation session with Gushi armed with two weapons: the first was the evidence already gathered against Gushi; the second was Stratton's knowledge of Gushi's reputation for not having guts enough to take an extended stay in jail, as demonstrated by his reported suicide attempts at Leavenworth. Stratton did not consider Gushi a natural informer. But faced with charges that could translate into years in prison, and shown the information already gathered, Gushi finally showed willingness to bargain for a new name, a short prison term, and a new start. But first he insisted that FBI agent John Oitzinger be called in while he told his story.

Stratton sent for Oitzinger and word went out that Gushi was going to talk. Through repeated pickups and questionings, the agents and criminals occasionally get to know one another — and the criminals pass the word around when they find an agent who is "trustworthy." From the criminal point of view, an agent is "honest" in three ways: he will level with you when the evidence is clearly against you; he won't pretend the evidence exists when it doesn't; and he will not misrepresent your talk with him by saying you said something you didn't say. Gushi trusted Oitzinger and felt safe talking to him.

Oitzinger arrived and was briefed on Gushi's interrogation up to that point, at which time Oitzinger was able to reassure Gushi that, yes, the evidence was clearly against him, and no, he wouldn't misrepresent what Gushi was going to say. The newspapers reported that for once Gushi was being selective in what he said instead of talking loquaciously, and one federal agent said, "Gushi is being pretty cute about what he tells us." But he *was* talking.

The Miami agents, meanwhile, were busily following Superintendent Tricker, who was onto the Marzano-DiFonzo bank trail. Although verification would come weeks later, Tricker had already succeeded in locating all the banks where Louie had opened new accounts.

On October 30, he and the recently arrived agents descended on the Holiday Inn just after Charlie and Louie had checked out. "Wouldn't forget that pair," they were told. "One of them turned the hotel upside down until he located a missing pair of pajamas" — Charlie's new ones, as it was later confirmed. "And they had a two-thousand-dollar bar bill — for just eight days. Paid."

Earlier that same day Stratton filed his full complaint against Louie, Charlie, and Tony. In essence, they were charged with stealing and intending to steal $1,165,204 described as belonging to the Merchandise National Bank of Chicago, but in the temporary possession of Purolator; with entering Purolator "used in part as a bank as agent for the Merchandise National Bank of Chicago" with intent to commit larceny; using explosives; and knowingly transporting money known to be stolen. Maniatis, Marrera, and Gushi were mentioned but not named in this complaint. The Miami FBI office was duly informed.

That same Wednesday night, an alert Laxa Airlines employee, Mike Adams, notified Superintendent Tricker that two men each with three suitcases had just purchased tickets for Costa Rica. According to Adams, the older man seemed nervous and "was puffing a big black cigar." The younger man identified himself as Mr. Stewart, and paid for both tickets — $98 each — in cash. When Adams asked for identification, they said they didn't have any. "That's when I got suspicious," Adams said, "and made my call." Twenty-five minutes later, only ten minutes before the flight for Costa Rica was scheduled to leave, the FBI agents and Superintendent Tricker arrived. Tricker asked the two men to identify themselves. They refused. Under Grand Cayman law, it is illegal to refuse such a request by a police officer. Thereupon, Tricker arrested them, took them back to Georgetown, and put them in his jail overnight.

On Thursday Tricker expelled the two men from his island by putting them on the first plane to Miami. To ensure their arrival, he sent one of his own constables on the plane, and the unarmed Miami FBI agents boarded as well. (Later, Charlie and his lawyer would argue that the FBI had no jurisdiction and had illegally removed them from the island. According to Stratton, Tricker did the removing; and the Supreme Court had previously ruled, in the case of Communist Gus Hall, pushed across the Mexican border, that it didn't matter how a "wanted' person was brought back, as long as excessive force was not used.)

Upon arrival in Miami, the head of the FBI office, armed, met the plane and put Charlie and Louie under arrest. They were quickly arraigned before Miami Federal Magistrate Peter Palermo, at which time one of the agents made an affidavit that a warrant of arrest for the pair was outstanding, a necessary procedure for keeping men in custody. Their bond was set at $1 million cash for Louie, $500,000 for Charlie, and then they were taken to a federal lockup to await the arrival of the official complaint and affidavit by mail from Chicago. A hearing for their return to Chicago was scheduled for a week later, on Friday, November 8. The documents were sent out Thursday, the same day as their arrest. The mail service being what it is, though, they didn't arrive in Miami until the Monday following. Meanwhile Louie and Charlie's attorneys were fighting their clients' "illegal removal" from Grand Cayman, and any further extradition from Miami to Chicago. But on Friday they dropped their objections to the transfer, and Charlie and Louie waived their Friday morning removal hearing. This paved the way for federal marshals to escort them back to Chicago. The marshals also brought the approximately $14,000 found on the suspects when they were arrested and it was earmarked for evidence in the trial. When they appeared later before Judge William J. Bauer and asked for return of the money because it could not be proved it came from the Purolator robbery, the judge replied that if they could show where it did come from he would indeed return it. The money was eventually included in the amount considered recovered.

And so the last wandering travelers were brought home.

26

Jail — Where the Upkeep Keeps Going Up

Last Saturday the back page of the *Tribune* was devoted to the scandalous overcrowding at Cook County Jail. If Jack Dykinga's pictures had originated in any other country, many Americans would have exclaimed about the lack of civilization in that foreign land.

— December 10, 1974,
Chicago Tribune

Bridewell, or Cook County Jail, an old building slightly resembling a castle, was built a little more than fifty years ago to house 1158 men. During the weeks that Tony was kept there it held some 2600 men — many of them sleeping on floors and tables.

Cook County Jail is separated from the back of the County Court House on Twenty-sixth and California Avenue by a large yard. Cars and paddy wagons are parked here, prisoners deposited and removed; friends, family, and lawyers crisscross from one building to another in a ritual as ancient as the buildings themselves.

When the booking procedure for Tony was completed at the FBI office, he and eight other prisoners were shuffled into a van, the door was locked behind them, and they were driven over to the jail yard. There the federal marshal backed their van up to a landing dock and Tony clambered out with the other men — "as if we're cattle," he muttered to the heavyset guy next to him. They were herded down a few steps to halt at a huge steel door with a small cracked window, its wire mesh a spidery pattern set at an uncomfortably high level. The marshal who had driven them over thumped hard on the door to get the attention of the guard inside. When he finally appeared, one marshal held up his badge and the door swung open. The thought of dungeons crossed Tony's mind as he was shoved inside.

Tony had been through what he called the "garbage process" before. First he would be stripped and given a cursory examination by the doctor, a few shots, and a plastic wrist band. "Just like a newborn baby," Tony later told J.D. "So they don't lose us."

This time, however, Tony's path through the process was interrupted. The guard on duty had seen the sheet of prisoners and knew that somebody from the Purolator job was coming in. When Tony arrived, the guard, a sergeant now, recognized Tony from the street and told him to sit on the side for a while.

"I'll get you a good tier," he told Tony, his mouth full of food. "C-1 if I can. Here, have some chicken sandwich." He sat down next to Tony.

Tony wasn't surprised by his friendliness. He knew the guards would think that the Purolator people had money to spare for favors. In Tony's case they were right, but not because of Purolator money. Tony always paid to go first class, if he could — even in jail.

Tiers C-1 through 4 were known as good tiers because

most of their inmates were federal prisoners (later, the federal government acquired its own jail), and were over the age of thirty. These men were considered to be from a higher class (at times these tiers held bankers and state employees), not wild young punks who killed people for a quarter. So Tony hoped the guard could help — with a lot more than a chicken sandwich.

Once through the garbage process, Tony was taken down another long corridor, past big cellblocks, to a huge holding room. Anywhere from forty to a hundred people waited in this room seated on benches that lined the gray walls. Occasionally someone used the one open toilet. At various intervals a guard appeared and called out ten or twelve names from a list.

Tony slumped onto one of the benches and waited for two hours for his name and tier to come up. An unsmiling guard led him and the others down still another hallway with signs over the locked doors indicating a tier and cellblock section. At C-1 the guard unlocked the door and called four names — Tony's among them — and sent the men up the stairway, locking the door after them. They climbed up one flight to another locked door, where they waited a few minutes — but the door remained closed. "Must be sprucing up the place for us," a man named Ernie said. Tony pounded on the door twice, then shrugged and sat down on the steps. Cold air drifted down from small broken windows with inset steel bars high up toward the ceiling. Tony and the other three prisoners alternately stood or sat shivering on the stairs for an hour and a half. Tony figured they must have heard about his connection with the Purolator score and they were thinking of the time when they could say, "Yeah, I came in with Marzano." Finally the upper door opened and another guard unhurriedly waved them in.

C-1 had other pluses. It was on the first floor, up a flight of stairs from the semibasement entrance, near the main offices and visiting area for lawyers and their clients. In this section, which included the warden's office and a pool of typists, narrow, wooden shelflike tables were set up between head-high partitions. Big wooden chairs faced each other across the table so that, when hunched forward, two people could meet in semiprivacy.

The visiting rooms for the other tiers were straight out of a zoo. In those, one person had to shout through a small screen into the ear of his visitor and vice versa, which meant they couldn't face each other. And because the stalls bordered a dayroom where a hundred or more men were pacing, talking, watching TV, and bemoaning their bad luck, conversation was almost impossible. Besides, the other prisoners crowded close to see if they could recognize any visitor, in which case they would bellow messages: "Tell him to get hold of my wife." "Tell Frank I'm still here and all right." "Find fuckin' Joe."

Tony had forgotten how wretched conditions were —even on the best of tiers. Blinking after the dim light of the stairway, Tony entered the large dayroom with its four big picnic benches and one blaring TV set.

"Hey, Tony. Over here." Tony turned to see a man named Albert, awaiting trial for hijacking, waving to him from the old kitchen carved into one side of the room, its dumb waiters from years past now sealed up. One old sink served as a basin to wash out socks or a shirt. Meals were served by a prisoner who acted as a straw boss and distributed the food brought upstairs on large steel trolleys. All the fixtures had been meant originally to serve about 75 people, but more than 125 now filled the forty cells and overflowed into the dayroom. Tony walked over to say hello to his friend, seated at a single small table in the kitchen, dealing out a hand of solitaire with yellowed cards.

"Don't worry about tonight," Albert said as Tony sat down across the table from him. "A guy I know's leaving and you can have his bunk."

"Thanks," Tony said and meant it. Those not lucky enough to negotiate for a bunk in one of the two-man cells had to find a mattress and sleep on the floor in the dayroom. A few men had a one-man cell because of their seniority. They were called "jailers" and they were still waiting after two or three years for their trials either to commence or to continue. You could always recognize a jailer immediately, without even knowing what one was. Men's features are altered in subtle ways — beyond prison pallor and prison wariness — by the efforts to prevent utter despair.

Tony looked around to acclimate himself. On the other side of the dayroom was the small washroom with one shower, a couple of toilets, and an old steel sink, above which hung a piece of aluminum that served as a mirror, although it reflected little. When a prisoner was to appear in court, he took a shower the night before and tried to shave in the morning, essentially in the dark, his face a blur in the gray metal.

Albert slapped his cards together and led Tony down the six-foot-wide hallway lined with twenty cells on each side, their doors never locked. The two-man cells contained an upper and lower bunk against one wall with just enough space for one small chair between the foot of the bunk and the cell door. Actually, four or five men took turns using these bunks, a few hours at a time, rather than sleep on the dayroom floor. To get to the top bunk, Tony first stepped on the toilet, then the sink, ducking under the clotheslines strung to hold jackets.

"Looks like a fuckin' tenement," Tony said.

"But we got art," Albert said, waving his hand at the pictures of naked girls pinned on the walls, some predating *Playboy*. Tony's pillow nudged a picture of a girl who had boobs as big as footballs. How could a guy sleep next to them?

A guard walk completely surrounded the tier, separated from it by iron bars. Visitors could circle the entire area, dayroom and cells, to observe the inmates. Sometimes a kitchen flunky strolled by to sell sandwiches and cigarettes with a well-rewarded guard's permission.

Later that night, even in his sleep, Tony could hear men talking and pacing inside and outside his cell, waiting their turn to sleep. At 3:00 A.M., Tony felt his shoulder being shaken. He tried to burrow deeper into the rock-hard bunk.

"Get up! Come on now," a voice said. "Get your fuckin' ass out."

Tony staggered up and out into the hall, stumbled past the pacing men and into the dayroom. In the dayroom, men were pacing, arguing, playing cards and cursing. The TV blared full blast twenty-four hours a day. It had no dials. A guard changed the channels with a remote control unit outside the cell area. There had been killings in the past when a prisoner changed a channel, or tuned in to an unpopular program. (Later, in Terre Haute, a maximum-security prison, during Tony's brief stay, one man smashed the TV and pulled a knife on another inmate who kept switching channels.)

Pandemonium never broke out. It was constant. Only money bought any kind of happiness. But money requires a friend on the outside as well as one on the inside, and Gino faithfully came through as life line to the outside, as Tony had done for him a few years earlier. First Gino saw to it that the sergeant who had arranged for Tony's assignment to tier C-1 was rewarded. Then he took Tony's twice-weekly food and supply order, which was shouted to him over the screams of the other prisoners. Gino's contact on the outside was a guard called the Chief. Gino delivered Tony's packages to the Chief, who brought them into the jail the next day. Gino also paid him for any privileges Tony had received, such as time to use the pay phone in the basement.

Characteristically, Tony did not order merely enough for himself and one or two friends. One supply box included twenty poor-boy sandwiches, a dozen grilled-pork-chop sandwiches from Tony's favorite place at Halstead and Fourteenth, assorted salami and pepperoni and beef sandwiches, and some provolone. Each delivery ran from $100 to $200. But the Chief balked at bringing in three quarts of vodka, Gino reported to Tony.

"Fuck him," Tony said. "Take some rubbing alcohol bottles and fill them with vodka. Then put them on the bottom of the next box, and put everything else on top."

Tony's bond hearings began almost immediately and always followed the same procedure — a process that Tony saw as debilitating, and calculated to elicit confessions from those too weak to see them through. Maybe turn someone into an informer.

The night before a court appearance, the prisoner tries to get cleaned up, which means a shave, a shower (where there is one shower to every hundred people), and some rest.

Prisoners are awakened at 5 A.M. and at 5:30 a guard appears to take them down to the bullpen as if they will be leaving momentarily. Here, as many as fifty people crowd together half standing up, yelling about their cases, discussing their chances, offering and giving advice. Bedlam.

At about 8:30 federal marshals arrive and call out the names of those prisoners going to federal court. They are removed, handcuffed, and put in a van. Then they are driven through the streets, where they can see people free and doing ordinary things. They pull into an area beneath the building, where only federal marshals and judges are allowed, unless the FBI is bringing in or removing prisoners.

Still handcuffed, they are herded to the twenty-fourth floor, where the marshal's offices are, through the offices to a long corridor of cells, mostly empty and curving around a corner so the prisoners are unable to see anyone else. There they wait in the cell until somebody takes them to the proper judge. Each judge has a cell outside his room where the prisoner waits until his case is called — any moment to the close of the day. The actual appearance before a judge could be as short as three minutes, during which the judge could continue the case, or hearing, until the next day. Then the procedure is reversed. The prisoner is returned to and locked in the marshal's cell until all prisoners have had "their day in court," and then they are herded back down the elevator, into the van, and back to jail, where they might have a two-hour wait outside the stairway door until the tier guard decides to let them in.

During this time, until you appear before the judge, your hopes and fears fight for equal time. Then, when it's over, you realize that you have to do it all over again whether you're going for bond, sentencing, or appeal. Even trial. Bailey tried to keep Tony's hopes up, but words don't mean much. Tony couldn't concentrate with people all around him screaming in the bullpen, asking questions about their cases, telling him what to do. He desperately needed time to think — away from the jail, in a less intimidating atmosphere, less crazy.

In the marshal's offices messages confused and tantalized. Call someone. Or the FBI wants to talk to you. (They can't unless you ask to see them — but the marshal can let the prisoner sit awhile in his offices before putting him in a cell, and someone could wander in and suggest, "They might be able to help. Just ask.") Bailey would call Tony out of the marshal's jail for a pep talk, but Tony despaired of making the $375,000 cash bond the judge seemed intent on requiring. And each day, going back and forth, he wondered if he would ever again be able to do what people did every day — drink coffee in a coffee shop, or just take a walk. Free. And his despair was matched by his main worry: "Where is everybody?"

Tony knew from the newspapers that he, Charlie, Louie, Pete, Jimmy, and Ralphie were appearing before the same Judge Bauer. Sometimes it was on the same day, but where were they? Which cell? When? What were they saying to the judge? And Ralphie coming in from Rockford. Was he still standing up? One day, as Tony was being taken to a marshal's cell, he walked past the one he knew was his, trying to see who else was there. Way down on the other side, around the corner, he saw a special-looking cell with two mattresses on the floor, ashtrays, cigarettes on little tables, two chairs, everything comfortable. "Hey," the marshal called to him, "get back here fast." Tony knew that cell was for Gushi and Jimmy — all the comforts of home to keep them talking.

On another day Tony saw a suit and tie hanging on the marshal's doorknob with Ralphie's name pinned on it. He asked one of the friendlier marshals to let him just wave to Ralph.

"Look," Tony said, "I know he's good people. He's not turning. I just want to say hello. Wave."

Quickly the clothes disappeared. "Sorry, I would but I can't. For no amount of money."

"Why?" This bothered Tony. "He's not talking. You know I'm *not*, or you'd be getting the government here." But the answer was again no.

Tony tried to yell as loud as he could from his cell to wherever Ralph was. But he got no answer. Usually if anyone is in a cell he answers. In the past Tony had yelled for Pete or Jimmy the Greek — but got no response either. He even called Ralph by name, said it was Tony calling, but no go. This seemed especially ominous — that they were being kept so separate. All of them appearing the same day before the same judge, yet never seeing each other. Even the lawyers worried about somebody plea bargaining before their client got a chance. Or turning into a witness and sending their guy down the drain.

By Saturday, November 9, a little more than a week since Tony had been arrested, he had finally settled into the county jail routine. He was visiting and (for a price) making plans with Gino in the main waiting room when suddenly there was a flurry of activity. Secretaries gathered in whispering groups and more guards than usual stood around doing nothing. The front doors opened and Charlie and Louie were ushered in by two federal marshals. Tony knew the boys were due in eventually because he had seen them on TV being picked up in Florida. He never missed a newscast if he was awake — the other prisoners kept him up to date on the broadcasts he missed. Tony nudged Gino's arm. "Go take care of the Chief so's they can get tier one with me," Tony whispered to Gino. "Make it worth it for him."

Gino slipped a hundred-dollar bill from the cash he always carried and sauntered over to the Chief, who was standing near the anteroom door. The Chief glanced at Tony and nodded. Then Charlie and Louie caught sight of Tony and waved glumly. Now the Purolator team was all inside; only the money was still outstanding.

Word went around C-1 that Tony's friends were on their way up. "Have a fuckin' reunion here," one of the jailers grumbled. Tony ushered Louie and Charlie to his cell when they had finally finished with the garbage below. A few men called out greetings, but mostly just stood back and waited for Charlie to make the first moves. Charlie came through the cell door first, looking around. Louie followed behind with a dazed expression on his face. Tony suddenly realized that neither Charlie nor Louie had ever been in jail before. No wonder they were so relieved to see him. Charlie slumped onto Tony's bunk as Tony brought out his supply box that had just arrived that day. It made them all feel a little better as Charlie related in a hushed voice the events of the few preceding days. Tony filled them in on some of the ways of staying O.K. in the jail. But two important people — Gushi and Marrera — were missing, so it wasn't really a reunion.

They hung out together for a while until finally the strain of being cooped up was getting to everyone. A week and a half later, when Charlie and Louie were still cheering themselves up with Tony's food, he pointed out that it did cost him money and why didn't they just chip in and help pay for extras? The next Sunday Tony had a new delivery of beef sandwiches and told Charlie and Louie to help themselves.

"No thanks," Louie said.

"We'll eat the food when it comes off the line," Charlie said. "We heard there's chicken today."

Tony stared at them in disbelief. "How you gonna eat that chicken with its feathers on?"

"I'm eating off the fuckin' line," Charlie insisted, and Louie once again agreed.

Tony couldn't help watching them when the cart came up and the straw boss, wearing plastic gloves, threw the food on the plates. Charlie and Louie, never meeting Tony's eye, cleaned their plates. Tony turned away in disgust, remembering all the fancy bottles of wine and special restaurant orders they'd consumed on the island.

He made one last try. "Hey, we need that guy's good will for phone calls."

"I don't want to make no phone calls," Louie said.

"Fuck the phone calls," Charlie said. "If *you* want to get

stuff in, pay for things, o.k. I'm not going to pay for nothing for other guys here."

Hey, Tony thought, we're supposed to be in this together. Charlie had brought him into it. Just count a little money. Got him in deeper. And now it wasn't "we" anymore. It's "you" — if you want to pay.

"Well, I need all those things," Tony told him. But he didn't argue later when Charlie and Louie still ate his food and made their phone calls and had a little drink on him now and then. They weren't much good for company, though. Louie said nothing most of the time and Charlie, too, kept to himself. When Tony needed distraction to get through the night, he joined Albert and Danny at the other end of the tier. Albert had a radio in his room and could always come up with three or four sticks. Tony would bring his vodka and some of the men would sit there, smoking and drinking and listening to music. Talking about women. Eventually the outside noise seemed to come from far off. Tony didn't want Charlie to catch him smoking, though, so he'd have one of the men check now and then to see if Charlie was pacing in their direction. He knew Charlie would call him a dope fiend and hassle him. On the outside, Tony rarely had a joint, but in here the resulting mellow mood made all the angry shouts of the men, their stories of innocence and frame-up rehearsed for imaginary judges, their bragging to imaginary girls, blend into the entertainment that had them falling off the bunks in laughter.

The ropes couldn't be learned in a week, and Tony soon discovered just how green he and his friends were. Every day half the tiers were allowed to trek to the commissary and sign for cigarettes, shaving cream, whatever they could afford from the money in their jail account. The guards would unlock all the doors that opened onto the stairways that led to the basement.

"Youse guys better go together," an inmate, one of the jailers, said. "Those hallways are open to the other tiers too, you know. People goin' up and down. Some guys wait around, and when they see you carrying stuff, they grab it, put the bags over their heads, punch you out, and next thing you know they're gone, mixin' with the other guys going up and down. You know — they're gone back to their own tiers." He pulled on his ear lobe. "And you don't follow, you know."

"Jesus," Tony said.

Several times they discussed where they were going to come up with bond money. Their bonds were still set outrageously high, even after many bond meetings. One judge had dropped Tony's cash bond to $375,000, then $225,000 after Judge William J. Lynch had turned down two earlier requests. But it was still way out of Tony's reach.

Meanwhile they had to raise easily accounted for visible money, so they couldn't be accused of using Purolator funds.

"I got legal contacts," Louie said.

"My family will put up property," Charlie said, but he didn't elaborate. "Do you think you'll be able to make it?" Charlie asked Tony.

Tony didn't like that turn in the conversation at all — there was that "you" again. They had taken all the risks together. Now he was winding up with nothing. His family didn't have enough. He had no property — just a little cash saved. He'd need fourteen paid-up houses to make a cash bond like his. As he saw it, the government wanted to keep them in forever with outrageous bonds. Tony knew Charlie and Louie had access to cash. Even Marrera had property he could sell or mortgage. So Tony suggested that maybe some of that money out there could be given to his friends or family up front, and then they wouldn't be taking such a desperate chance mortgaging themselves to the hilt. They would be covered — protected.

"No," Charlie said. "There isn't any necessity for that." Louie nodded in agreement. Tony couldn't believe it. Here he was, one of the main guys taking all the weight. What the hell was going on? Why did he have to find his own money — and where? What Charlie was telling him was he was willing to let Tony sit there forty years if he had to.

When they weren't discussing bond procedures, Charlie's main litany was "Nobody should plead guilty. They can't prove anything."

"You gotta be kidding," Tony said.

"Gushi won't testify," Charlie said.

"Look," Tony said, hunching forward in the dim light of the cell so he could see Charlie's face. "Everybody's in jail; word is that Gushi is singing his heart out, whether you want to believe it or not. They followed our fuckin' footprints all over Grand Cayman."

"But they can't get anything out of the banks," Louie said. "It's against the law." Tony rolled his eyes.

"And they can't get anything out of Marrera either," Charlie said. "He's been through it before — he just gets to stonewalling. So they got exactly nothing."

"They got Gushi the Mouth," Tony repeated.

"Gushi won't testify," Charlie said, shaking his head. "Talkin' ain't testifying."

A few days later, Charlie said that Pete Gushi's cousin had come to see him and told him not to worry, that Pete wasn't going to testify in court.

"Whoever he is," Tony said, "he's lying. Or he thinks he's talking to babies. That we'll believe Pete will change his story and do a hundred years. After he went bad in the beginning. Pete couldn't even hold off a month — give us a chance to breathe." Tony suspected Charlie wanted him to believe everything was going to be great, Pete not testifying and all. Just so Tony wouldn't think of doing anything foolish.

Another time, Charlie said that someone came to his and Louie's lawyers and said the government was willing to give Charlie seven years, and Tony and Louie three apiece.

Tony knew he was lying, but he didn't want to say it right out. So he said, "Someone's lying to you. If we could, why not? We won't even have to leave jail. We can plead guilty right now."

"Nah. We're going to beat this," Charlie still insisted.

"Listen, tell whoever told you that that I'll take three and three — I'll do six. If we can get off like you say. In fact, they can let everyone off and I'll do ten by myself."

Charlie didn't say anything more then.

Meantime, Tony checked with Bailey because rumors are rumors. Bailey confirmed his suspicions. "Never. With over four million missing. Three years? What would the public, the government say?"

Friction between Tony and Charlie grew. Charlie had all the money and everybody tied up tight with him. And he continued to say stupid things, trying to make sure Tony would stick with him down to the last day, but not willing to let loose of a penny to help him make bond, or set things up on the outside for his family, or any needs he might have now. You just don't do that — bring someone in on a deal, get him in deeper. Then he's supposed to be a standup guy when he doesn't get one cent.

Tony tried not to let his feelings show. But he knew that if he had been dealing with his usual friends, J.D., or Gino, they all would have cooperated — pooled their money, worked out some deal together, some compromise so nobody got hurt too much. That's the way men were supposed to deal with each other in this business.

Louie didn't even listen to Charlie and Tony's arguments. He just looked as if he couldn't possibly be where he found himself, and what might happen couldn't possibly happen. He didn't mix, just stayed close to Charlie. Tony avoided both of them when he was feeling down.

In the meantime, Chicago was still fascinated with the biggest heist in American history. Front-row seats in the jail dayroom were taken hours before the "Two on Two" television broadcast November 16. Tony, Louie, and Charlie sat together. Bill Kurtis had flown down to Grand Cayman for his 6:30 P.M. Saturday report. Walter Jacobson held down the Chicago front and Gene Siskel, the *Tribune* movie critic, reviewed the burglary as if it were a high-budget movie. They showed the seven miles of white sand beach, the luxurious Holiday Inn where the trio had stayed. Kurtis held the microphone up to a nervous young desk clerk who said, "Yeah, they wanted to make sure they had the best rooms. Had a bar bill of almost two thousand dollars when they checked out." The dayroom cheered and someone hit Tony on the back in congratulations. Then Kurtis stood by the swimming-pool bar and explained how the customers didn't have to get out of the water to have a drink in the tropics. An Italian tourist who was now occupying the room that Tony and Charlie had was told to "look under the bed; they might have left something behind." The cameras zoomed around palm trees and panned in on a few sun-bathers and again brought cheers from the prisoners. Tony particularly enjoyed the mini-interviews with the people on the Chicago streets — hair blowing in the windy city, nervous, grinning — saying they wished the guys had gotten away with it. "They pulled it off," said one man in a three-button pinstripe suit. "No violence, no Watergate tapes, just money."

"Everybody's got a little larceny in their hearts," another man said.

"Better hope they're on the jury," someone called back to Tony. Speculation as to sophisticated burglary tools was wild. And finally a shot of Gushi and Maniatis with their arms over their heads, and the parting queries as to where the money is now.

To Charlie the show was one more bit of proof that nobody knew anything.

The days dragged on with few diversions, but Cyrus Feeder, forty, whom Tony knew by name from the streets, provided the most memorable one. Feeder was awaiting trial for allegedly killing Anthony Raymond, a Hillside policeman. Supposedly, Feeder and two other men had abducted the patrolman on October 1, 1972, when he stopped their car minutes after a restaurant holdup. Feeder was charged with burying the body on Feeder's sister's farm in Rhinelander, Wisconsin. The body was found in August 1973, and showed signs of having been covered first with lye to speed decomposition. If convicted, Feeder could expect 300 years. He was, therefore, usually in a bad mood as he prepared for his court hearings and trial. His cell was filled with notes from his lawyer, a common practice of long-time inmates, some of whom learned to write decent minibriefs to aid their cases.

One day Feeder left for court after borrowing another inmate's brand-new boots. "I have to look nice," he explained. He returned in a fury. "They won't let me even see the fuckin' witnesses accusing me," he ranted. "They put hoods over their heads and something to change their voices." He sat down at one of the picnic tables and pulled off the boots. "Fuckin' hoods. Can you believe it? This could only happen to me." He retired to his cell still cursing, the boots left by the table for their owner to retrieve.

The next day he began mumbling about somebody going through his cell, looking at his private papers. "Some nosy thief in here," he would holler from the doorway. "Somebody can't fuckin' leave my stuff alone." At around 5:30, when the food was coming up, the men had lined up leading from the dayroom all the way to the end of the corridor. Feeder walked past all the inmates until he stood at the front.

"I want your attention," he yelled. "I got somethin' to say."

A sort of silence fell, in deference to his reputation and jittery behavior.

"Somebody was in my cell looking at my fuckin' papers. I don't know who." He looked down the line of men. Then he pointed to a large garbage can. "See that drum of garbage? If I find out who it is, I got enough on my mind with those fuckin' hoods. If I find that guy, I'm gonna cut him up and put his pieces in that drum over there like they say I did that fuckin' cop. That's the way this guy would be."

He paused. "Thank you for your attention." Then he walked to the end of the line.

Tony had never heard the dayroom so quiet.

"Jesus," one guy said. "There could be agents planted here. Even a guy who'd be willin' to turn informer. Be another witness against him."

"And wearin' a fuckin' hood," another voice added.

But there was more shaking of heads than laughter over the terrible risk, as they saw it. It just made Tony's tooth hurt worse.

His tooth eventually provided Tony's other diversion while in jail — a visit to the dentist. The pain wouldn't go away even when he was drinking heavily. Eventually he complained to his lawyer that he had to get his tooth fixed before he could talk anymore. His lawyer relayed the message to the judge, and shortly thereafter two federal mar-shals appeared as escorts. Tony was ushered out of jail and into the offices of a Michigan Avenue dentist whose spe-cialty was welfare payments at supposedly low cost to the county.

"Not surprised they're hurting you," the dentist told him. "You need four teeth filled. Two uppers on each side. If you can handle it, I'll do them all at once."

"Go ahead," Tony said. "Give me lotsa of Novocain. They can add that to my bar bill. I wanna be numb. It just makes me numb, right?" Numb was what he wanted to be, anyway, as he lay back in the chair. And wouldn't Charlie be happy that the fillings were done for free.

27

Finders Keepers

Three ILIC undercover agents were introduced to Jerold (the Bomber) Casio, a crime syndicate figure, while they were checking reports that a major burglary was being planned. The introducer, in what could be mobdom's social faux pas of the year, was Gushi. Gushi, unaware of the agents' identity, introduced them under their play-acting names as specialists in securities thefts.

— November 17, 1974,
Chicago Sun-Times

The papers were full of the Commercial Union Insurance Company's frustration in its attempts to learn the names and amounts of the Grand Cayman bank accounts.

On Tuesday, November 5, as Charlie and Louie were being returned to Chicago, Grand Cayman's acting attorney general, Roderick N. Donaldson, in a secret session before the island's Grand Court Judge Locksey Moody, sought an unprecedented order forcing Eric Cranston to identify the five banks that had received deposits from DiFonzo and the Marzanos. Prior to this meeting, Cranston had refused, stating that the lawyer-client relationship barred his disclosing this information. Judge Moody ruled otherwise, and Cranston named the following banks: the Swiss Bank and Trust Corporation, the Royal Bank of Canada, the Bank of Nova Scotia, the World Banking and Trust Corporation, and the Cayman National Bank.

Superintendent Tricker had located Cranston earlier for the FBI after questioning cab drivers, hotel officials, and bank clerks. He was anxious, as were other Grand Caymanians, to do whatever was possible to settle the matter and move the conflict out of the international news. They deplored the publicity that their haven was receiving and insisted that nobody on the island wanted his bank filled with "dirty" money. Cranston said that, as far as he knew, Di-Fonzo was supposed to be associated with the Boston law firm of Joseph Oteri (Oteri later was one of DiFonzo's defense attorneys — an association of sorts).

On Thursday, November 7, in his second surprise move, Attorney General Donaldson sought another order from the Grand Court, Grand Cayman's highest tribunal, that would force the banks to reveal the exact amounts deposited. The FBI hoped that the amounts disclosed would equal the burglary loot that DiFonzo had brought through customs. If the amounts were the same, the Commercial Union Insurance Company would immediately file suit to recover the cash.

As much as Grand Caymanians wanted to wash their hands of the whole affair, they were caught in a sticky clash of interests: Purolator's stolen money versus the island's banking secrecy laws. Since the 1966 Bank Secrecy Act, Grand Cayman had become an internationally known tax haven that had attracted big foreign deposits to the island. Therefore, for nearly two weeks the bankers and business community contended that if any of the island's more than 170 banks was forced to reveal how the estimated $1.4 million was divided into deposits by the Purolator suspects, it would cause a mass exodus of existing depositors and potential depositors in the direction of Hong Kong or even Liechtenstein. They therefore wanted the Grand Court to reject Donaldson's request that the banks be required to wave the protection of the secrecy act.

Meanwhile, Tony, Charlie, and Louie were shuttled back and forth from Cook County Jail to federal court in the Dirksen Building for hearings of their own to get their bonds reduced so they could make bail. Each hearing so far had brought the amounts down, but the figures were still out of their available cash range.

Before they succeeded, Stratton got a break. An informer provided Stratton with a key piece to his puzzle, and of course he knew exactly how to use it for maximum effect. On Thursday, November 21, 1974, at 5:15 P.M., Stratton finished writing a thirteen-page affidavit stating why he needed to search a certain building. Then he waited for U.S. Attorney Thompson to return to his office to read it. Thompson approved it even though his assistants disliked the phrasing of several paragraphs. Stratton immediately delivered his affidavit to Federal Magistrate Balog's home north of Sandburg Village and collected his search warrant. (This affidavit would be suppressed later by Balog to conceal the name of the informant.)

True to his pledge of cooperation, Stratton then invited the IBI and Chicago Police to accompany him on the search. One IBI agent had to be out of town that night. "Can't you hold off for one day?" he pleaded with Stratton over the phone. No, Stratton could not. Shortly thereafter, Stratton and his agents left. Their destination: a plain brick bungalow at 2045 North Natchez, owned by Dorothy Marrera, grandmother of Ralph. The informer had said "Marrera's grandmother's house," but it was discovered that four grandmothers were living — Marrera's two and his wife's two. Stratton settled on the North Natchez location when investigators found that Marrera had been maintaining it ever since his grandmother had left about two years earlier.

At 8:50, the group, now numbering about eighteen, armed with search warrant, weapons, and sledgehammers, gathered on the porch and steps as one of Stratton's agents picked the lock. They filed quickly through the first-floor rooms and descended the basement steps. There they found concealed beneath some cardboard boxes a freshly poured four-foot-square area of concrete, still with the light powder of dry new cement on the surface.

"This is it," Stratton said as agents, IBI investigators, and policemen gathered around. Stratton handed a sledgehammer to Special Agent Maureen Higgins, the only woman on the FBI staff at the time, and suggested she take the first crack at the concrete.

"She gave it a good clop," Stratton said later. "She's a strong woman." Taking turns, other agents eventually finished the job, battering through five inches of concrete reinforced with chicken wire. When they had cleared away the rubble they found five green duffel bags filled with packages of ten- and twenty-dollar bills.

"This is it. This is it," Stratton said, bending over the money, as another agent whistled.

"They got it counted," someone said as Stratton poked one of the tags marked in crayon.

"What's the total?"

"Counting up the tags it's two million twenty thousand."

"Hey, there's something else in there," another agent said, pointing into the hole. Again, the group closed in as bags of silica were retrieved from the bottom of the pit. Marrera must have placed it there to absorb moisture and protect the money from the earthly elements.

"He sure did a lot of work — for nothing."

But not for nothing. Thompson later announced that $2.2 million had been recovered — a simple matter of a misplaced zero, an easy error when staring at a table full of one-foot stacks of money — and easy to correct. But the final total, when actually counted, was less than $2.02 million. About half a million less. (Stratton figured that back on October 21, when Marrera disappeared from Purolator, he must have skimmed that amount off before burying the rest, not bothering to correct the tags.) But even though the recovered amount turned out to be only $1,454,140, Thompson was delighted. Early in the case, he had said he thought it unlikely that any sizable amount of the Purolator cash would ever be found. For once it was great to be wrong.

Neighbors of the North Natchez house, just two blocks from where Thompson grew up, were interviewed in the following days. They stated that they had noticed recent activity at the house — lawn cutting, digging, and rubbish removal. One neighbor thought the men were "fixing a valve," which necessitated construction work in the basement. The house sits only twelve feet from the sidewalk, four feet from the homes on either side, and across the street from the Simonds Cutting Tools Division of Illinois Gear-Wallace Murray Company. Cecil Pigg, a watchman for the company, said, "Who would have thought there was two million dollars in there?" He said a man used to drive to the house daily about 2:00 A.M. in a station wagon to check if the door was locked, but he never went in.

And now, as many of those same neighbors gathered to watch the unusual amount of activity surrounding an empty house, Stratton's agents lugged the green duffel bags out of the basement and into a waiting car, which was sent on its way under heavy guard back to the FBI offices.

There the money was dumped on a long conference table,

and reporters and photographers gathered to take pictures and statements from various federal and Chicago authorities as they contemplated the still rubber-banded stacks of cash. A radio reporter arrived late, and Stratton, years later, said he'd never forget the way the man's eyeballs snapped — just as if they were stretched cartoonlike from their sockets on elastic threads. One of the published pictures shows Stratton looking tiredly at the money, still gloomy from his supervisor's anger over the fact that Stratton had taken a state's attorney along on the search. But FBI chief Kelley in Washington had already wired his congratulations for a job well done.

Back at the county jail, Charlie still maintained they couldn't prove anything. Even when the TV blared the news about finding money in Marrera's grandma's basement. "How'd they know where it was?" he muttered to himself. Tony knew Charlie was thinking "Who told?" because he was wondering that himself — including "Who knew?" They made jokes about all the lawmen trying to get their mugs into a picture with the money. But mostly they shook their heads and watched in silence. The next day's newspaper accounts didn't make things any clearer. Yes, there was an informer, they had already figured that, but no one said who or how. Still Charlie insisted that there was no way Marrera's money could be tied to the money in Grand Cayman. Tony figured that Charlie felt even surer now that lugging the money to the island had been a good idea.

Louie didn't comment at all. He'd put all his faith in his lawyers. All he did was set up some corporate accounts. Marrera was none of his concern.

Early Friday, the Commercial Union Insurance Company's lawyer arrived in Chicago and was greatly relieved when Stratton told him he could have most of the money back. They both understood that the daily interest on such a sum tends to add up. Stratton had already instructed his men to don gloves and remove the top and bottom bills from each money stack. They would be carefully examined for fingerprints and any other markings, possibly from Hawthorne racetrack or even the partial outline of a bank stamp, if a rushed teller had missed the three-quarter-inch slip of paper that separated the larger stacks into smaller sections. (No such paper wrappings were ever found.)

It seemed obvious to Stratton that the Marzanos could not have had sufficient time to separate the individual bills in the period between 8:30 P.M., when they probably took the money, and 5:20 A.M., when they rendezvoused with Gushi and DiFonzo at Denny's Restaurant. So they had been forced to count by stack. Therefore, they would have touched only the outer bills. Those came to $23,000, for which the FBI gave the insurance company a receipt until they were able to return it some months later.

Then Stratton and the insurance company hit a bureaucratic snag. The U.S. attorney's office wanted to hold on to all of the $1 million–plus to be used as evidence. (Every small-store owner who has ever been robbed is aware of this little holdup. Not until the alleged assailants have had their day in court do the stolen goods or money find their way back to the original owner. In fact, one shopkeeper suggested unsuccessfully that he give the police a check to hold in place of his hard-earned cash.)

But storing all that money is a problem. First thing Friday morning, once Stratton's agents were finished, the money was transported to the First National Bank to be counted by its machines to get a rough estimate. The bank counted to approximately $1.5 million and then refused any further responsibility for it — in fact, emphatically refused to keep it even over the weekend; thus it ended up back in the federal offices. Rob Wrobel, credit officer and assistant to the president of Amalgamated Trust and Savings Bank, at 100 South State Street, was quoted as saying he got a frantic phone call from Jim Thompson about 4:30 Friday afternoon saying he hadn't realized how late it was and he needed to store a considerable sum of money that was on his desk. He asked Wrobel if his bank would store it in the vault over the weekend.

"I figured he was referring to the Purolator money. So I said I'd try to work something out." Wrobel then got hold of Larry Bloom, senior vice president of the bank, who set the wheels in motion to receive the money — if the FBI would add guards to supplement the bank's personnel. Wrobel then went to the lobby to await the FBI agents. He paced back and forth worrying about what might have happened on the way over.

"But shortly before 5:00 P.M. I was approached by a guy who showed FBI identification," Wrobel said. "He told me the money would be carried into the bank through the Monroe Street entrance. I went out to the street and there I saw a sight that looked like it was out of some 1930s movie. Three cars stood parked near the entrance. Out of the first car jumped several agents in dark raincoats, who began shouting and directing traffic away from the area. Then agents jumped out of the second and third cars and began unloading five huge mail sacks from the trunk of one of the cars. The agents began hauling the sacks into the bank, but they were so bulky that one of the men and his sack got stuck in the bank door. After much pushing and shoving he was freed, and things went along pretty smoothly after that. During the last little obstacle, I remember one of the agents turning to me and saying 'That damned money is cursed. It's given us nothing but trouble since this whole burglary business began. I'll be glad to get rid of it.' "

Wrobel said the money was placed in a safe within the vault and that the agents had a key to the safe. "They'll be taking the money out Monday," he added, "and I'll be glad to get rid of it, too. What a way to start a weekend."

True to his word, Stratton supplied agents, drawn from squads other than bank robbery, to take on guard detail in eight-hour shifts. He also assured the bankers, who worried about an attempt to get the money if its whereabouts were learned, that the FBI still held ultimate authority — and responsibility.

But the U.S. attorney was annoyed that Stratton wanted to hand over the money to the insurance company.

"Where would you keep it?" Stratton asked.

Why couldn't they get the bank to keep it as reserve money?

The bank representative emphatically said no. They might have to go into their own reserves and an employee could use that money by mistake. And, as it was, they didn't like having a *roughly* estimated $1.5 million in their vault.

Stratton finally said, "It's my search warrant. I represent the FBI. We have the money and we're not going to be responsible for it any longer than we have to. I'm turning it over to the insurance company now and that's all there is to it." Then he swung around to ask the insurance company's attorney for a formal "hold harmless" agreement. The man immediately dictated one to a secretary in the office. Essentially it said that if someone sues the government for that money, the insurance company would step in and defend the action. Four assistants in the office then rewrote it six times until the final version, according to Stratton, was *exactly* as the lawyer had written it in the first place. But none of the government assistants would sign it, other than as witnesses, so Stratton again stepped in and signed it on behalf of the United States.

On Monday morning the Monroe Street scene of cars and

agents replayed itself. The money was again transferred, this time to the Northern Trust, where the insurance company had an account. This was done over the strenuous objections of the accounting department because no one could give an exact figure. Once more Stratton put his name to a paper asserting that the money came from what he called "grandma's basement."

For three days, two tellers counted steadily — first one would add a stack, then the other would recount it to double-check. When they finished on Wednesday, November 20, sick of Alexander Hamilton and his wig, they entered the amount of $1,454,140 on a deposit slip in behalf of Commercial Union Insurance Company of New York.

Less than a week after his grandmother's basement was invaded, Marrera twice tried to kill himself. The first time by hanging; the second, a scant hour later, by putting his head in the prison toilet and flushing it. Stratton refused to accept the latter as a viable suicide attempt, but Marrera was removed from the Winnebago County jail on November 29 and taken to the Cook County hospital-jail in Cermak Hospital for observation. The following events were never entirely agreed upon by everybody, except for the central fact that on Wednesday, December 4, Marrera went into a coma, ran a temperature of 106 to 108 degrees, and the night-duty nurse could not awaken him. His stomach was pumped, and his life saved, but for a while speculation as to the cause of his illness raged as wildly as his fever. The media quoted suspicions of everyone from the mob to the unknown mastermind behind the Purolator score. Ultimately, the conclusion was that Marrera had had an unfortunate allergic reaction to the tranquilizer properly administered to him by a legitimate staff member.

Nevertheless, on Tuesday, December 10, Marrera's family, "fearing for his life," succeeded in having him transferred to Northwestern Memorial Hospital. He supposedly had some lucid moments, but lapsed back into a dazed condition.

Meanwhile, five Grand Cayman banks admitted, after being named by Cranston, that they had received deposits from DiFonzo and the Marzanos, but continued to maintain that the secrecy act prevented them from opening their books and declaring exact amounts. They were supported in this stance by Magistrate Frank Field, who turned down Donaldson's request for full disclosure saying it was "premature." Field contended that, since no one was as yet convicted in the Purolator burglary, the government had no grounds for its request. Donaldson said he wasn't content with the decision and was going to pursue disclosure through other avenues — such as a possible filing of local criminal charges.

In Chicago, Stratton's painstaking scrutiny of the money paid off. Of the $23,000 examined, about $15,000 had markings from a dozen of the Hawthorne racetrack employees. And one fingerprint turned up — that of William Anthony Marzano. This print figured heavily in Tony's decision to plead guilty.

Stratton was gratified at how neatly this piece of the puzzle fit into the larger mosaic. It connected place and person — fitting the race track to Purolator to Marrera to Marzano to Grand Cayman to grandma's basement. Then, as Stratton was checking through "belated" Chicago Police reports he suddenly found the last missing link to his puzzle — the actual results of the lie detector test given the Wells Fargo employee on October 21. He immediately dispatched agents to pick up the young man, who not only was an Indian citizen, but also had a ticket home for the *next day*, where he would be beyond the reach of any United States subpoena.

The Chicago Police showed that the Wells Fargo employee had flunked the lie test, and on the following day he admitted he had lied. He then recounted that on a number of Sunday nights, as the records confirmed, the alarm had gone off showing that the Purolator vault door had been opened. But every time the Indian had phoned, or sent a man over to Purolator, Marrera assured them that everything was fine. So they assumed it was a malfunction or intermittent voltage drop, and returned to their jobs, first resetting the alarm.

On the Sunday night of the robbery when the alarm went off, the Indian board watcher had saved himself and Marrera a call and had *reset the alarm without even checking in with Marrera.* The next Wells Fargo man to come on duty after the Indian heard the Purolator fire alarm go off and this time set the proper wheels in motion.

Stratton reinterviewed the young man in the U.S. attorney's office, and had him taken before the grand jury, which lifted his passport until he could testify in the late spring. Then Stratton, angry that a vital piece of information had almost disappeared forever, phoned the upper echelons of the police department. He was assured of better cooperation in the future.

And now Stratton, fitting the final puzzle piece, felt that his suspects had just been forced to pick the card marked DO NOT PASS GO. DO NOT COLLECT ANY MONEY. GO STRAIGHT TO JAIL. Even the totals worked nicely. Charlie and Louis had escorted more than $1.1 million to Grand Cayman. Marrera had buried $1.4 million. Gushi accounted for $400,000. Only a little more than $1 million of Purolator's $4.3 million was unaccounted for. Considering they had not expected to find or recover any amount of the money, the lawmen were elated.

"I feel like a couple of million bucks," one of Stratton's men said. Stratton agreed.

28

Trials of That Old Gang o' Mine

Gushi's whereabouts is being kept such a closely guarded secret — and his court appearances are so curtailed — that Echeles referred derisively to Gushi in court Thursday as a "ficticious defendant."

— January 10, 1975,
Chicago Daily News

Tony's twenty-eight days in Cook County Jail (later credited toward time served) cost him nearly $1500. After fourteen hearings, his final bond for release was set on November 25 at $50,000. The bond was a secured bond requiring only 10 percent cash rather than the previous cash bonds, which demanded the entire amount be raised. This meant that Tony could get out of jail on the $5000 raised by his aunt, mother, sister, and friends. Toward the end of the month, news had come that Marty's cousin was so embarrassed at the way Marty had treated Tony the night before he turned himself in that he was ready to put his house up if Tony needed it. Gino, too, had offered his help.

Tony was barely home when the state sent another indictment through the mail saying that a state bond was necessary, too, because the state's attorneys, in spite of Carey's agreement that the federal government should prosecute, were continuing their own charges. He was told to "please stop in and make bond on the charges we have outlined." "Don't worry," Bailey told Tony. "When they ask you by mail to come in, it can't be too big an amount."

Early Monday morning, Louie and Charlie, who had received the same notices, and Tony all showed up. To their dismay, the state asked for a million-dollar cash bond each.

Just a minute, the lawyers argued. They're already out on bond. The government let them out. They're not going anywhere.

Finally the judge agreed to $50,000 each, 10 percent in cash.

At this point the lawyers and their clients adjourned to a separate room. Charlie and Louie had just the amount they needed. "Sorry, Tony," Charlie told him. "We got just enough for us."

"Maybe I can find some cash around the halls," Julius Echeles, Charlie's attorney, offered, obviously uncomfortable about Tony's situation.

"I'll call my sister," Tony said. Then, "Therese said she'd be right down."

"He'll be all right," Charlie told Echeles. "You'll be all right won't you, Tony? Can't take your sister an hour to get here. You can wait an hour. Won't hurt you. We gotta go."

"Sure," Tony told him. "She just has to get a car. Then she'll be down." But Tony was disgusted. They could have put the money up for him. Then they could have all gone back to his sister's, since they were heading in that direction anyway — and gotten the money from Therese immediately

if they were so worried about it. And not forced her to drive
to that neighborhood — leave her home and come rushing
down. But he waved them out. Sure, he could wait an hour.
Charlie wasn't coming up with anything new.

The double set of charges had everyone involved marching back and forth from one courtroom and building to
another for the various state and federal hearings. The state
continued to refuse to drop its own charges, indicating it in-
tended to try the alleged burglars after the federal trial was
over. (The state's charges were eventually dismissed when
Judge Philip Romiti of Cook County Criminal Court ruled
that double jeopardy was involved.) Continuances piled up.
Finally the case was put on the boards and assigned to
Judge Bauer, the next judge in line.

As the government began to prepare its case, Stratton had
reason to believe he had dotted every *i* for the most near-
sighted juror. He was leaning heavily on a federal law that
says a principal offender "tars all." In a "joint venture" all
principals in a crime are considered participants and equally
guilty. Once Marrera, who "allowed" the money to be
stolen, was tied to the money and to Marzano, Stratton was
confident that the proof and the law were as plain as Tony's
fingerprint.

Stratton felt equally confident of the conspiracy charge.
He recited from memory the General Federal Conspiracy
Statute, U.S. Title 18, Code Section 371, the nemesis of
many thieves because it covers two or more persons who
conspire to commit an offense against the United States —
and commit one or more overt acts. A meeting itself can be
the overt act, even if the crime never takes place. The
"beauty of conspiracy" as Stratton terms it, is that the act of
one participant is binding on another. If you have a meeting
with someone to plan a crime, and then you borrow a car
for the crime, that act is binding on all the participants, even

if they were not present at the time of the car borrowing, an overt act.

"It's a tough statute," Stratton admitted. "The lawyers have been trying to get rid of it for years. It's so easy to prove conspiracy. All you need is an informer, or even one of the conspirators, to testify to the object of the conspiracy, plus one or more overt acts — even if the crime never takes place." The statute was passed during prohibition, when the proof could be dumped, but the smell and machinery would still be there. And it has always been upheld.

At the judge's discretion, a conviction of conspiracy can add up to five years to a bank-robbery penalty, which carries a twenty- to twenty-five-year sentence itself. A suspect could pick up a thirty-year jail term — a weighty lever in the government's arsenal for prying information or pleas loose. So Stratton began applying pressure.

Shortly after Christmas, Bailey, Tony's attorney, called him to come in to his office for a talk. A friend waited for Tony across the street in a bar. Bailey and Tony discussed the conspiracy charges, the fact of Tony's fingerprint, and the possibility of pleading guilty. Bailey said he'd been talking to the FBI and asked Tony if he'd like to do five years. Bailey was all excited. This was almost like a win — especially with a hundred years staring them in the face, with Gushi as informer. Tony could tell he was really pleased.

Tony joked a bit. "What about the state?" Maybe Bailey could get them to run the same period?

Bailey brushed that aside. "Forget about the state. What do you want to do?"

"Hey, try for three," Tony said.

"Forget it," Bailey told him. "The only way you'll get less than five is if you're a witness — so forget it. That'd be crazy going out on a limb like that. Take five if you can get it. Five won't hurt and you'll be out right away." Tony was glad Bailey didn't try to talk him into testifying — that he understood the price of turning was always too high — no matter how many years they gave you off.

"I'd like to do it right now, if possible," Tony said. He knew parole could reduce the years in jail to less than three. Tony thought three instead of thirty a pretty good deal, although that day he told Bailey he wanted to wait a little to "see if something comes up."

Charlie and Julius Echeles refused to consider a guilty plea. Charlie saw the choice as zero days in prison versus maybe a maximum of seven years (with concurrent terms and parole). Besides, Charlie was still confident that he would not be found guilty because nobody could prove he was ever inside Purolator and he did not have to explain money in Grand Cayman any more than he had to explain breakfasting with an old friend, or collecting alarm manuals.

Louis DiFonzo was getting different advice from his attorneys. He had hired (relinquishing a Rolls Royce as retainer) Boston attorneys Thomas Troy, Martin Weinberg, and Joseph Oteri — primarily the latter, whom Stratton believes to be one of the best criminal lawyers in the country. Oteri advised Louis to plead guilty in exchange for a three-year probationary term — something the government refused to agree to. Echeles convinced Charlie that he could get him off, and Charlie prevailed on Louis also to go to trial.

Throughout this time, Tony continued to assure Charlie, and all federal representatives, that under no circumstances would he testify for or against anyone. Under no circumstances would he implicate anyone else, or give one single piece of information to anyone. But he had to decide about his plea soon, Bailey told him. If Tony was going to plead guilty he had to do it before the jury was selected and the trial begun. Otherwise it would make it difficult for the other defendants to begin with three defendants and then have one disappear. Tony still wanted time to think it over.

Charlie continued to say the most idiotic things. Like when they were driving to the Y to play racquetball.

"We can only get ten years. Don't worry."

Tony slammed on the brakes, almost killing them both. "What do you mean? The bank robbery charge is twenty years by itself. What kind of stupid nonsense are you telling me? We could get a hundred ten years if you add them up. Interstate transportation of money, fifteen. Explosives probably twenty, and on and on. Who do you think you're talking to? A little kid?"

"My lawyer told me."

"I don't care what he said. You better do some thinking on your own." Tony knew what Charlie was telling him — don't do anything wrong. A double insult — first to his character, as if he'd turn like Gushi. And then to his intelligence — as if he couldn't see through it. Christ, his own cousin.

Charlie just laughed as Tony added, "I only wish we'd get ten years. I'd grab it."

A few days later, Tony appeared for one of the hearings, which ended in yet another continuance, wearing his messiest jeans and oldest shirt, and with an unshaven chin. Charlie was waiting in the hallway when Tony came by and was annoyed at Tony's appearance — especially when Stratton called, "Hey, Charlie, can't you loan some of that money to your cousin so he can at least afford some blades and a decent haircut?" Stratton didn't know Charlie.

The next time Tony ran into Stratton in the hall, the FBI man had something else on his mind. "Hey, Tony," Stratton asked, "do you know Roberto Lopez?"

Tony hadn't answered. He and Roberto had grown up

together, but he hadn't seen Rob in more than a year. And he wasn't telling Stratton anything anyway.

"Well?" Stratton wasn't deterred. "We know he's an old friend of yours."

This time Tony spoke. "So what? I haven't seen or heard of him in years."

"Got a little information for you," Stratton said. "A strange thing happened. We had him locked up with Pete Gushi, same place. He tried to kill Pete with a pipe. You should have heard Pete screaming about being put in with a killer, somebody insane, when he's supposed to be under protective custody for helping us out." Stratton walked away shaking his head.

Tony watched him disappear into the courtroom; he was too stunned to reply. Why would Lopez care if Pete was talking about Tony? Had that been his reason? And why was he even in the same place with Gushi? (Tony found out afterward that Lopez had been taken into custody four or five months earlier. But not until a few years later did he learn that Lopez had first been caught in Ohio with a list of names of people to hit, and with silencer-fitted pistols. With thirty to forty years staring him in the face, he had agreed to testify against a couple of really big Mafia figures, Carl Stone and Ben Falconi. So Tony didn't get it — why would one guy who ratted try to kill another guy who did the same thing?) As it turned out, the FBI kept Lopez in protective custody for three or four years before trial. Tony sure couldn't see giving up all that time. For what? He always figured you served your time like a standup guy, and put in for early parole. Then you can still go home to your friends and family. "Where's your roots if you've talked to the law?" Tony said. He wondered how guys like Pete with new names and faces made it — new name, new town, but still looking over your shoulder all the time. That would never be for him. Stratton had Tony figured that way too. He said he knew from the beginning that Tony would never be turned into an informer. So after their first encounter he didn't even try. Pete had been a different story. A change in Marrera's situation occurred next, as his lawyer and psychiatrists declared him unfit to stand trial. Stratton was so unconvinced that Judge Bauer finally asked if he would be satisfied if the judge himself chose another doctor to investigate. Stratton agreed. The new psychiatrist reported back that Ralph Marrera indeed was unfit to defend himself or testify in a trial. Stratton accepted the decision on legal grounds, but his gut still told him otherwise. (Two years after the trial was over, Stratton told a couple of men to watch Marrera's house, inconspicuously so as not to upset the neighborhood or family, who might charge harassment. "Just see if you can see him," he ordered. In six weeks of watching they never saw Marrera once — either leaving or entering his house. Stratton believes that he was out somewhere looking after his "millionaire" status. But as late as 1978 Marrera's federal file showed that a doctor testified in still another hearing that Marrera is not always aware of the month or day, and shuffles about like an old man.)

During the months that passed before the Purolator case actually came to trial, Judge Bauer was elevated from the district court to the court of appeals. To Stratton's gratification, however, Bauer kept the case and tried it. "He's one of the better judges, a really good legal mind," Stratton said, "and probably the best U.S. attorney Chicago ever had." Stratton remembers when Bauer was appointed to the district court after being a U.S. attorney; he knew he was losing the best U.S. attorney he'd ever worked with but gaining a judge with a fine legal mind. He had been an FBI man too long to hope to have both.

As the actual trial date drew near, a new indictment was

handed down superseding the first. All the participants except DiFonzo were charged with bank larceny, bank burglary, and use of explosives in committing a theft. Marrera and the two Marzanos were named as the actual thieves, with DiFonzo and Gushi named in the transportation of stolen property across state lines. Gushi and Maniatis were also charged with abetting and advising the theft. Marrera's name was never removed from the indictments. In fact, Stratton pointed out, in a sense Marrera was tried even though he wasn't there. DiFonzo was also indicted for conspiracy to steal the money because of the reported meetings with Gushi and Charlie where a big score was mentioned during the conversations. In underworld parlance, that always means stolen money.

The attorneys for DiFonzo and Charlie Marzano originally had asked for separate trials and were denied. Federal rules say that when the same offense is committed at the same time and same point of participation, one trial will do, thus saving the government time and money. That economical view is also behind much plea bargaining, including Tony's eventual assertion that by pleading guilty — even though he wouldn't testify — he was saving the government the expense of a trial. Those in favor of plea bargaining believe, as Stratton sees it, that it avoids "the risk of a stupid jury." Those against say only a judge should have the authority to determine sentencing. Plea bargaining is allowed in federal court, but the judges are not allowed to promise to honor the agreement between the government and the defense attorneys — although the judge usually indicates he is willing to accept something along the lines suggested. Sentences are never handed down anyway until the probation department finds out everything it can about the defendant — past record, character, and so on. The judge reviews this information and then determines the sentence. The defendant must say under oath that no promises were made to him, in order to protect the record in case of an appeal. Thus the attorney's promises are merely a strong suggestion for an agreeable judge. Gushi and Maniatis obviously took advantage of plea bargaining to trade information for years.

On Monday, April 14, as the jury selection drew near, Tony prepared to plead guilty to all charges. Still trying to give Charlie the benefit of the doubt, he met Charlie for breakfast before going to court. But Charlie had to ask the accusing question: "You're only going to plead guilty aren't you? Not do anything wrong?"

"Now what kind of logic is that?" Tony demanded. "Would I be here in the restaurant with you? Gone this far? What kind of crazy thinking do you do?"

"Well, listen," Charlie said. "Do you want someone to drive your car back? You might not get out — be coming home."

"Now how the fuck you figure that? I'm out on bond. They don't sentence you the same day. Your lawyer still telling you this stupid stuff?"

So they went to court and Tony pled guilty to all eleven counts — in front of Charlie and Louie waiting their turn, and with the reporters writing furiously. Bailey even said loudly that he wanted it printed and noted that "we're pleading guilty, but want it on the record before the judge that my client will not be a witness for either side, and if forced to appear will take the Fifth Amendment."

On April 23, after the jury selection of nine men and three women, the Purolator trial finally began. Reporters lined the front seats with a few more spread out along the wall behind the prosecution. No pictures were allowed in court, but each day one or more artists sketched the tense scene for later TV newscasts. As one faced the room, the prosecutors' table was on the right. Seated there were the three government attorneys, James Breen, Gordon Nash, and Michael King. Stratton attended every trial day; he sat at this table along with Michael Balgley, who kept the federal exhibits in order. The defense sat on the left — Charlie Marzano and Julius Echeles, Louis DiFonzo and his three lawyers. The reporters took voluminous notes recording the defendants' carefully prepared appearance: Charlie looked like "the maître d' in a second-class restaurant," and Louie's hair was "so perfectly coifed that it must require the attention of a hairdresser each morning."

All the while the trial went on, Charlie never called Tony or tried to get in touch with him. And Tony never tried to get in touch with Charlie either. Bailey had told Tony to stay away from the courtroom just in case the jury spotted him and wondered why he wasn't on trial. It could work to Louie's and Charlie's disadvantage. Even so, a week later, when Bailey had to enter the courtroom on a totally different case, Charlie and Louie and their entourage eyed him as if he were about to come up with a certain witness. They were still jittery and distrustful—right down to the very end, Bailey told Tony. Some friends.

The parade of witnesses began. Larry Callahan, who had done undercover work for the IBI while he was working for Gushi, was one of those called. He testified that Gushi often talked of his part in the heist, and that, prior to the burglary, Gushi said he was going to have four carbines and rifles and if any cop got in the way he was going to take care of him. Callahan further quoted Gushi as saying that he was going to be dead or alive, but he didn't want to be poor anymore. He also testified that Gushi had bragged about killing Tony Dichiarinte with an ice pick, that he had driven through Dichiarinte's alley and grabbed him when he was emptying his garbage. The defense attorneys elicited this testimony in an attempt to discredit Pete Gushi as a state's witness. At any rate, Tony's suspicions had been on target — Peter Gushi's past had given the FBI a lot of bargaining power. In a sense, however, they got more than they bargained for, because Gushi's three days of testimony were to uncover some of the most interesting and bizarre twists in the trial.

One area of Gushi's testimony focused on his disposal of $300,000 of the $400,000 given him by Charlie Marzano for safekeeping. Gushi maintained that he had given the money to threatening strangers in the night. His story was that no sooner had he opened his store on Thursday, October 24, than a boy about eleven or twelve years old handed him the torn back of a matchbook cover. On the cover was a telephone number followed by the words "In ten minutes." "Where'd you get this?" Gushi said he'd asked. "A man gave me a dollar across the street," had been the boy's reply. Gushi said he'd turned and seen a car with two men in the front seat pull out of the National Supermarket lot and drive west on 111th Street. He dutifully drove to a liquor store a couple of blocks away and used its pay phone. A male voice had answered and asked where Charlie was. When Pete had asked "Who is this?" he responded, "These are the two partners that got left behind. You replaced one of us. You know who we are." Then Pete recounted for the jury how he told the man he couldn't get in touch with Charlie and of the man's threatening reply. "Now listen to me real good. There is going to be blood. It is going to be Charlie's ass. It is going to be yours and anybody else's that is involved. We got two million dollars coming. Half of that money belongs to us and we mean to get it and we do not care who you run to. Now how do you want to do it — the easy way or the hard way?"

Gushi said that when he continued to profess ignorance the man suggested they meet at nine o'clock that night, that Gushi would recognize some people who might persuade him better. Gushi stalled, saying he had only a small amount in a suitcase and that he'd call back in ten minutes. After composing himself and thinking, Gushi testified that he'd called back, checked to find out if his caller knew where he lived, then instructed them to come by his house about four o'clock in the morning, driving slowly. They were to drive by twice, Pete told them, then on the third round, "Give me your brights and dims and I'll put the suitcase with the money in it out there behind the fence."

When Gushi's attorney in direct examination asked him "What was the significance of the phrase 'We don't care who you run to'?" Gushi replied, "Obviously no one was going to be able to help me and obviously a call wouldn't have come if someone didn't tell them it was O.K. to call."

The rest of the day, Gushi recalled, he tried to reach Jerold Casio. Pete, the reputed mob enforcer, was not about to accept a "collect call" for $300,000 without checking with his long-time friend and mob protector, Jerry Casio. Casio refused to see him and, according to Gushi's testimony, said only, "You are going to have to use your own judgment."

"I am going to have to use my own judgment," Pete said he had repeated.

"That is right. You are on your own," was Casio's alleged reply.

"I am on my own," Pete remembered saying again.

"You are on your own."

At another point in Gushi's testimony, Julius Echeles wanted to know why Gushi had responded so docilely to a matchbook cover. The transcript reads:

ANSWER: I decided to respond.
QUESTION: Why?
ANSWER: Why?
QUESTION: Why?
ANSWER: My mind told me that I should call.
QUESTION: Why?
ANSWER: I was curious.
QUESTION: Curious about what?
ANSWER: A great many curious things were happening about then.

No less curious was Pete Gushi's description of the $300,000 transfer of funds. He testified that while watching from his bedroom window around 4:00 A.M. he saw first one car, then another about half a block behind it, come down the street, two men in each car. They were driving about ten or twelve miles an hour, he said. When they passed his house the first time, he recalled how he got the big suitcase and his revolver and stood by the back of the house near a weeping willow tree where no one could see him. The cars came by a second time, and then a third, blinking first their bright lights and then the dims.

"So," he testified, "I flipped over the fence, put the suitcase about four feet behind the fence and two feet off of the sidewalk, went back over the fence, into the house, and down to the basement." He then watched the first car stop near the house, its lights out, and the second car stop half a block away — its lights still on. One man got out of the back door, picked up the suitcase, and got back into the car. They pulled away, then turned on their lights.

Gushi told the jury he'd kept about four or five bundles of money, packing his attaché case about two-thirds full. The rest he had put in the suitcase that was carried off by the mysterious strangers.

According to Stratton, Gushi's story held up under three lie tests. But there is still another kind of test — credibility. As Tony Marzano sees it, nobody knew that Gushi had that money. Charlie had not originally planned to give it to him to hold. That had been a last-minute decision made in Denny's parking lot when someone didn't show up to claim the suitcase. Furthermore, Peter and Jerry Casio were close friends — Pete at one time bought a house across the street from him. Tony believes it is probable that Pete called Jerry and asked him to hold the money — just come and get it at four in the morning. Where safer? Would Charlie go sniffing around the mob asking for a refund? It was probably worth splitting $300,000 with a friend versus netting $50,000 — especially if the friend might have "suggested" it first. Fooling the lie test would be easy for Pete if the facts were so close to the truth. All actions would remain the same — only the motives would be changed to protect the whereabouts of the cash, some of which Jerry might have even handed over to his associates for further safekeeping.

As it turned out, members of the jury later admitted to a reporter that they never believed anything Gushi said, even when the evidence itself backed him up, including his own phone bill documenting his early morning call to DiFonzo about the meeting at Denny's the morning after the burglary.

In fact, the defense lawyers did their best to bolster the jury's low opinion of Gushi's reliability. Oteri spoke softly and infrequently, but Stratton noted that when Gushi or the jet pilot, or a cab driver, was asked to identify DiFonzo, Oteri had apparently instructed Louie to rise instantly to indicate he obviously had nothing to hide. And Louie never denied on the stand that he had escorted the money to Ohio, Miami, and Grand Cayman. The whole point, as Oteri tried to make clear through questioning DiFonzo, was that DiFonzo never knew the money was stolen. He was hired, he testified, for his knowledge of corporate bank accounts and the workings of a tax haven. And if he now and then used an assumed name (although not on the island when registering at the Holiday Inn), in what way is it a crime, his attorney courteously inquired, to employ other names for multiple business transactions?

Echeles, too, attempted to discredit Gushi in the jury's mind. Gushi in earlier testimony had repeated a statement that he had made to an assistant state's attorney that "Charlie is going to get all fucked up and I will be the one to do it to him." In recross-examination Echeles tried to show that this statement could be interpreted to mean Gushi might be lying in order to get Charlie "all fucked up."

Echeles asked Gushi, "Why didn't you just say, 'Because of my testimony, Mr. Marzano might get convicted if anybody believes me.' Why didn't you say something like that?" And Gushi replied, "I wasn't feeling very articulate at the time. I just uttered what came to my mouth."

Adding insult to injury, Gushi also touched upon Charlie's knowledge of alarm systems. He admitted telling an FBI agent that Charlie did such a lousy job installing his alarm system at the store that he had to get a regular alarm man to complete the job. Echeles, in his closing arguments to the jury, said of Gushi, "His middle name should be Judas instead of James."

The trial continued with various other witnesses for the prosecution — people from Purolator, Hawthorne racetrack, sundry cab drivers, a jet pilot, and even Superintendent Derrick Tricker from Grand Cayman, Mr. Law himself. Stratton had been alerted by the Miami agents that Superintendent Tricker would probably welcome a drink or two while waiting to testify. Tricker could not be subpoenaed from a foreign country, so the Chicago FBI office wanted to keep their "volunteer" happy. The agents met Tricker at the airport and dropped him at the Palmer House with a half-gallon bottle about one in the afternoon. At 5:00 P.M. Stratton and his men joined the superintendent for a predinner visit and drink.

Tricker, "a little bitty-banty rooster kind of man," according to Stratton, bounded up, ready to go. Stratton, wanting to get home as soon as possible, suggested they have a drink in the room before going out.

Tricker held up the bottle — empty. Stratton silently acknowledged that the Miami agents were not given to exaggeration. They retired to the cocktail lounge downstairs, Stratton noting the man's thin legs, full chest, sharp movements, and alert gaze. He wondered where the liquor went.

On one of Tricker's visits to the FBI office, he saw some agents wearing Purolator guard hats and instantly wanted one.

"We call them 'Percolator' hats," he was told as he slapped his gift on his head.

Tricker's day in court was more spectacular than his cast-iron constitution. When he was called, up he marched to stand front and center to Judge Bauer's bench. There he gave a deep bow and bellowed, "Good afternoon, M'Lord," in a clipped British accent that reverberated throughout the courtroom.

Judge Bauer, lips twitching, informed the superintendent that in the United States he is known as a judge and the form of address "Your Honor" suffices.

"Yes, M'Lord," replied Tricker just as loudly as before, and took the stand. After tracing the actions of Marzano and DiFonzo as his investigations had revealed them, he bounded down from the witness stand to face the bench again. In the same declaiming tones he announced, "Good afternoon, M'Lord," and marched out.

Eighty witnesses in all, twenty from out of state, were to testify in this trial. On April 30 the attorneys finally presented their closing arguments and the prosecution rested its case.

Now the waiting began. The jury retired for three hours of deliberation during which time Oteri, at his insistence, treated both the defense and prosecution to dinner at Binyon's Restaurant. Judge Bauer finally sequestered the jury at 10:00 P.M. when they were unable to come to an immediate decision. They reconvened early the next morning for a four-hour session of deliberation.

At last it was announced that the jury had reached its verdict. Court was reconvened and the jury filed in. The foreman presented the judge with its findings.

Stratton knew immediately that something had gone wrong when he saw a deep flush suffuse Judge Bauer's face as he silently read the verdict. Bauer handed the papers over to the clerk of the court, who slowly intoned the decision that Charles Marzano was guilty on eight counts and Louis DiFonzo was not guilty.

Everyone was incredulous — but for different reasons. Charlie Marzano, his wife, and his attorney remained impassive. Louis DiFonzo's wife burst into tears. Everyone began talking. The gavel came down as the clerk demanded order or the room would be cleared. Judge Bauer, his face still dark with anger, curtly dismissed the jury. And the jurors, who didn't know that it is customary for the judge to congratulate them or at least thank them for their efforts, merely filed out. Then the judge gathered up his papers and swept from the room, his robe billowing behind him.

Reporters and friends of the defendants scrambled for phones. Julius Echeles said nothing, just sort of grinned. Louie DiFonzo, unable to control his relief, broke down and cried, as he started for the attorneys' room as soon as the judge had left the bench. Stratton stopped by to congratulate him on defeating justice — he remembers being dumbfounded to see his worst nightmares about juries come true.

Minutes later, a now jubilant DiFonzo left the courthouse

and started down the street with his equally jubilant attorneys. Stratton watched from a distance as they all stopped, stunned — a red, white, and blue Purolator truck was coming down the street. In an unparalleled opportunity for the comment of the year, Louie raised an eloquent finger and shouted, "That to you guys. That to you."

29

A "Peerless" Jury for a "Perfect" Crime

Crime pays — till you get caught.

— J.D.

"I couldn't believe that jury," Stratton said later. "That they would convict Charlie of taking the money and then acquit him of planting the bombs. The two are inseparable. Did they think Marrera lugged the bags of gasoline in with him when he showed up for work? Did they think he ran around filling them up after Charlie and Tony had cleared out?" Stratton said, "The jury appeared to be well satisfied with their verdict at the time. It was only after the news media began questioning them that they saw how stupid they had been — and not many admitted it even then." One reporter posed questions similar to Stratton's for a juror and Stratton overheard him admit that the problem was simply that there were no eyewitnesses! No one saw Charlie set those bags in place. Or light a fuse. *No one saw him take the money either,* Stratton wanted to reply, but didn't. The newspapers would do that soon enough. At least the jury believed that Charlie had entered Purolator with a van and left with it full of money — and found him guilty of that.

Stratton had long agreed with the suggestion made by Judge Julius Hoffman that jurors should be trained professionals employed to serve at trials. Louis DiFonzo's acquittal only confirmed Stratton's opinion of jurors. They evidently saw no criminal intent and no conspiracy. They apparently didn't think it was DiFonzo's legal duty to inquire into the sudden source of so much well-wrapped cash. As another juror said, "There was nothing definite. Just inferences and you can't go on that." How was DiFonzo, a reputed financial wizard, to recognize stolen money when all money looks alike? The jurors could not get rid of their reasonable doubt. Stratton later remembered that he had been uneasy when the jury foreman was elected by his fellow jurors. The man had seemed to Stratton to display a show-me attitude. Stratton said he felt as if the foreman was saying throughout the trial, "If I didn't see it, you won't convince me of it." He didn't seem to understand, Stratton said, that especially in criminal trials you have to *infer*. What was equally galling and mystifying to Stratton was the final realization that the jurors never believed Gushi at all.

Tony was out on bond during the trial, trying to crowd each day with enough sunshine and laughs to buoy him during his prison term. He was still feeling friendly enough with Marty and friends to join them at a new singles complex near O'Hare Airport. On the day the jury reported back, Tony's group had been swimming in the pool, and eventually went into the bar for drinks. Tony flicked on the TV to catch the news and the verdict blared out at them. Their reaction was stunned silence. When Tony caught the others glancing at him, he just shrugged. But he was thinking, that's the way a jury is. You can't ever figure them. He preferred leaving decisions up to a judge, as he had in the first FBI cartage case against him. As he saw it, if you have a case that makes legal sense, an ordinary man might not understand it.

But he was really glad Louie got off. His respect for the younger man had increased a hundredfold when he and Charlie had found him on the island, all the money intact. He could have taken off, never to be found again. But Louie had turned out to be one of those who kept his word.

Of course, he was certain that Louie's acquittal would probably increase Charlie's sense of personal injustice. He was already mad at Tony for not standing trial. Tony had pleaded guilty to twelve charges (the original ones being divided into separate ones for each bank, Jewel Tea, Hawthorne, and so on). And in turn he had been advised that the main sentences, divided five, five, and seven years, would run concurrently, which meant he would serve not less than five years nor more than seven — even though he had emphatically refused to testify. "Once you start testifying," he had said, "they want it all. Can you picture it? With all my relatives in the courtroom? The feds are crazy. No way do I testify against anybody. Or for 'em."

On May 9 the Purolator case had faded from page one and from most people's minds, but not all. Tony appeared with his lawyer to be sentenced to, he thought, five years. However, to Tony and Bailey's surprise, Assistant U.S. Attorney James Breen held out for seven years. Tony glanced at Bailey and understood the message. Keep quiet. In sentencing Tony, Judge Bauer read from the parole officer's report, which said that William Anthony Marzano, who had no previous convictions, apparently had tried to avoid associating with criminal elements. "It's a pity he failed and became involved in one of the most daring, outstanding, and carefully planned crimes that has ever come to my attention," the newspapers quoted Bauer as saying. Eight months later, as Bailey had promised, he asked for a review before Judge Bauer and explained that Tony had been told he would draw not less than five years. They had understood that phrase to mean five, not seven. Stratton also appeared and agreed that such had been the language used and such would be the usual interpretation. Bauer concurred that the phrase was ambiguous and reduced Tony's term to five years.

Pete Gushi was given a three-year sentence, of which he served fourteen months — just long enough to give the FBI time to provide him with a new identity and a new home.

The elderly Jimmy Maniatis pleaded guilty and was given eighteen months by the federal government for procuring the van. He then served extra time added by the state for his other "services" in Gushi's employ. He told the court he had never been in jail before. "Then at least you started big," Judge Bauer said.

On May 29 Charles Marzano was the last to be sentenced. He received twenty years: ten for bank larceny, ten for the other charges, and five for conspiracy, the latter to run concurrently. He was also held responsible for court costs, which included the price of the transcripts, court reporters, and the expenses of eighty witnesses — twenty from out of town. Judge Bauer rejected an argument by Julius Echeles that the amount of money involved should not be a crucial factor in the sentence. Echeles asserted that the character of a crime "remains the same whether four thousand or four million dollars are involved." But Judge Bauer replied, "There is a difference in the magnitude of a crime. The mind boggles at the amount of money involved."

Thus, the seven years that Charlie had gambled against had grown to twenty. But his indignation lives on in his appeals. The first — that his attorney had not been given sufficient time to examine witnesses — was denied (with

Louie's acquittal cited as proof that time was obviously ample for his successful defense). In the next appeal, Charlie's attorney asked for a reversal on the grounds that not only had Charlie and Louie been arrested and brought out of Grand Cayman against their will, but except for the FBI telling Tricker about them, he would never have known they were suspects in a robbery and therefore would not have arrested them. Appeals Judge Cummings shared Charlie's point of view. But Assistant U.S. Attorney Breen argued that if they were using the "but for" rule, but for the burglary, they never would have been on Grand Cayman in the first place. The other two appeals judges agreed with Breen.

Another of Charlie's appeal arguments concerned the length of his sentence, which was more than Tony's by fifteen years. Charlie's lawyer indignantly pointed out that Tony had pleaded guilty while Charlie still declared himself innocent. Should a person who seeks to prove his innocence by trial get a longer sentence than a person who admits he's guilty? Although the planner is apparently considered guiltier, Charlie's sentence was reduced from twenty to fifteen years. (As late as June 1979, Charlie's lawyers questioned the retired Ramon Stratton for several hours seeking information for still another of Charlie's appeals to overturn or lighten his sentence.) When Charlie's attorney tried to implicate Tony in a deal with the FBI, Stratton bristled. "The government paid no money to William Marzano. He was not cooperative. He would not testify or anything," Stratton said afterward. "Charlie and his attorneys didn't get anything because there is nothing to get."

He suggested, however, two possible reasons for Charlie's appeals strategy. One: it gets him out of a distant prison, and a forced occupation of some kind, and into Chicago where he is near his lawyer and his family. And second: there is no more Purolator money on Grand Cayman, so he can't offer to return it in exchange for fewer years. Why was this latter information never revealed before? Stratton shrugged. Nobody asked. But if they had, they would have learned from him that six months after the trial was over, the FBI called the insurance company and said a check was waiting for them on Grand Cayman in the amount of approximately $1.6 million — about $500,000 of it in accrued interest. How was this accomplished when Grand Cayman Court of Appeals itself turned down requests to open the bank's books? Did the FBI bring unknown pressures? Did Lloyd's of London, one of the main insurance carriers, apply pressure through its own sources in the British Parliament? Stratton shrugged. These questions he won't answer.

In the post-mortem period of the Purolator burglary, various opinions emerged concerning the original plan. Although caught, the burglars contend their methodology was sound. It took an informant (as in all major crimes) to catch them. Ironically they had believed that *they* wouldn't have that problem. Again, because the burglars were caught, the police and FBI attitude was that the original plan was flawed — informants aside. Or, as one policeman said, "Charlie was just a burglar, not too many smarts."

The two main areas of disagreement concerned Marrera's role and the disposal of the money — Grand Cayman versus grandma's basement. One point neither group emphasized is that the fire was supposed to burn everything up, including all evidence of a burglary. It should have been merely a problem for the fire department — to put out the fire — and for Purolator to decide how much money had been burned. The burglars had used the combination, so there were no signs of forcible entry to give them away. The missing ingredient was oxygen — not money. The burglars had also known of and counted on the vault air vent — sufficient for breathing with the door closed and, they thought, sufficient for a fire.

The police also view Marrera as a fool for staying on the premises even though he didn't expect the burglary to be discovered. He would naturally become (as he did) the number-one suspect. "He should've broken a leg and been in the hospital," says one deputy chief. "But then the lie box would get him anyway."

Tony and his friends view it differently. Marrera had to be there to send the other Purolator employees home. He also had to play his charade with Wells Fargo in case they decided to check up on things when Marrera opened the vault door, setting off the alarm at Wells Fargo. If Marrera had stayed away, Tony and Charlie would have had to get past the guards with threats and guns — and this wasn't their style or preference. "Marrera could have stonewalled it," Gino said. "Flunking a lie test is no big deal. They can't use the test in court, anyway."

Tony's friend Mickey Vena agreed. "It was better that Marrera did hang around until the thing was discovered. It made it so they had to prove he was guilty."

Actually Marrera did stonewall, and did flunk the polygraph by sticking to his unlikely story. He was never put to the final test because he was unfit to stand trial, but, with a little luck and the jury that acquitted DiFonzo, who knows what might have happened? Even his decision to bury the treasure wasn't a bad idea, the police observe — though grandma's basement was the wrong place and, obviously, the wrong neighbor caught a hint of the operation.

It might be said that this great amateur robbery was neat and clean up to the point when the men pulled out of the Purolator garage that autumn night. Homemade though it was, the plot had the right mixture of shrewdness — lifting the vault combination out of the vice president's desk and using the old Aesopian moral about the boy who cried wolf — and a good deal of luck. Shortly thereafter, the machinery began to show marked signs of strain. And that was because no one in the plan had been capable of imagining the sheer bulk of the paper money. It could not be disposed of quickly. Some 700 pounds of paper had to be counted and sorted out into Marrera's cut and the complicated set of drops. Then the remaining mass of paper had to be lugged down to the Caribbean.

It was, of course, remarkable that this unlikely team of the Marzanos, Gushi, and DiFonzo could have smuggled their carload of bills out of Illinois, across the country, and finally into a Grand Cayman bank without any evident pursuit or hindrance by authorities of the law anywhere. In a reasonably plausible heist movie, it wouldn't have been so easy.

There is another school of thought about all this. Tony's friend Mickey, for instance, says, "You got a million dollars, you bury it. Then you got no state lines to cross, no nosy FBI, just the state to worry about. No sweat. And who needs interest?"

Not at all, Tony says. There was nothing very far wrong with the plan except Pete Gushi. He talked a lot beforehand. He couldn't arrange for the boat in Florida. Then he talked a lot afterward.

Whatever the critiques, there is one area of agreement: the authorities recovered some $3 million in cash and some $1.4 million is still missing. But there are still more mysteries. According to the tags found with the money in grandma's basement, $700,000 had been skimmed off that cache — but did the packets contain $5000 each or $2500? Tony still isn't sure. Did Pete Gushi really give $300,000 to some strangers in the night? In any case, somebody else has discovered the magic trick the Marzano crew might have longed for — how to make a bale of paper currency invisible. Or at least no more visible than a figure on the bank statement of a numbered account. In a Grand Cayman bank, for example.

Almost Everybody Wins

There are still secrets — nothing illegal, no dirty tricks — but
that is just the way the law is.

— Ramon Stratton

On July 14, 1975, Tony Marzano turned up at the gate of
the Terre Haute, Indiana, maximum-security prison to start
serving his term. Later he was transferred to Sandstone in
Minnesota and then, at his request, to Eglin, a minimum-
security prison in Florida.

The prison is on the grounds of Eglin Air Force Base, the
largest in the world, and most of the prisoners are employed
in jobs for the air force. Tony, for instance, worked on the
construction of a new golf course. Life was not bad there.
After six months in some old barracks, Tony was moved
into a new dormitory. He had a bed and a desk in his own
cubicle. The floors were carpeted; air conditioners kept out
the Florida heat; there were ice machines and televi-
sions — and no one got knifed for changing a channel.

As for social life, there were the off-base Alcoholics Anonymous meetings Tony attended, the Toastmaster's Club, and
the picnics. Prisoners were permitted to have family picnics

on the grounds. Stan, his friend and fellow con, had a wife; the wife had a girl friend named Connie; Tony had ways of getting an I.D. for Connie to pass as a friend's wife.

The Toastmaster's Club, too, offered outside activity. Some of the meetings were held in Pensacola, Fort Walton, or Panama City — and that meant a chance to get off base. But the most interesting thing about the club was its leader, who lived in Tony's dormitory unit. His name was Howard Hunt.

"Very smooth and interesting," Tony described him, "but with a kind of sneaky look you'd expect from a CIA man." Hunt worked in the prison laundry. In his spare time, he did paintings or worked on a book he was writing. Most of his friends were the Chicago police officers — sergeants and lieutenants — who had been caught shaking down establishments in Tony's favorite Rush Street area.

But the great event of the social season was Howard Hunt's address on the subject of Watergate. It was given, on the last Saturday night preceding his release, before a crowded auditorium of 500 people. No reporters, note takers, or tape recorders were allowed. Tony remembers it as a stirring event. For an hour and a half, Hunt held the audience mesmerized, beginning in a controlled, quiet tone and gradually rising in volume to an eloquent rage. Hunt spoke about the president who had given him a special mission and, along with it, an assumed name and an office in the White House. He told of his loyalty during his first months in jail, his confidence that the boss he had trusted would find a way to get him released. And, even after he knew he'd been betrayed, he'd kept silent. But now he would no longer be silent.

At the end, there was a hush and then resounding applause. This audience knew exactly the kind of loyalty and betrayal he was talking about.

At about four o'clock the next Monday morning, Tony woke up to see Hunt, with a small suitcase under his arm, about to leave the dormitory. Guards were following with the rest of his belongings. "Good luck, Howard," Tony said, and Hunt nodded. The man had class.

It was a CIA-style exit. Reporters had gathered in front of the prison early, had waited for nearly three hours, and finally had set off in chase of a laundry truck that sped out of the prison gates. But Hunt was long gone by that time. Guards had taken him the back way through the woods to the lake, where a boat was waiting. A smooth operation, Tony thought.

Tony was released after a total of twenty-eight months in detention, his debt to society paid.

In the end, who won and who lost?

Russell Hardt thinks Purolator lost. Both he and Joseph Woods resigned their jobs shortly after the burglary. All of the supervisors at that time left the company within three years. The strict new security rules put everybody under suspicion, Hardt feels, and lowered morale.

Tony laughs. "Purolator had an $18,000 deductible insurance policy," he points out. "They got off cheap, considering." And was the Purolator image hurt? "Everybody thought they made those dinky oil filters," Tony says. "We gave them a big-money image." Purolator's stock went up after the robbery and the company had a 6.5 percent increase in volume the next year.

It seems a fair assumption that the Commercial Union Insurance Company lost. Still, contrary to U.S. Attorney James Thompson's prediction, it did get some money back — $3 million, the largest sum of stolen money ever recovered.

James Thompson came out ahead. The press coverage undoubtedly helped in his winning campaign for governor in 1976.

As for Tony, he decided to go home to Chicago and, following in the footsteps of the fellow prisoner at Eglin he had so much admired, to write a book.